mass communication in india
a sociological perspective

J.V. Vilanilam

SAGE Publications
New Delhi • Thousand Oaks • London

First published in 2005 by

Sage Publications India Pvt Ltd
B-42, Panchsheel Enclave
New Delhi 110 017
www.indiasage.com

Sage Publications Inc 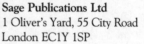 Sage Publications Ltd
2455 Teller Road 1 Oliver's Yard, 55 City Road
Thousand Oaks, California 91320 London EC1Y 1SP

Published by Tejeshwar Singh for Sage Publications India Pvt Ltd, phototypeset in 10/12 Goudy Old Style by Prism Graphix, New Delhi and printed at Chaman Enterprises, New Delhi.

Library of Congress Cataloging-in-Publication Data

Vilanilam, John V.
  Mass communication in India: a sociological perspective/J.V. Vilanilam.
  p. cm.
Includes bibliographical reference and index.
1. Mass Media—India—History. 2. Mass media—History. I. Title.

P92.I7V55   302.23'0954—dc22   2005   2005017388

ISBN: 0-7619-3372-7 (Pb)   81-7829-515-6 (India-Pb)

Sage Production Team: Rrishi Raote, Rajib Chatterjee and Santosh Rawat

contents

preface

*b*ecause of the proliferation of the mass media in India in recent years, there is a great need to look at them from a fresh perspective. Journalism has been in existence in India for at least 225 years if we take the first printed newspaper, namely, *Hicky's Bengal Gazette* or the *Calcutta General Advertiser*, started by James Augustus Hicky in 1780, as the starting point. Although communication has always existed, to equate what is transmitted or received through the mass media with genuine communication is a philosophical and epistemological fallacy.

There is an etymological problem too: communication implies a two-way exchange and mutual or common understanding whereas mass communication is mostly one-way. What the mass media always do is to convey information without giving the recipients a chance to react or exchange ideas with the person who conveys the information through the media.

Again, mass communication has been equated with communication not only in India but also in other countries. The distinction between the two is brought out in this book, citing authorities in the discipline of communication/mass communication.

There was a time when we used to categorize the media into 'print' (newspapers, magazines and other periodicals) and 'electronic' (radio, television and film). Modern technological advancement has led to an obliteration of this differentiation. All media are now electronic, except the traditional media of singing, dancing, advertising through hoardings and other means of oral and graphic publicity. Today, even graphics and cartoons are generated electronically.

The other major development in recent decades has been the advent of the computer and the binary system. As Paul Gilster, a communications expert has said, something 'protean and profound' is happening to our world now, whether we call it 'a digital revolution, an information super highway or a grand convergence of the media'. It is a digital world that many of us are living in now; everything can be turned into the binary and everything can be broken down into electrons, protons, neutrons, mesons, etc. All the major media (except the human agents of communication) operate electronically, digitally and virtually.

In our digital age, the power of the new media is seen through the computer, especially the personal computer (PC), which has become the central feature of modern life.

Many foresee that today's computerized DTP systems, DVD systems and digital systems will 'open out to the digital archives of our species'; a second Renaissance through the new media is predicted. 'What is fantasy, what is real?' asks one expert. Another says that 'with the development of the Internet, and with the increasing pervasiveness of communication between networked computers, we are in the middle of the most transforming technological event since the capture of fire'. Perhaps the 21st century will prove that human beings are not designed genetically to live at the speed of light, although, as Marshall McLuhan once wrote, they are now capable of communicating at the speed of light.

The electronic, digital revolution and the consequent communication revolution is certainly a fact of life in the 21st century. But almost half the world's population has been left out of this revolution. More than 50 per cent of the world's population has never used a telephone, not to speak of more modern instruments of communication such as the Internet. The natural tendency in human beings is to utilize superior knowledge to keep others inferior.

There is a great need for developing technologies that are essential to remove the ignorance, poverty and misery of the people of the backward half of the world, who are still struggling to eke out an existence at less than a dollar a day, or perhaps slightly more than a dollar a day.

Progress and development, technological revolutions and the improvement in the standard of living of a sizeable section of the world's population are certainly great achievements, but the other half or more are not experiencing any significant improvement in their lifestyles. Technology has to have a human face if the world is to be a less dangerous place for all its inhabitants.

In an earlier book, titled *Communication and Mass Communication in India*, I reached out to students just embarking on the study of mass communication. My focus therein was on the difference between communication and mass communication and the evolution of communication since the beginning of time. While the present book also traces the progress of communications technology from primitive times till the present day, it does so from a historical and sociological perspective. It also points out that substantial numbers of people are not living electronically, digitally or in a wired world. This historical truth has to be acknowledged by policy-makers in both rich and poor countries. There is an unstated fact in all deliberations: the prosperous in the global village try to market their products and the more prosperous among the poor sectors of the world try to popularize those products, sometimes forgetting their own national priorities.

Communication scientists and media sociologists can reduce the disparities between the sectors, if not totally eliminate them. If this does not occur, communication will, no doubt, continue to be one-way. As stated earlier, this is a negation of the very basic meaning and goal of communication, which is bringing people together on the basis of a just, humane, equal and peaceful order.

I do not deny the marvellous achievements of science and technology but only wish to stress that the fruits of development must also go to those sections of humanity that have been bowed by the weight of centuries of poverty, oppression and the unjust social and economic systems sometimes imposed by the 'more knowledgeable people in the information society' on the 'less informed and less knowing people'. The idea of progress is certainly good, but not good enough for substantial sections of humanity. Progress without any thought for the absolutely poor of the world or of India is a mirage, a temporary glitter.

This book is the result of a few years of observation and analysis of media performance and media content in various parts of the world, including India. I have written it in the hope that I will not be misunderstood as a scrooge unwilling to enjoy the fruits of modern development! Nor am I a Luddite decrying all the progress already achieved in telecommunication, space travel, or modern medicine. I want to emphasize that communication, in order to be free and unfettered, and aimed at the peaceful transformation of society, cannot be left to the big business conglomerates trying to monopolize all systems of public communication in an attempt to influence people in certain directions, purely to amass profits and social prestige. Communication must become a vital tool in the hands of ordinary people who can make use of conventional as well as modern systems to transform society.

I wish to express my sincere thanks to those who assisted me in the preparation of this book, particularly my daughter-in-law, Lulu, and my wife, Annie. I also thank Sage Publications for all the encouragement given to me, not only in the publication of this book but also in the publication of other books from the late 1980s onwards.

Trivandrum   J.V. Vilanilam
August 2005

list of abbreviations

3-D	three-dimensional
9/11	The terrorist attack on the twin towers of the World Trade Centre in New York on 11 September 2001
ABC	American Broadcasting Company
AFP	Agence France-Presse
AIR	All-India Radio
AOL	America Online
AP	Associated Press
AP-DJ	Associated Press–Dow Jones
APW	absolutely poor of the world
AT&T	American Telephone and Telegraph Company
BBC	British Broadcasting Corporation
CATV	Community Antenna Television
CBS	Columbia Broadcasting System
CD	compact disk
CD-ROM	compact disk read-only memory
CGI	computer-generated imagery (imaging)
CIS	Commonwealth of Independent States
CNN	Cable News Network
CNNfn	CNN-financial news
CNN/SI	CNN/Sports Illustrated
CNS	central nervous system
CPB	Corporation for Public Broadcasting
CRT	cathode ray tube
DD	Doordarshan
DPA	Deutsche Presse Agentur
DTP	desktop publishing
DVD	digital video/versatile disk
EDUSAT	Educational Satellite
EMR	electromagnetic radiation
ENAJ	Europe, North America and Japan
ENG	electronic news gathering

ESPN	Entertainment and Sports Network
FAO	Food and Agriculture Organization
FCC	Federal Communications Commission (USA)
FSN	Full Service Network
GB	gigabytes
GDP	Gross Domestic Product
GE	General Electric
GNP	Gross National Product
HDTV	high-definition television
HPT	high-power transmitter
I&B	information and broadcasting
IBM	International Business Machines
ICT	information and communication technology
IGNOU	Indira Gandhi National Open University
INSAT	Indian National Satellite
ISRO	Indian Space Research Organization
IT	information technology
ITU	International Telecommunication Union
LPT	low-power transmitter
MB	megabytes
MGM	Metro Goldwyn Meyer
MIT	Massachusetts Institute of Technology
MP	Madhya Pradesh
MTV	Music Television
MVT	magnetic video tape
NASA	National Aeronautical and Space Administration
NBC	National Broadcasting Corporation
NCL	News Corporation Limited
NCNA	New China News Agency (same as Xinhua)
NRS	National Readership Survey
NYT	*New York Times*
Op-Ed	opposite-editorial page in newspapers
PBS	Public Broadcasting System
PDA	personal digital assistant
PTI	Press Trust of India
RCA	Radio Corporation of America
RGTU	Rajiv Gandhi Technical University
SAC	Space Applications Centre, ISRO
SC	scheduled caste
SITE	Satellite Instructional Television Experiment

SR	Stimulus-response (theory)
ST	scheduled tribe
TASS	Telegrafnoe Agentsvo Sovetskogo Soiuza (now, ITAR-TASS: Informatsionnoe Telegrafnoe Agentsvo Rossii—Telegrafnoe Agentsvo Sovetskogo Soiuza)
TV-G	Television for general audience
TV-MA	Television for mature audience
TV-Y	Television for young persons
TV-Y7	Television for children above the age of 7
UGC	University Grants Commission
UHF	ultra high frequency
UNDP	United Nations Development Programme
UNESCO	United Nations Educational, Scientific and Cultural Organization
UNI	United News of India
UNTV	United Nations Television Unit
UPI	United Press International
UP	Uttar Pradesh
VCD	video compact disk
V-chip	Violence chip
VCR	video cassette recorder
VDT	video display terminal
VHF	very high frequency
VR	virtual reality
VTR	video tape recorder
VTU	Visvesvaraya Technological University
WMD	weapons of mass destruction
WSJ	*Wall Street Journal*
WTC	World Trade Centre
WWW	World Wide Web (also termed W3)
YCMOU	Yashvantrao Chavan Maharashtra Open University

communication and society
an overview

C ommunication is as old as humanity itself. As the MacBride Commission, set up by the UNESCO in 1978, observed in its report in 1980:

> Communication maintains and animates life. It is also the motor and ex-
> pression of social activity and civilization ... [T]he task of communication
> has become ever more complicated and subtle—to contribute to the libera-
> tion of mankind from want, oppression and fear and to unite it in commu-
> nity and communion, solidarity and understanding. However, unless some
> basic structural changes are introduced, the potential benefits of technologi-
> cal and communication development will hardly be put at the disposal of
> the majority of mankind. (1980: 3)

The structure of a particular society will influence the nature of communication in it. If the society under discussion is not a free society, but one that
is dominated by certain groups, the content and media of communication
will be so organized that the messages will perpetuate the dominance of
interested groups. Communication in such a society will negate the very
meaning of *communication*, which etymologically implies sharing, a community of interests and social cohesion based on social justice.

There are three varieties of communication: *Intrapersonal* (taking place
in the brain and physiological systems within the individual); *Interpersonal*
(between individuals, groups, etc.); and *mass*.

We shall discuss the first two cursorily and bring out the essential differences among the three varieties. We shall study the third in detail because
that is what has created a great deal of discussion in recent years. Moreover,
mass communication has gained immense social significance because of mass
media, which touch the lives of millions of people all over the world.

Naturally, this raises the important distinction between *communication* and *mass communication*.

The mass media that act as social instruments or as organizations shaping social life through their repetitive appeals to different sections of society, wide popularity and pervasiveness are perhaps exerting more influence than other social institutions. Virtually every section of society is influenced to some degree by the messages disseminated on a regular basis through professionally produced and technically perfected programmes. Fast changing aspects of Indian society are brought to the attention of media users who are in turn influenced by the messages.

Influential political and economic groups are trying to spread ideas through the mass media (mainly newspapers, radio, television, film, audio and video tapes) for their own particular ends. Various issues, for example, elections to various democratic institutions, national issues such as the Babri Masjid demolition, erosion of secular values in public life, persecution of minorities and women, communal and caste conflicts, violence against vulnerable sections of society, terrorism in the country and the world, decisions of the World Trade Organization and their effects on trade and agriculture in poor countries, revival of religious fundamentalism, pseudo-religion and superstitions, gender inequality, unequal access to primary and secondary education, unemployment and lack of attention to the generation of employment, etc., can be brought to the attention of people through the mass media.

There is practically no section of important socioeconomic, political and cultural life that is not dealt with in media reports, features, editorials, letters to the editor, magazine materials, video clips and programmes including films, telefilms, interviews and talks, though media may not find it practical to present everything that individual media users find interesting, useful or necessary.

The messages reaching the audience through various channels are likely to influence different sections of society differently but, in general, those who watch or listen to particular programmes or read certain kinds of material in print media are likely to develop a soft corner for the ideas expressed in those media.

The Five Components of Communication

Communication, whether interpersonal or mass, will be based on five components: *communicator*, *communicatee* (the person who receives the communication), *medium* (channel), *message*, and *feedback*.

Of these, feedback is the factor that distinguishes interpersonal communication from mass communication. In the latter, there is very little feedback, except in the case of print media such as newspapers and magazines which publish letters to the editor.

There is also a negative factor, namely noise, which may be technical or sociological. When there is disruption caused by various reasons, the process of communication becomes incomplete. The sociological noise is generated by the pronounced status difference between the communicator and the communicatee. It can be created by the barrier of language too. Whatever creates an obstruction between the sender and the receiver of the message is a noise.

Communication will also suffer when those who are engaged in it try to influence each other unduly. A certain degree of mutual influence is necessary, desirable, and even justified, but when one communicator tries to influence the other for personal gain, the process is vitiated and real communication does not take place.

The word 'communication' has the Latin roots *communis* and *communicare*, meaning sharing of meaning and understanding based on friendship, mutual respect, equality and a feeling of oneness. The basis of human communication is, and ought to be, sharing of love and understanding. It rests on the fundamental principle that all human beings are essentially the same, fed by the same Nature and nurtured by the same Creator.

Most theorists agree that communication has three shades of meaning: exchange of information verbally, non-verbally and verbally and non-verbally, for promoting understanding. The message or messages conveyed will also be known as communication, as in the sentence, 'There has not been any communication from Mr X.' Again, in its plural form, *communications* signifies the means of communication: for example, *the mass media of communications*.

But a mere sending of messages from one end to another in a linear or circular fashion does not necessarily lead to communication. There should be sharing of ideas, meanings, thoughts, feelings—these are at the base of the communicative act or the communication process—and this sharing must lead to action.

In this Age of Information, we have to look at the process from the perspective of information and communication. All ideas, meanings, thoughts and feelings are basically pieces of information.

Thus it is not wrong to modify our definition of communication to 'the exchange of information between and among human beings for the promotion of mutual and common understanding and desirable social action'.

Some experts represent the process of communication as in Figure 1.1.

Figure 1.1
A Simple Model of Communication

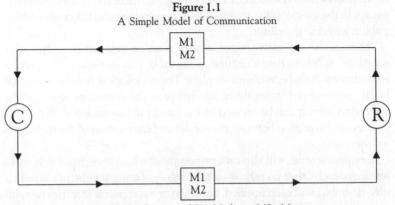

Notes: C=Communicator, R=Receiver, M1=Medium, M2=Message.

The process continues cyclically until the intention of the sender coincides with the understanding of the receiver, and vice versa (Orlik 1992: 3). However, this model is not complete. The medium or channel through which the message is conveyed is also an important component of the model.

In the Universal Model of Communication, Figure 1.2, medium M is included. However, since this M should not be confused with the M of message, we use M1 and M2 for medium and message, respectively.

Figure 1.2
The Universal Model of Communication (UMC)

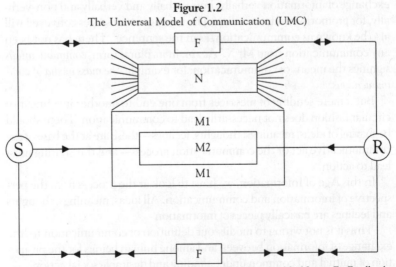

Notes: S=Sender, R=Receiver, M1=Medium, M2=Message, N=Noise, F=Feedback.

In oral communication, *air* and *language* are the two media. In non-verbal communication, message is conveyed through signs, symbols and gestures; there is no *speech* involved. In certain situations, sound conveys meanings; for example, a cry signifies pain. But even for the sound to be heard, air is essential, since a vacuum will not convey sound. Although usually taken for granted, air is essential as a medium to convey sound; and words, after all, are representations of sounds.

However, *non-verbal communication* is highly significant because it conveys meaning to others without the help of words. A smile is a universally recognized sign of goodwill, welcome and acceptance, not an indication of hatred, ill-will or non-acceptance, certainly not of suspicion. And a cry expresses pain, sorrow or fear, whether in Manchester or Mattancherry.

A friendly handshake could mark the beginning of good relations between individuals. Anthropologists tell us that the practice of greeting with open hands, a handshake or folded hands, as in *namaste,* started long ago when humans wanted to reassure other humans that their hands were not hiding weapons.

But non-verbal communication cannot go much beyond gestures, handshakes, winks, and so on, which are sometimes likely to be misinterpreted by others. The thoughts behind these actions of the initiator cannot be explained without words. Every human action has a cause or causes, which cannot be fully conveyed non-verbally, although psychologists tell us that certain actions are accompanied by bodily movements of which the actor (or speaker) is unaware, but which are visible to others. In other words, there are automatic, involuntary reflexes which reflect the actor's state of mind. For example, the ginger steps of a young man appearing for a job interview may reflect his lack of self-confidence; his sitting at the edge of his chair may also indicate the same. Some people hold their hands in a defensive position when they face someone unfamiliar.

In common parlance, non-verbal communication is referred to as *body language* and includes gestures, facial expressions, body movements, looks, clothes and even shoes, which send messages to others. There are popular books on how to read a person like an open book, how to interpret every move of an individual and how to guess the mind of a person from her looks, etc. The study of human behaviour based on individual body language is becoming increasingly popular.

But to interpret every movement of the body and to decide on a course of action based on it is as foolish as ignoring it all together. It is safer to acknowledge that human communication is not entirely verbal or non-verbal. It is a combination of both, although over-emphasis on the non-verbal is likely to make communication mysterious and even dangerous. People of a particular locality who use a common language understand its grammar and usage; but gestures and body movements do not follow any common language of signs and symbols or rules of expression. Judy K. Burgoon, a professor of communication who has spent many years studying the intricacies of non-verbal communication, has made the following observation:

> Just as a coding system must have semantic and syntactic rules, so must nonverbal signals as they are combined to form messages—if they are to be treated as a coding system. This assumption delimits the nonverbal domain to the extent that it excludes behaviours that lack consistent meanings and behaviours that fail to be combined in systematic, grammatical ways with other nonverbal signals. (Burgoon 1994: 231–32)

Certain gestures and movements have specific meanings in certain cultures and the opposite meanings in other cultures; but language common to both cultures will not have great dissimilarities, although there are likely to be minor variations. In language mode, the ambiguity is likely to be less, whereas in gesture mode, it is likely to be more. Non-verbal communication is thus more culture-specific than verbal communication.

Receivers are not Passive

The communication process has to be two-way, but at least up to the 1960s, it was assumed, even among scholars, to be one-way, from those who had something to say, show or convey in words or pictures to those who were supposed to receive the information. It was also assumed that those who had the means to communicate could influence those who received the message.

The Stimulus–Response (SR) Theory Early research in mass communication, primarily to measure the effects of communication on recipients of messages, was based on the *SR model*. This theory has to be associated with effects research. Mass communication was seen by those who owned newspapers, radio and television stations, film studios and advertisement agencies as an efficient device to deliver their messages, particularly about products and services, to very large numbers of consumers. They thought that these messages would reach media users directly and make them respond immediately, thus acting in a manner predictable by the message senders. Media users were seen primarily as buyers of products, as targets for messages, particularly commercial messages. Only later was it found that the message receivers responded on the basis of several personal factors and that responses to identical messages varied greatly. Audiences may receive some stimulus from the media but such stimulus need not necessarily lead them to buying action. It was also found that messages did not always reach the audience directly but via opinion leaders in society (Lazarsfeld and Katz 1955).

A variation of this model was the 'hypodermic needle model', also called the 'magic bullet model'. The underlying assumption in all these approaches to mass communication was that mass media messages acted like a hypodermic needle or magic bullet on users and brought about changes in their behaviour. This approach was considered useful not only for economic and business ends but also for military purposes. Much World War II propaganda was based on this theory.

Meaning is not simply conveyed by the message sender and her words and gestures; it is also constructed by the message receiver. The construction of meaning depends on the receiver's cultural, social and economic background. Communication is thus not only what is detected on the surface of an interaction or transaction.

An interaction or transaction is completed and meanings fully constructed on the basis of the internalized thoughts and habits of the message sender and the message receiver. For example, a person from Asia will instantaneously recognize a *namaste*—the greeting through folded palms—but not so a European, American or African, especially if he or she lives in the rural areas where interactions with the outside world are few and far between.

Similarly, students in Western countries do not stand when the teacher enters the classroom, because they are not used to such a practice. But as a mark of respect and admiration for a musical performer, the Westerner rises and claps his hands. In the East, people meeting a great performer may bow their heads in veneration. These are practices followed by people living in different parts of the world. There is no uniformity in cultural practices; There is God's plenty in the world, and variety is the spice of life.

In all processes of communication, therefore, the various components will discharge their functions according to their basic acculturation. The extent to which communicatees can be influenced depends on the *intrapersonal* storehouse of information built in all those who are associated with the process of sending and receiving messages.

The Pyramid of Communication in Society

We have already indicated that communication takes place in society at three levels: the individual (intrapersonal), social (interpersonal) and mass society (mass communication) levels. Another categorization of communication is based on the medium used—verbal and non-verbal. There may be occasions when all forms of communication are used. The process may involve words, gestures, signs, symbols and pictures, at the interpersonal level and the mass level. Both the interpersonal and mass level communication are the results of intrapersonal processing of information. This is why our pyramid of communication has as its base the intrapersonal segment. In fact, the bulk of our communication results from our intrapersonal processing of information. Then comes interpersonal communication. Mass communication occupies only the apex of the pyramid, accounting for perhaps 10 per cent of the area. The largest area is occupied, no doubt, by what is going on in our central nervous system (CNS), our brain.

The base of people's attitudes, beliefs and opinions is formed at a very early stage in life. People are not robots; they absorb information from the environment from childhood onwards through interactions with parents, siblings and others at home, and later with fellow students, teachers, neighbours and others. Tastes, likes, dislikes, opinions, ethics and morals are formed in the course of such early interactions. As Orlik has observed,

> Attitude comes into play in any human transaction because it is improbable for people either to send or receive messages without encasing them in an opinion-suggesting wrapping. People ... make evaluative judgments in the transmissions of other people. (1992: 3)

It is, however, through intrapersonal communication that the basis of people's opinions and reactions is formed.

Let us look at the communication pyramid (Figure 1.3) provided by McQuail (1994: 7).

The Psychological Base of Communication

Our brain makes up less than 2 per cent of our body's weight but it uses up 20 per cent of the body's energy. Our body obeys the commands given by this extremely complex organ, which acts like a supercomputer. Nerve impulses travel along neurons (nerve cells) at speeds of up to almost 15,000 cms per second.

Scientists tell us that the brain contains between 10 trillion and 100 trillion neurons. Each neuron is linked by what are known as synapses to thousands of other neurons. Information passes through this complex system and part of it gets stored in the brain. Although a computer can do arithmetic faster than the human brain, the latter can do more things than any computer yet invented.

Figure 1.3
The Communication Pyramid (modified model)

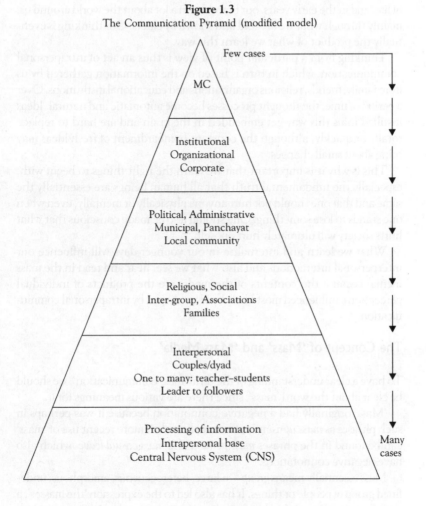

Few cases ──────

MC

Institutional
Organizational
Corporate

Political, Administrative
Municipal, Panchayat
Local community

Religious, Social
Inter-group, Associations
Families

Interpersonal
Couples/dyad
One to many: teacher–students
Leader to followers

Processing of information
Intrapersonal base
Central Nervous System (CNS)

Many
cases

All our organs and their movements are controlled by the chief organ, the brain, which flashes messages to every corner of the body via the nerves. The brain and the nerves thus make up the nervous system network. This network carries information from all parts of the body to the brain and vice versa.

The brain is not only the body's central control but also the storehouse of information. It can do lots of things at once, and do them fast. Our actions depend on what our brains let us know and remember. In the very first year of life, and in the early years, our brains learn a lot about the world around us, mainly through what we are told and shown by elders. Our thinking is eventually the product of what we learn this way.

Thinking from a particular point of view is thus an act of intrapersonal communication, which in turn is based on the information gathered by us from family, friends, religious organizations and educational institutions. Over a period of time, the thought processes become automatic and natural. Ideas instilled in us this way get embedded in the brain and are hard to replace totally or quickly, although the constant bombardment of fresh ideas may bring about small changes.

This is why it is important that we learn the right things to begin with, especially the fundamental truth that all human beings are essentially the same and that one should not hurt anyone physically or mentally, even when one stands to lose something. One should also be made conscious that what hurts society will ultimately hurt oneself.

What we learn and internalize in our younger days will influence our interpersonal interactions and also what we see, hear and read in the mass media, because the contents of the media are the products of individual perceptions, influenced most likely by ideas shaped by intrapersonal communication.

The Concept of 'Mass' and 'Mass Media'

To have a clear understanding of the term 'mass communication', we should be clear about the word 'mass', since there are various meanings for it.

'Mass' originally had a negative connotation because it was perhaps in such phrases as *mass uprising* and *mass upheaval*. A more recent use of 'mass' can be found in the phrases *mass petition* and *mass casual leave*, which also have negative connotations.

Mass essentially means *group*—a large, heterogeneous, amorphous, undefined group of people or things. It has also led to the expression 'the masses', a shapeless, usually unruly or undisciplined group of people, almost equivalent to a *mob*. The word *masses* means *common people*. The masses live a life that is different from that of the middle class or the aristocrats. *Elite* versus *masses* is a common system of comparison.

The phrase 'mass movement' indicates a movement by a very large number of common people for the fulfilment of some political or social demand.

But the most common connotation of *masses* is the lower class, often the ignorant, illiterate, uneducated, unruly, irrational and even violent groups of people. With social revolutions succeeding in many countries, the term *mass* acquired the positive sense of ordinary people engaged in movements for political, economic and social equality, and for liberty. However, the dominant sense has been unflattering as it indicates amorphous, even faceless or anonymous groups of people. One dictionary defines mass as an aggregate in which one's individuality is lost.

McQuail (1994: 36) has summarized the concept of mass in four brief points:

- large aggregate
- undifferentiated (bulk)
- mainly negative image
- lacking order

What, then are the mass media? Here the meaning is slightly different. Mass media are those means of communication which help

- Transmit messages (news, entertainment, information of all kinds) simultaneously to large, heterogeneous, anonymous masses of people living in different regions of a locality, nation or the world.
- Transmit messages rapidly and instantaneously.
- Large groups of people in different locations to receive the same information in the same language, although translations of the main points can simultaneously be displayed in subscripts or superscripts on the television screen or in voice-overs on the radio or in parentheses in print.

Here, 'large' means immensely large, to be counted in the millions rather than in the thousands.

The mass media include large-circulation newspapers, magazines, form letters that go to hundreds of thousands of customers, books such as J.K. Rowling's Harry Potter series, radio and television programmes, films, CDs, DVDs, and audio and video tapes sold in the hundreds of thousands or millions. The criterion here is the number of users. Newspapers and magazines read by a few thousand people are not considered mass media.

Although some radio and television programmes may be heard or watched only by a few hundreds or thousands, radio and television are always considered mass media (as are films). This is because these media, as a whole, reach millions of users.

E-mail and the Internet are on their way to becoming mass media in a certain sense. Nevertheless, there are experts who do not consider them mass media because of the lack of uniformity in the messages they transmit.

Interactive e-mail, fax and the Internet carry personal messages and news digests. Strictly speaking, they are interpersonal media, despite their capacity to deliver messages by the million and despite their technical capacity (particularly of the Internet) to display newspapers and magazines and transmit radio programmes and pictures.

One special characteristic that distinguishes the audiovisual from the print media is that the messages they transmit are transient in nature. To have hard copies, one has to capture the contents on magnetic tapes. For ordinary consumers or media users, such taping and re-use involves a great deal of expenditure and effort; hence the messages are for all practical purposes, transient. Print media messages are long-lasting, especially when they are preserved on microfilm and microfiche, at much smaller expense; and such messages can be used over and over again by ordinary people.

After having examined the meanings of mass, mass media, and mass communication, let us now look at another commonly used term that sometimes causes confusion among students and media workers. And that is 'journalism'.

Some think that journalism is what editors and reporters, photojournalists and feature writers are engaged in, in the world of newspapers and magazines or, in general, all print media. They try to keep the term exclusively for use in the print media. This is an erroneous approach, especially in these days of *media convergence*. Journalism is not simply print journalism alone. There are different varieties of journalism: radio journalism, magazine journalism, newspaper journalism, film journalism, television journalism, and so on. What then is journalism?

What is Journalism?

Writing a book is different from writing a journal article, and the latter is different from the writing of a news report. There are certain conventions associated with newspaper writing. Daily newspapers generally carry reports on events of the previous 24 hours; they also carry feature articles on events, personalities and issues of contemporary relevance. Timeliness is associated with journalistic writing in a daily, as opposed to writing for a weekly, monthly or other periodical.

Journalism is popularly defined as 'a report of things as they appear at the moment of writing, not a definitive study of a situation' (Agee et al. 1979: 11).

Etymologically, a journal is a record of events, almost a diary where the journal-keeper enters salient points of daily occurrences. The journalist is associated with two things: reporting the news, and offering interpretations and opinions based on news.

The journalistic writer is different from the creative or imaginative writer. The journalist's writings may be entertaining but its entertainment value is only incidental. Facts are more important than the style or manner of writing, although the appeal of such writing is enhanced if the facts are presented in a certain order, to capture the attention of readers and maintain their interest.

As Harold Lasswell of Harvard put it almost 60 years ago, three major functions of the journalist are:

- Surveillance of the environment
- Correlation of parts of society through interpretation of the events reported
- Transmission of cultural heritage from generation to generation (1948: 37–51).

To these has been added the function of *entertainment*. It was Charles R. Wright who saw the growing use of radio, television and film (RTF) for entertaining mass audiences and pointed out that entertainment is a major function of the mass media (1959: 15–21). However, entertainment is largely confined to RTF while mass media can be used for mass dissemination of news, mass mobilization of people for good causes (or bad ones), and for the promotion of democratic participation, as Denis McQuail (1994) has pointed out.

The account given by a journalist in a news report must be accurate, factual and free of personal or social bias. It should be impartial and of social significance. However, statement of opinion and interpretation is also part of journalistic duty and practice, and it should be identified as such. This is why all newspapers have one or more editorials and a couple of editorial page and 'opposite editorial' page (op-ed page) articles.

Newspapers have entertainment pieces as well, tongue-in-cheek *middles*, reviews of films and other entertainment activities (drama, dance, etc.), comics and cartoons. But more than surveillance, mobilization or democratic participation, the major goal is entertainment as far as the RTF contents are concerned.

Reporters, editors, feature writers, columnists and reviewers are identified as journalists. So are those who write for syndicates, press associations and magazines. They are all part of what is generally termed 'the press', that is, the print media; but news reporters, commentators and others on radio and television are also journalists. Sometimes, photographers and videographers are identified as press photographers or photojournalists and television reporters. And these days, the term 'press' covers not only print media journalists but journalists from all media.

Thus, the distinction between one form of journalism and other forms is artificial. Journalism enhances not only the print media, but all media. What Agee et al. (1979) suggested decades ago is applicable to today's journalism:

> News reporting and commentaries delivered by television and radio are equally a form of journalism, as are public affairs documentaries, direct broadcasts of news events and filmed and videotaped documentaries. The reporters, writers, editors and photographers in RTF area point out that the general descriptive term 'the press' applies to them as well as to the print media people, when they are dealing with news and opinion. But they tend more often to identify themselves with the name of their medium than with the collective word 'journalist'. So do others in the list of 'communicators— photographers, book editors, advertising specialists, industrial editors and so on.

Another way of describing those who work in various media is to use the phrase 'media personnel'.

Media Convergence: The Interrelationship among the Media

Watertight compartmentalization of the various media is a futile exercise since all media are interrelated technologically and sociologically.

First of all, we now live in a world of global communication, a world of electronic mail (e-mail) and the Internet. News reporters, feature writers, editors, photographers, cinematographers, commentators, writers of magazine article, book publishers and book editors, ad copywriters, PR writers, graphic artists, sound and picture technicians, technical writers, science writers, film directors, choreographers and artistes all work working with the help of electronic devices.

Film and video editing is done electronically. Advertising agencies and PR firms make use of electronic processing of data; and book publishers use electronic processing, editing and printing, including desktop publishing (DTP) systems.

Microelectronics, photophonics, holography, virtual reality, miniaturization, digitalization, electronic news- and data-gathering, processing, storing, retrieval and dissemination, and software management are all part of the modern world of communication. What was considered science fiction 50 years ago is now reality. The 'global village' which Marshall McLuhan spoke of in the 1960s has become a reality, at least in the technical sense, in the richer parts of the world.

Every medium is related to every other medium. Electronics is part of the print media as reports are processed on computers and transferred electronically to a main information bank from where they can be recalled and edited, processed again, photo-composed and made part of the page to be electronically prepared for offset printing.

The phenomenon of compunication (computerized communication) is part of every medium's operation on the practical plane. Most pieces of equipment in the modern media world are electronically operated.

From another angle, the fact of convergence can be seen as an operating reality in the media world in that people working in one medium can move into another medium without much retraining because of the basic similarities in the media. A newspaper reporter with a good voice can become a radio commentator, and a radio reporter can become a television reporter if he or she has good looks, presence of mind, fluency, correct pronunciation and accent. Obviously, the radio reporter appeals more to the ear than to the eye; the television reporter appeals both to the eye and the ear. The news reporter's vocabulary and phraseology, her style of writing and order of narration or exposition, as the case may be, will have to be appealing to the readers, and accord with their educational background and the intellectual standard of the newspaper as a whole.

In a sociological sense too, there is interdependence in the media. All the mass media lean heavily on advertising. Round the clock TV programming is impossible without the support of advertising. Radio too depends on commercials. Half or more of the total space in commercially successful newspapers is occupied by advertisements. In magazines, more than 60 per cent of space is given to advertising.

Films do not depend on within-medium advertising, except in theatres where screen space goes for advertising at the commencement of a movie and during the intermission. The income from the exhibition of ad slides goes to the theatre owners, and not to the film producer. However, TV channels sell time for on-screen products and messages displayed even when a TV programme is running. Many films depend on sponsors. Not only are the films advertised, but so are the film-makers, film studios and sometimes the theatres where the films are exhibited.

PR agencies put out a steady stream of stories on movies, movie-related products and movie personalities. Certain newspapers have a special day for supplements carrying movie material. For example, the *Hindu*'s 'Friday Review' has four pages every week. This is in addition to regular newspaper stories (news and features) on outstanding movies and artistes.

The interdependence of the media becomes visible on another plane. A magazine may carry an illustrated feature based on a report in a newspaper (often a sister publication), which may lead to a film, a TV serial or a telefilm. There could be a novel; and soon a comic serial may appear in a magazine. Dance-dramas, *harikathas*, *burrakathas* and other folk forms may also appear on the same theme. There may be radio dramas, book reviews and television reviews on various renderings in different media. The likelihood of such duplication is heightened if several different media are owned by the same media group. This leads us to the very important area of media ownership.

Media Ownership

There are various types of media ownership. A single owner or proprietor may operate one small medium—a small-circulation periodical, even a small daily; a small radio station (this is not yet relevant to India, although private ownership of a frequency-modulation [FM] radio station by a single owner is a possibility in the future); or an advertising agency or PR firm run on a small scale.

We are, however, concerned here with ownership of mass media. There are four major types of ownership of mass media: chain, cross media, conglomerate and vertical integration.

Chain Ownership　means the same media company owns numerous outlets in a single medium: a chain of newspapers, a series of radio stations, a string of television stations or several book publishing companies. A series of radio or television stations owned by the same company will have the main station in a prominent city and hundreds of affiliated stations in other cities and towns. For example, there are four major networks of radio and TV stations in the US: the National Broadcasting Corporation (NBC), Columbia Broadcasting System (CBS), the American Broadcasting Company (ABC) and the Public Broadcasting System (PBS). Under each of these, there are hundreds of radio and television stations operating throughout the country. In India we have a national telecasting system called Doordarshan which has several dozen Kendras and relay stations, and a national broadcasting system called the All India Radio (AIR) having hundreds of transmitting stations in different cities and towns.

Chain ownership in India applies mostly to newspapers. There are many publishing groups in India which fall into this category, such as the grou~ headed by the *Times of India, Hindustan Times, Indian Express, Statesman, Anandabazar Patrika, Eenadu, Hindu, Telegraph, Asian Age, Malayala Manorama, Mathrubhumi, Dinath Thanthi* and the Living Media Foundation. All these groups, until recently, had only newspapers and magazines, but some of them have now entered the field of film, audio and videotape production and distribution. A few of them are trying to establish their own radio (FM) stations and possibly some TV stations with or without foreign participation.

Each of these groups has, besides newspapers and magazines for a general audience, several publications for specific sections of society—women, children, the working class, general-knowledge seekers and students and job seekers.

Cross Media Ownership   is when the same company owns several media outlets—radio and television stations along with newspapers, magazines, music labels, dotcoms, publishers and so on. In the West there are many media companies with this ownership pattern. For example, the Washington Post Publishing Company owns radio and television stations along with the newspaper. Rupert Murdoch's News Corporation Limited (NCL) owns all kinds of media, both print and electronic.

Conglomerate Ownership   means the ownership of several businesses, one of which is a media business. For example, when a publishing company owns a newspaper along with chemical, fertilizer, cement, rubber or plastics factories, or a liquor brewery or distillery; or a major corporation has controlling shares in a number of media-related businesses; the pattern is conglomerate.

In a conglomerate, there will be interlocking of directorships, which means the same persons will be directors of a media company as well as of manufacturing industries or financial corporations. In fact, several transport or lorry company directors are directing the destiny of newspaper, television or film production companies. Their main business will be a high-profit industry, but they run a media company for prestige or to exercise social and political influence on decision makers in the private or public sector and in the government of the day. Such a conglomeration may not always support an unbiased or dispassionate presentation of events, issues and personalities.

Vertical Integration indicates that a media company monopolizes the production of the ingredients that go into the making of media products. For example, a newspaper publisher may own several hundred acres of forests where the major component of a newspaper, namely, wood for newsprint is cultivated. Some other newspaper company may own a factory that produces the bulk of the printing ink or presses used in the newspaper industry. Certain film companies may own studios or industrial units producing film stock, or even a chain of theatres where the films are exhibited.

If the present trend of cross media, conglomerate and vertical integration ownership continues, monopolization will result, which will ultimately lead to the phenomenon of suppression not only of media freedom but also of the unbiased presentation of various points of view. Dissenting voices will vanish from the mass media scene.

Editionalization and Circulation War

There is a new trend in the newspaper world in India and that is *editionalization*. This means the same newspaper that is published at the newspaper headquarters is brought out from other towns by making use of the modern technologies of facsimile production. The *Indian Express* and *New Indian Express* are the leaders in this, having a total of 22 editions. The *Hindu* has 12 editions, *Malayala Manorama* has 13, the *Times of India* has six. Almost all successful newspaper companies in India publish multiple editions. In a way, the trend is good, but there are criticisms against it because these so-called editions differ from the headquarters edition only in a few local pages. Critics see this as a method employed by the newspaper companies to canvass advertisements from more towns and increase revenue. They point out that newspaper companies are not trying to bring out genuine local editions that focus on local issues.

We cannot ignore the fact that India is passing through a period of circulation war between major newspapers and magazines, which are less interested in highlighting the concerns of the common man than in fulfilling certain international standards of production, distribution and advertisement revenue augmentation. There are some critics who take the extreme view that the media in India are not serving the political, economic and cultural needs of the people but rather amassing wealth and promoting their own prestige and that of their owners. With every change of government, the established media try to please those in power in two ways: by ignoring the genuine needs of the people but promoting narrow party and personal interests advantageous to the media owners, and by harsh or oblique criticism of every pro-poor step taken by a new government, especially when that step seems to go against the economic interests of the media conglomerates. Most big, established media are huge economic organizations with extra-media interests. Avowedly committed to the public interest and the public sphere, conglomerate media's private economic interests are promoted through various media outlets. Senior journalists of many newspaper companies are posted in New Delhi and in state capitals as liaison officers to lobby on behalf of their newspaper publishers, who also happen to be chairmen or managing directors of conglomerate companies.

Conglomeration and corporate mergers seem to be the order of the day, particularly in the US. For example, Time-Warner and America Online (AOL) have merged. NBC is owned by GEC (The General Electric Company) which has entered the real estate and finance businesses apart from its conventional business of energy production and distribution. CBS and ABC are owned by Viacom and Capital Cities, respectively, which have non-media interests. Murdoch's News Corporation Limited (NCL) has the following media interests in the US:

- The 20th Century Fox Film Corporation
- Fox Broadcasting Company, which has 157 full-time TV stations and 42 secondary stations.
- A cable TV service called FX
- HarperCollins Book Publishing Company
- TV *Guide* magazine
- News America FSI, Inc.

NCL also has huge media stakes in the UK, Europe, Australia and New Zealand, besides substantial financial interests in Asian media. (For more details, see Chapter 9.)

The phenomenon of conglomeration and ownership concentration is found in the movie world too: Warner, Disney, Viacom and Fox produce and distribute more than three-fourths of the movies of the world.

As for newspapers in the US, Gannett, Knight-Ridder, Advance Publications and Cox Enterprises control most of the circulation, although independent newspaper companies such as the *New York Times* and *Los Angeles Times* have a lot of clout and high circulations.

Recently, in May 2003, the Federal Communications Commission (FCC) of the US passed new ownership rules that furthered the consolidation of the media in the hands of a few conglomerates. The FCC had in its own survey found that despite all the innovations in recent years, the vast majority of Americans did not get their news from cable or satellite channels. The majority (56 per cent) relied primarily on terrestrial TV for their news and information, 23 per cent relied on newspapers, 10 per cent on radio, 7 per cent on cable and even less on the Internet. The FCC's decision to support conglomerates went against the grain of Americans' media habits. What the *Business Week* of the US said in an editorial in its issue of 26 May 2003 is worth citing here.

> More consolidation of the media is likely to lead to less access to diverse sources of information. Many news outlets already recycle news from network radio broadcasts and newspapers. In radio, the lifting of ownership caps has already cut the diversity of music played. (p. 126)

Mere diversification of ownership, however, will not ensure diversity of news, views and programming. The BBC (British Broadcasting Corporation) is not privately owned. It proclaims neutrality and impartiality and claims that other than during World War II, it has taken a non-partisan position and maintained neutrality. Yet, the BBC itself cannot be absolutely impartial when it has to deal with British foreign policy, as happened in the recent Iraqi crisis (April 2003). The BBC repeated the British Foreign Secretary's assertion and the Prime Minister's declaration that Iraq had stockpiles of weapons of mass destruction (WMD) on the eve of the US–UK attack on Iraq. Of course, the BBC has taken up the David Kelly issue seriously, but that is no consolation to the thousands of Iraqis who have lost their lives and property; nor is it any consolation to the families of hundreds of US soldiers killed in Iraq.

In June 2003, the BBC took exception to the British Prime Minister's declaration in April and highlighted his prevarication. Although it is to the BBC's credit that the PM was challenged after two months, it is not creditable that it rushed with undue haste in April 2003 to support official British foreign policy based on 'imaginary' threat of non-existent weapons of mass destruction. Reports of the UN weapons inspectors and the CIA's own revelations in September/October, 2003 established the non-existence of WMD in Iraq. This is what usually happens on the international scene. The media of a country more often than not support its official foreign policy. (This has been corroborated in the case of the reporting of the Iranian Revolution in 1979 [Vilanilam 1989].

If this is the case with an autonomous and non-profit institution such as the BBC, we cannot expect more neutrality, impartiality and objectivity in the news and views presented by wholly private agencies that operate strictly for profit. Conglomeration and consolidation of media ownership will only make the situation worse. It will not help the cause of truthful dissemination of facts among citizens.

The media ought to serve the cause of truth and public interest, and not bend the truth for private advantage. The present system of concentrating ownership in fewer and fewer hands is not conducive to such a principle. The decision-makers of the world are in a way wired to 24-hour news channels such as CNN and BBC.

Many consider even those who work in the commercial media socially useful elements providing competition of thought. According to McNair, 'The media supply information forming the *public sphere* (a phrase used by Jürgen Habermas), communally accessible communicative spaces in which information, ideas and opinions can be debated and exchanged as a precondition for rational collective decision-making.' However, he also suggests that this dominance paradigm or liberal pluralism is the basis of the practical performance of the media in capitalist systems and it is characterized by exploitation, injustice and inequality (McNair 1998: 21).

In the economic system that prevails in India, social communication does not serve the bulk of the citizenry, but the dominant, private, selfish interests of about 10 per cent of the total population. Indian society is stratified along lines of caste, class, sex and ethnicity. The communication system in the country seems to be promoting the interests of the rich, the male and the members of the higher ethnic groups, who try to imitate lifestyles in affluent societies without much regard for the large majority of the population who continue to be poor, illiterate and unaware of their human rights. Some of the educationally forward sections of the backward communities (the so-called 'creamy layer') try to imitate the rituals and practices of the higher social groups for social acceptance. M.N. Srinivas called this process of upward mobility 'sanskritization'. The media sometimes promote the social myth of caste superiority, through appropriate messages in films, television serials and newspaper features that give wide publicity to purely mythical and irrational rituals and superstitious practices—all in the name of religion. The numbers of full-page advertisements of local and regional religious festivals in national newspapers (local editions) and of sponsored television programmes have increased several-fold in recent years. This clearly indicates that the media exploit the 'religious fervour' of forward sections of the backward castes as well as the hidden agenda of forward communities to augment advertising revenue.

Some of the media are owned and operated by the nouveau riche who have amassed substantial wealth from *abkari* and other businesses where shady dealings are not uncommon, with the result that the principles that motivated journalists of a previous era often no longer apply to their work in practice.

Recruitment of media workers is also not always above board. Even in old, established newspaper organizations, young men and women belonging to the privileged sections of society are recruited and given in-house training aimed at making them sellers of a product rather than upholders of serious socioeconomic principles. Business management principles are more applicable in such situations because what counts in media organizations these days is profit.

What linguists and sociologists such as Noam Chomsky have described as the propaganda model of media is also true of most Indian media, as they are subordinated or pressed into service to uphold the values of the elite. Chomsky, for example, has written:

> The media serve the interests of state and corporate power, which are clearly linked .... The mainstream media not only allow the agenda of news to be bent in accordance with state demands and criteria of utility; they also accept the presuppositions of the state without question. (1989: 5)

However, the media owned and controlled by the rich (both individuals and companies) have varied content these days because they try to reach the maximum number of people in order to fix higher advertisement rates for commercial matter and thus earn greater revenue (rates are related to the circulation numbers and reach of the media). This competition for varied content has great import for media freedom.

Although there is more pluralism and variety in media content these days, the media are also under pressure from different social determinants. These determinants include proprietorial demands, market forces, commercial priorities, political pressures of the ruling and opposition parties, government censorship and lobbying and regulation. They also include new and constantly changing technological imperatives such as electronic news gathering (ENG), the Internet, editionalizing, computerization, professional culture (ethical and aesthetic codes and conventions), and subjection to a hierarchy and chain of command based on a 'pecking order' and to strategies of news management by public relations outfits having close connections with proprietorial interests. Thus mass media in India, like media in other countries, are affected by the socioeconomic, political, technological and cultural environment in which they function. All these environmental forces may not work all at once on a given medium; rather, a few of them may come into play, depending on specific situations and the interests at stake.

Communication is never neutral. Like other organized human activities it is essentially ideological. The media construct a reality based on their own values, beliefs and priorities. Communicators' depiction of truth is influenced by these environmental forces. Their accounts may lack the 'empirical depth and methodological rigour of science' (McNair 1998: 11). We have to set the different media products within this larges context.

Media Output

The sociological view of all media output is that all of it, despite claims of truthfulness and a realistic reflection of society, is more a construction than an exact reflection of reality. And this constructed reality has the stamp of the intellect, technology, economics, politics, culture and history of the environment where it is constructed. Despite their claim to the contrary, journalists and other communicators in society are not entirely 'free agents' as they cannot be totally free from their professional and social environment.

Finally, we cannot ignore the extra-media social actors (that is, persons or their organizations which are not themselves part of the media) who exert their pressures on media organizations and media professionals. This group includes politicians, lobbyists, religious heads, sports and cinema celebrities, the police and the trade unions. All of them compel media workers to publish their viewpoints.

We have examined in some detail the impact of various socioeconomic and political forces on the media and their institutional set-up. We have also discussed the functions of the media of mass communication. Let us now look at the dysfunctions of mass communication.

Dysfunctions of Mass Communication

In the 1950s, Robert Merton, an American media sociologist, suggested that in addition to functions, the media also have dysfunctions. He said that some consequences of communication were manifest, and others were latent. Not all of these consequences were positive. Undesirable consequences of the media, although unintended, had their dysfunctional effects. He cited the example of a public health campaign, which is basically good and desirable, but can have the opposite effect by triggering public confusion and fear. Some people might be frightened about the results of a medical check-up; for such people, the public health communication can become dysfunctional (Merton 1957).

Mass communication bestows 'prestige' or 'status' on certain individuals, whose news or photographs appear in the media. On the other hand, there are people who chase the media and media workers for publicity. Paul Lazarsfeld and Robert Merton (1948) spoke about the *status conferral function* of the media, which really is a dysfunction. Those whom the media publicize include not only celebrities, but also manipulators of publicity and, on occasion, criminals of various hues.

Lazarsfeld and Merton also refer to the 'ethicizing' function of the media. They draw attention to the fact that the media enforce as well as reinforce social norms. This can become a dysfunction since norms are sometimes reinforced in such a manner that social change becomes almost impossible. (1948: 95–118). The socioeconomic, religious and communal interests of media controllers may cause them to emphasize certain norms in the media and enforce them through repetition—this too can be a dysfunction.

The mass media's status-conferral function is at the base of publicity and public relations. Ethicizing, as critics point out, is the basis of social control by the controllers of the media.

In fact, every function can also become a dysfunction in certain situations. For example, surveillance is beneficial in most circumstances but it is threatening under a dictatorship. In most cases, 'unconnected news [i.e., not relevant to the media user] about the world potentially threatens the structure of any society', said Charles Wright.

Wright also says that unfiltered news about conditions prevailing in other societies can motivate locals to clamour for a change, whether that change is sought through rebel action or other means.

Even a fictionalized account of an event can foment panic, as demonstrated by the classic example of Orson Welles' dramatization of H.G. Wells' *War of the Worlds*. Welles' radio rendition of the novel caused several hours of panic in the US. Listeners drove into the hills for safety, believing that there really had been a Martian invasion! An unexpected consequence of mass communication, indeed!

Another dysfunction is 'narcotization' or 'desensitization'. Repeated reporting of heinous crimes in the media can desensitize people who are fed an overdose of crime news; they get fed up and stop reacting to such crimes as long as they are not individually affected. Social problems no longer move citizens to righteous indignation; citizens become benumbed.

Media, more often than not, try to cater to the tastes and opinions of a diverse public and thus please all and sundry. This naturally makes them keen to avoid controversial issues. Social criticism becomes rare, although individuals are eulogised, or penalized selectively for media proprietors' personal gains or out of spite. Because of their lukewarm attitude to real social problems and the profit imperative, media may choose to take extreme positions—such as supporting socially divisive practices in the name of religion or nationalism—in the search for greater circulation or viewership. 'The consumer of predigested ideas, opinions and views becomes an ineffectual citizen, less capable of functioning as a rational man', says Wright (1959: 21).

The mass media take it as their duty to transmit culture through entertainment and news and features. Can they also handle the process of socialization? Can they take up the responsibility of character-building, education, defining normal social behaviour and so on, which are matters usually handled by parents, family elders, teachers and local social leaders? How far can the media go? Is social activism healthy for, and to be expected from, the media? Do the media appeal to the baser instincts of media users in order to deliver the maximum number of clients for the advertising fraternity? Do the media exist for the people or for the advertisers?

Some Experts' Views on the Media

Before we close this chapter, let us briefly examine the opinions of some famous journalists and media sociologists of the 20th century. Many people think that a newspaper or TV news programme gives all the important news of the previous 24 hours. This myth has to be broken. Any news organization in the world will testify that there is a vast selection process going on every single day under the supervision of trained personnel and what they finally select, process and present is what we read, see or hear. What comes before media users is not raw news, it is constructed by a large team of professionals.

Walter Lippmann, a famous journalist of the early 20th century, once said:

Every newspaper when it reaches the reader is the result of a series of selections as to what items shall be printed, in what position they will be printed, how much space each shall occupy, what emphasis each shall have. There are no objective standards here. There are conventions. (1922: 268)

Another sociological truth is that the media are as much influenced by society as society is influenced by the media; the impact is mutual and continuous. As Melvin DeFleur has said:

The communication process is utterly fundamental to all of our psychological and social processes. Without repetitively engaging in acts of communication with our fellows, none of us could possibly develop the human mental processes and human social nature that distinguishes us from other forms of life. (1970: 76).

But when society ignores the fundamental aspects of communication and concentrates on mass communication, several important fundamentals of social life are either totally evaded or distorted. We have already seen how mass communication occupies only a small segment of the Communication Pyramid.

Communicators, according to sociologists, have to answer basic questions such as:

- Does communication have any role to play in bringing about structural changes conducive to the liberation of human beings from centuries of oppression, misery, poverty, ill-health, illiteracy, unemployment, non-utilization or under-utilization of natural, God-given talents in human beings?
- Does communication through the mass media currently contribute to the strengthening of political and social oppression, economic misery, cultural stagnation or psychological subjugation to feelings of fatalism and inferiority in a large section of the population?
- Does it promote social harmony, egalitarianism and communion among human beings?
- Does it promote willingness to share one's extra resources with others who live in worse circumstances for want of adequate social mechanisms based on social justice?

If social communication subjects itself to 'technological imperatives' that have from the Industrial Revolution onwards affected the course of human history, it cannot extricate itself from the mammoth media organizations directed and controlled by small but powerful segments of society.

Mass communication is of comparatively recent origin in the history of humankind. It is, as stated before, only one of the levels at which human communication takes place. All communication efforts are connected to the socioeconomic, political and cultural environments in which they are made. But additionally, mass communication is global and the messages conveyed through mass media sometimes appear to be aimed at manipulating or preserving the status quo.

Mass communication is communication of mass-produced messages to mass audiences consisting of millions of people who do not gather at any particular place but individually receive the messages sitting at home or in their offices. The messages are produced by trained professionals in organizations specially formed by private entrepreneurs or public/government/ autonomous bodies that invest millions of dollars for the production and dissemination of those messages.

Mass communication is the product of modern science and technology, which are themselves products of the capitalist system. It employs the latest technology for the production and transmission of messages involving vast and complex networks of electrical, electronic, cable, fibre-optic and satellite-based systems of communication. It also employs huge social science research mechanisms, which use sociodemographics and psychographics to assess the best methods for capturing the largest audiences for particular messages.

Mass communication did not evolve in a natural way in many media-poor countries, including India. It aims at capturing markets, especially elite sections of the population who can afford the thousands of products advertised by the mass media. Because of the global character of all mass media, local media focus on the priorities set by the global media. The primary objective of the mass media seems to be to influence its users, economically, politically or culturally. Herbert Schiller believes that the media carry 'messages that intentionally create a false sense of reality and produce a consciousness that cannot comprehend or wilfully rejects the actual condition of life, personal or social' (1973).

George Gerbner looks upon mass communication as a process that is entirely different from that of communication, and draws our attention to 'the rise of the industrial and centrally managed discharge of massive symbol-systems into the mainstream of common consciousness'. According to him mass public communication is carried on through messages that are 'largely mass-produced and/or distributed by complex industrial structures'. He thinks that the members of a public born in a particular cultural context select and interpret messages in a certain way. Their selection and interpretation depend on the system of messages that regulate social relationships. Such cultivation and public acculturation is carried on through the massively mediated messages which over a long period of time provide a 'functional perspective of *existence* (what is), *priority* (what is important), *values* (what is right and wrong) and *relationships* (what is related to what)' (Gerbner 1985: 13–25).

The media of mass communication, according to Gerbner, are in fact ways of selecting, composing, recording and sharing stories, symbols and images. In the long run, they become social organizations acting as 'governments' or authoritative decision-makers for the people. They may even assume the role of dictators of norms for media users, and act as the cultural arms of powerful business corporations.

In the context of India, a country of millions who are impoverished and information-poor, the same media are 'instruments of conquest' (in Paulo Frier's terminology) for the elite. This small minority of educated, socially superior, economically better off people are heavy media users and they sustain the mass media system. Their interests, values, priorities and relationships are reflected in the messages frequently transmitted through the media.

It will not be incorrect to assume that mass communication in the context of media-poor countries is communication 'from the few to the few' whose interests are identical. Its messages are normally intended to protect and maintain the social order, which unfortunately goes against the interests, needs and priorities of the many.

Thus the socioeconomic environment is an important determinant of mass communication activities and media institutions. The social aspects of communication/journalism can be approached within the twin perspective of the social structure and its effect on the media, and the social effects of the media on society.

Social Structure

Indian society consists of five basic groups: Three groups are considered high caste—Brahmins, Kshatrias and Vaishyas, traditionally the priests, military class and business people—and the fourth group consists of the low-caste Shudras, who until recently were considered untouchable but even now suffer various social handicaps.

Brahmins are still considered the highest caste, and the Kshatrias by virtue of their royal status (although royalty has been abolished) are still powerful. A sizeable percentage of the members of the Indian Parliament and state legislatures is either Brahmin or Kshatria. Vaishyas, being members of the business community are, by and large, financiers and industrial magnates. There are, however, regional differences; in the south, there are powerful business houses run by people belonging to all castes. Shudras are mostly labourers, agriculturists, small farmers and petty traders. They are not big landowners. Much of the cultivable land is under the ownership of the higher castes although there are Shudra landowners in some parts of the country.

In addition to these four groups there is a fifth group of the casteless, meaning they are outcastes, mostly menial workers such as scavengers, who are often treated as slaves. Although they are listed in a schedule of the Indian Constitution and earmarked for special treatment along with tribals, the attitude towards the lower castes among the higher castes, even today, is one of superiority.

The purpose of giving special treatment to certain groups such as the scheduled castes (SCs), scheduled tribes (STs) and other backward communities (OBCs) was to reduce the impact of the handicaps that have historically held them back and to bring them up to the level of the other caste groups, at least socially. Unfortunately, the objective has not been fulfilled. Instead, more and more groups are nowadays agitating for their inclusion in the schedules for access to privileges. Thus a very haphazard categorization of human beings is going on in India. This has a certain influence on the Indian media. They prefer to highlight all the caste agitations but ignore the root economic causes.

Pseudospeciation[1] seems to be the delight of the media, which have forgotten all these decades to look at human beings as human beings. Even during government elections, religion, caste, sub-caste and other social factors are given a great deal of emphasis, as evidenced by media reports during the 2004 elections; issues of governance get a lower priority. The class character of the media may have something to do with this kind of media treatment. The problem of pseudospeciation is compounded by reservations in college admissions and government jobs for certain caste groups. This unhealthy practice in Indian polity will perpetuate caste and religious rivalry for decades to come.

Women, who form half the population, also suffer many handicaps. Although the Indian Constitution does not allow discrimination against any individual or group, in practice many millions are treated as unworthy of moving with 'caste' people. Unfortunately, women happen to fall into this lower category. Women do not have sufficient representation in the Legislative Assemblies and Parliament.[2]

The media do not oppose social reform movements in different parts of the country, but when policies which will bring about meaningful structural changes, such as land reforms in particular, are discussed, their enthusiasm diminishes. The media generally try to please all caste groups and political

---

[1] A well-known term first used by Erich Fromm. It means looking at people belonging to groups other than one's own as 'other species'.

[2] The new Indian government elected in May 2004 has announced its intention to introduce the Women's Reservation Bill, which promises to reserve 33 per cent of the seats in Parliament and the state legislatures for women. In this, the government is treating women as candidates for affirmative action, like socially-disadvantaged caste groups.

groups by publicizing even unimportant activities. Their attitude to religious revivalism and irrational practices is also ambivalent, to say the least. They give high visibility to social ceremonies to please individuals and leaders of social groups who have an axe to grind. Even when some space in the print media or time in the electronic media is given to social problems, there is no attempt to bring media users' attention to harmful social practices in a sustained manner.

Serious issues such as the rehabilitation of people displaced by development projects, the improvement of primary and secondary education, developing a scientific attitude to religious and social practices, discovering the underlying causes of communal clashes, and so on, do not receive substantial attention in the media. What seems to be more important for the media is often a series of spicy reports and pictures, advertisements and interesting or entertaining tidbits.

The Indian media, like media in many rich countries of the world, love controversy and indulge in 'statement journalism'. They print or broadcast opposing statements without attempting to investigate and bring out the truth. Statements from various self-styled 'spokespersons' create a smokescreen and confuse media users who do not have the will or the time to sort out all the statements. The truth gets obscured by a volley of hot controversial statements. The main issues are thus forgotten; side issues, unwanted arguments, unimportant sidelights and even trivia appear centre-stage.

The Indian media are of, by and for the urban (more specifically, metropolitan) people. They are owned by the affluent and run by people whose major interest is in capturing the advertisement market. They turn to the countryside and the rural poor only during elections and when something sensational or something that challenges the established order occurs.

The major part of the circulation of the print media and the reach of the electronic media is confined to the four or five metropolitan cities, two dozen state capitals and a few big industrial towns. But most Indians live in small towns and villages. The media report or cover mostly politics and government activities. Their surveillance of the political and socioeconomic environment is quite useful to the business and industrial sectors. Their interest in restructuring Indian society in accordance with the goal set out in the Constitution is purely incidental. Priorities change according to the agenda set elsewhere by global financial institutions.

Though there is a great deal of McLuhanese in decision-makers' pronouncements, such as 'global village', 'think globally and act locally', the full implications of such catchy phrases are not explained by the media to the media users. Offering realistic interpretations within the Indian context ought to be one of the major duties of Indian media, especially in the current environment of liberalization, privatization and globalization.

The top 10 per cent of Indian society enjoys more than 75 per cent of the nation's wealth. The so-called 'middle class', consisting mainly of salaried people, takes up 15 per cent of the wealth. The remaining 10 per cent of the wealth is shared by almost 90 per cent of the people! It is in such a lop-sided development scenario that the media of communication are placed. Without recognizing this vital economic truth, there can be no realistic discussion of social communication through the mass media.

The phrase 'social communication' was first used in the Vatican document *Inter Mirifica* (December 1963). It embraces not only the mass media but all instruments or means of communication including public announcements, posters, advertising, audio tapes (videotapes became popular only later), gramophone records and so on. It stresses human communication—interpersonal, individual as well as group. It stresses the limited meaning of communication as exchange of messages using traditional or modern technical means but avoiding the intrapersonal aspect. It looks upon the media as God-given instruments to attain the social goal of communitarianism and communion.

A warning given by the Norwegian scholar Johan Galtung is worth noting in this connection. While recognizing the importance of social communication, Galtung points out that the emphasis is still on the producer of messages, the media, and that the producer has not changed. The producer's concept of news, for example, has not undergone any change despite the sea changes that have occurred in the recent history of humankind. 'News' is what the news producer decides or characterizes as news most of the time. Criteria such as timeliness, relevance, proximity, and socioeconomic, cultural and political status may influence that decision. Since, however, thoughts like 'What will appeal to the media user?', 'What is important to the media user?' and 'Give the public what it wants' predominate in newsrooms, the ultimate criterion in the selection of news is 'saleability', as decided by the editor or editor-publisher.

The product of social communication has also not changed, whatever the medium used. 'There is', says Galtung, 'more elitism, personism and negativism than ever before'.

> The front page of a newspaper degrades itself, its journalists, its readers and all those concerned, when it represents rape and murder as the major constituents of world society. And this is sometimes called the personal touch! (1984)

The media, unfortunately, support negative rather than positive thinking.

We have discussed in this chapter the meaning of communication and mass communication; we have also presented the sociological implications of concepts frequently encountered in our field, namely, mass, journalism, the structure of Indian society, the modern systems of electronic transmission of ideas, and the impact of communication on society. We have examined the functions as well as the dysfunctions of mass communication and the sociology of the mass media. It is within this conceptual framework that the historical evolution of mass communication in India is treated in the following chapters.

early years of the print media

*t*he earliest known journal was the *Acta Diurna* (Journal of the Day) which was the name given to the handwritten news bulletins distributed in the Forum Romanum. The Forum was Rome's meeting and market place. This was in the 1st century B.C., during the time of Julius Caesar.

The first printed newspaper appeared in Peking (Beijing) in the 8th century A.D. The Chinese did the printing using separate wooden blocks for type, which could be used over and over again. Pi Sheng (Bi Sheng) invented printing from movable type almost half a millennium before Johann Gutenberg, considered the inventor of movable type printing in Europe.

Although the Koreans followed the Chinese in the art of printing from movable type, for some reason printing did not receive wide popularity in Asia. The other requirements for printing, namely, printing ink and paper, were developed in China and Egypt. But the whole process of printing had a stunted growth in Asia. The Europeans, on the other hand, used the new process on a large scale.

Europe benefited from the popularization of printing, which led to the advent of affordable books and popular newspapers. This also led to the democratization of communication. Knowledge began to move out of the precincts of the priests and the aristocracy and into the hands of first the middle classes and eventually the artisans and merchants who became empowered during the Industrial Revolution.

Printing led to the third major revolution in communication, the first having been the development of human speech some 35,000 years ago and the second the art of representing sound in written form using an alphabet.

With the spread of printing, libraries and schools sprang up. Books, libraries and higher education—all these led to major political, socioeconomic and cultural changes in Europe.

The new modes of agricultural and mechanical production, migration of people from rural areas to industrial towns, rapid changes in social and cultural life and scientific and technological inventions led to new methods of communication among people. Ideas once considered sacrosanct and hence inaccessible to the lower rungs of society began to be questioned and knowledge seeped through the different layers to the lower levels. Democratization of communication meant strengthening of democratic ideas. Political democracy led to economic democracy and social reorganization, step-by-step. Dissemination of ideas was part and parcel of this sociopolitical and economic change.

In all this, the newsletters produced in various sizes and at different frequencies played an influential role in Germany, Holland, France and England during the 16th, 17th and 18th centuries.

By the early 18th century, political leaders realized how powerful an instrument the periodicals were for spreading ideas. Many of them began to produce their own papers to propagate their ideas and influence people. A new force was detected in society, namely, the force of *public opinion.*

Most of the newspapers of the 18th century were political and were owned by different political parties such as the Whigs and the Tories in England. Political parties also ran newspapers in the US. Consequently, the journalism of the period was largely political in nature and thus the impression, justifiable to a great extent, was created that journalism was an adjunct of politics.

The first regular printed newspaper of Europe is considered to be *Avisa Relation oder Zeitung,* which commenced publication in 1615. The first newspaper of England was the *Weekly News,* that lasted from 1622 to 1641. The next paper there was a fortnightly, the *Daily Courant,* that started publication in 1702.

The first printing press in the Americas was established in South America by Juan Pablos, a Spanish printer, in 1539. Here, too, the growth of printing and journalism depended on political, social (including religious), economic and cultural activities.

Boston, capital of the Massachusetts colony, became an active centre of printing in the 17th century. The Puritans imported the first printing press to New England in 1638 to supply printed materials to Harvard College. Soon colonies on the eastern seaboard of North America became great centres of political and religious activities. The earliest newspapers of the United States appeared towards the end of the century. Massachusetts, Pennsylvania, New Jersey and New York became active centres of education and journalism, books and pamphlets were printed and libraries established.

The very first newspaper in the US was *Publick Occurrences—Foreign and Domestic,* published by Benjamin Harris, a bookseller in Boston, in 1690. Harris could not continue publication as he was imprisoned by the British authorities for printing without 'prior consent'. Then came another newspaper, the *Boston Newsletter*, in 1704. James Franklin, brother of Benjamin Franklin, published the *New England Courant* in 1721.

One of the remarkable contributions made by English writers to early journalism was the essay, political or otherwise. Famous English essayists such as Joseph Addison, Richard Steele, Dr Samuel Johnson and others either contributed essays to their own publications or to periodicals published by others. They wrote on contemporary issues besides literary topics. Similar contributions across the Atlantic were made by Benjamin Franklin, Thomas Paine, Thomas Jefferson, Alexander Hamilton and others.

These early journalistic efforts had serious political significance, as they led to revolutionary political thoughts and movements both in England and the US during the 17th and 18th centuries. The Glorious Revolution in England (1688), the American Revolution (1775-76) and the French Revolution (1789) owe much to the radical and rational thoughts of people such as Hume, Locke, the Pitts, Robespierre, Hugo, Voltaire, Rousseau, Jefferson, Franklin, Paine, Hamilton and others in England, France and the American colonies. These eminent men had their own journals to spread their ideas, or contributed articles to journals published by friends and well-wishers.

Suffice it to say that books, journals and newspapers in Europe and America served to widen the outlook of people and reorient their thinking towards democratic restructuring of their societies.

Let us now turn to what was happening in India during the early centuries.

Emperor Ashoka's pillar inscriptions and rock edicts in different parts of the Mauryan empire during the 3rd century B.C. are considered examples of imperial political communication to the informed and literate sections of the population. Even before Ashoka, a system of news-gathering is referred to in the *Ordinances of Manu* though news-gathering was perfected during the Mauryan period (circa 321-185 B.C.). The Mauryas used it as an intelligence organization of great administrative and political significance under Kautilya's (Chanakya's) supervision (Khurshid 1956 : 9).

Ashoka (272-232 B.C.) used the Prakrit language in his communication on ethics and morals as evidenced by his inscriptions. Prakrit was the forerunner of Sanskrit (the language of learning, refined from Prakrit).

The learning of languages was confined to the high castes, the aristocracy, priests, army personnel and landowners. The majority were illiterate then as even now and the early communication efforts in India did not bring about any change in the social structure. There was no democratic approach even among the top classes. Social, political and economic power was concentrated in the hands of princes and plutocrats and their high-caste advisers, who were also the leading landowners.

Another feature of communication in ancient India was the emphasis placed on oral and aural systems. Learned people were *bahusrut* (people who *heard* and memorized a lot). Of course, writing was done on palm leaves using a stylus, but the written documents were considered too sacred to be touched or used by the lower classes.

The ruling class used certain methods for coding, transmitting and decoding messages secretly through the network of spies employed by all princes, to glean information about neighbouring enemies. The system initiated by the Mauryan emperors continued into later periods. For example, in the 10th century A.D., the Ghaznavi dynasty which established its rule over the Punjab had a system of news collection that was a source of intelligence about the princes of neighbouring areas, the course of battles and the personal lives of generals.

The news-gatherers and news-carriers were part of the administrative and military intelligence system under the Mughal dynasty established by Babur in 1526. According to historians of journalism, news was collected in a well-organized manner under Akbar the Great. In 1574, Akbar established a recording office that helped later medieval historians gather materials for chronicles. The recording office had a number of copyists on its staff, who wrote abridged versions of documents and presented them to the Waquiah Navis, or the newswriter of the court (Khurshid 1956: 9).

Such newsletters were sent through messengers to different army commanders and other important government functionaries. Between these newsletters and modern newspapers was an intermediate phase in news communication, namely, private manuscript newspapers organized by former newswriters who were unemployed. The manuscript newspaper was extant during Aurangzeb's time when soldiers were supplied with such newspapers. There were also other private newsletters written by newsagents employed by merchants and others (Wordsworth 1968: 188–200).

European Connection

A long European era in Indian history was inaugurated towards the end of the 15th century when Vasco da Gama, the Portuguese explorer, landed on Kappad beach of Calicut (Kozhikode) in 1498, six years after Columbus landed on the American continent. Da Gama had landed along with two shiploads of adventurers and traders and one missionary. There is historical evidence for a visit of Roman Catholic missionaries to northern India during the 14th century on their journey to China, but that visit was for a short duration and it did not lead to any long-term intellectual and cultural relations in the region.

The Portuguese developed cordial relations with the Zamorin of Calicut, but eventually moved their headquarters to Goa. They also developed strong centres in Cochin and Ceylon (Sri Lanka) but they had no influence in the interior parts of India. Eventually, they were displaced by the Dutch whose Dutch East India Company had already established trade and military posts in different parts of India and Sri Lanka. The Dutch were ultimately supplanted by the British. What is important for us here is the establishment of the first printing press in India during the Portuguese period.

The First Printing Press in India

According to the historian J.B. Primrose, and the letters of Jesuit missionaries, the first printing press arrived in India on 6 September 1556, and was installed at the College of St. Paul in Goa (Primrose 1939: 242). The letters also mention that the press was originally meant for Abyssinia (Ethiopia), but the Abyssinian project was abandoned for some reason. Some say that a storm forced the ship to land in Goa. Whatever the reason, the first press and the subsequent ones were brought from Portugal. They were used mainly for printing religious literature—tracts, song-books, catechism, pictures—and not for commercial, social or political information, or for newspapers.

The First Indian Newspaper

The first printed newspaper of India was in English, edited and published by James Augustus Hicky, an ex-employee of the East India Company. It was a weekly carrying news of interest to the small community of European, mainly British, settlers in Calcutta. This newspaper, *Hicky's Bengal Gazette or the Calcutta General Advertiser*, also known as *Hicky's Gazette*, the first issue of which came out on 29 January 1780, carried only classified advertisements on the front page, a practice prevalent in newspapers in England.[1] The *Times* of London and many other newspapers stopped the practice only by mid-20th century. The *Hindu* of Madras, too, published only advertisements on its front page up to 1953–54.

---

[1] For details of the advertisements in *Hicky's Bengal Gazette*, see Mishra n.d.: 3–12.

A year and a half after it was first started, *Hicky's Bengal Gazette* was forced to fold up when Hicky published a news item that was scandalous and offensive to Warren Hastings, the Governor-General of the East India Company, and his wife. He was jailed and fined and his newspaper was proscribed.

Many other English language newspapers appeared in the three major provinces of Bengal, Bombay and Madras which were all in the form and style of *Hicky's Bengal Gazette.* Some of them were: *Calcutta Journal, India Gazette, Bengal Harkaru, John Bull, Bombay Herald, Bombay Courier* and *Journal of Commerce.* These newspapers were all weeklies and their circulation did not exceed 400 copies at the most. They dealt mostly with personal news and carried classified personal advertisements. Most publications of the time, with the exception of the *Calcutta Journal* edited by James Silk Buckingham, dealt with the arrivals and departures of Europeans, the timings of the steamers and the personal domestic needs of European settlers in the three major metropolitan cities, Calcutta, Bombay and Madras. According to Moitra many of them were scurrilous and scandalous publications (1969: 3–12).

Buckingham's paper was a model for later financial and commercial publications. However, there were great similarities in the news content of all Anglo-Indian newspapers. According to Margarita Barnes (1940), newsletters from London, Paris, Stockholm, Vienna and other major cities in the world appeared in the Anglo-Indian newspapers of the time.

English newspapers of the period run by Indians primarily for English-educated elite Indians are called Indo-Anglian newspapers. The first newspaper of this kind was the *Bengal Gazette* started in 1816 by Gangadhar Bhattacharya, a learned disciple of Raja Rammohan Roy. This wholly Indian venture, a weekly, lasted for nearly four years. Bhattacharya marked a trend which became powerful in the latter half of the 19th century; the expression of nationalism through the medium of English to draw the attention of British administrators to the cultural history and philosophy of India. The nationalist editor aimed also to educate his readers about the best in European philosophical thought, without sacrificing the essential tenets of Hinduism and the Hindu way of life. But neither Bhattacharya's paper nor Roy's English fortnightly, the *Brahminical Magazine,* dealt with political or economic issues, although Roy deserves credit for fighting social evils such as *sati* and, human sacrifice. Roy's attempts succeeded when Lord Bentinck banned these social evils in 1829.

English journalism in India rose out of the needs and interests of an alien population in the metropolitan cities that were the headquarters of the British provinces. When it was taken up by Indians it still maintained its orientation towards European life and culture, with an added flavour of Indian culture, religion and a bit of Indian cultural nationalism in the initial years. Later, when the Indian nationalist movement became strong, Indo-Anglian newspapers became totally committed to Indian national needs and political freedom.

Indian language journalism, on the other hand, was wholly oriented towards religious communication in the initial years as it was sponsored and promoted by European missionaries. While recognizing the commendable pioneering efforts of the European communicators in establishing not only the printing press but initiating the process of printing books and journals in different languages of India, compiling dictionaries, vocabulary lists, proverbs and manuals and laying the foundation of journalism in almost all Indian languages, the historical fact remains that the native population did not take to journalism as a useful means to inform different sections of the population about the events and issues that were of importance to them. Coupled with this indifference of the native elite was the view that scholarship was to be judged by the ability of the scholar to memorize the sacred *slokas* and the degree of emphasis laid on *bahusrut* (hearing a lot), as mentioned before. Modern Western knowledge was totally excluded from the realm of scholarship. Moreover, there was opposition from certain quarters to printing and printed material as it was considered *mleccha* and hence untouchable since the ink used for printing contained animal fat.

The Major Indian Language Newspapers

Digdarshan (World Vision) was the first Indian language newspaper. It was started in April 1818 by the Serampur missionaries William Carey, Joshua Marshman, and William Ward, who also started another journal in June of the same year, the *Samachar Darpan* (News Mirror). The latter lasted for 34 years and covered general news as well as items of special interest to local Indian Christians. Besides these two Bengali weeklies, the Serampur trio brought out an English journal, the *Friend of India*.

These efforts aroused the journalistic interest of many Bengali intellectuals such as Rammohan Roy who brought out periodicals in English, Bengali and Persian. Some of Roy's papers were *Sambad Kaumudi, Brahmanical Magazine, Mirat-ul-Akhbar* (Mirror of News), *Bangadoota* and *Bengal Herald*.

Roy (1772–1833), the founder of the Brahmo Samaj, was the leader of the Bengal Renaissance which inspired many intellectuals in different parts of the country to take up social reform movements that culminated in what historians call the Indian Renaissance. Neverthless, the missionaries were the prime movers of Indian-language journalism in most parts of the country. The leading newspapers in various Indian languages are discussed below.

Assamese

Arunodaya, a distinguished journal in the Assamese language, was started in 1846 under the editorship of the Reverend Oliver T. Cutter. About this journal Nadig Krishnamurthy, historian of journalism, has the following comments:

> Besides news items ... [it] contained pictures produced with wood-cut blocks. [It] was published for over 36 years. Learned articles from many eminent writers such as A.R.D. Phookan, Hem Chandra Barua and G. Barua ... adorned this journal. (1966: 284–85)

Gujarati

The newspaper with the greatest longevity in India, *Mumbai Samachar*, was also the first Gujarati newspaper. Established in 1822, it will celebrate its bicentennial in 2022. The paper was started by Fardunji Marzaban as a weekly, and became a daily in 1832. In those days, the present states of Gujarat and Maharashtra were part of the composite British province of Bombay, also called the Bombay Presidency.

Hindi

In 1820, the first bilingual paper, *Gospel Magazine*, came out in Bengali and English and it carried a notice that extracts of the magazine would be available in the Nagari script (used in Hindi). The only copy of 'extracts from the *Gospel Magazine*' printed in the Khari Boli dialect of Hindi is available in the British museum. This is the earliest example of Hindi journalism, if not the first Hindi journal, according to Vedalankar (1964: 76).

The first regular Hindi publication, however, was *Oodunt Martand*, a weekly published by a Kanpur businessman, Pandit Jugal Kishore Shukla, who was settled in Calcutta. Its first issue came out in Calcutta on 30 May 1826. *Oodund Martand* thrived for some time on the controversy between the Bengali magazine *Samachar Chandrika* and the upcountry traders in Calcutta. Although Shukla expected some help from the government, he could not get it and his paper was closed down on 4 December 1827.

Among the early Hindi Newspapers were *Samachar Sudhavarshan* (Calcutta, 1854) which was, incidently, the first Hindi daily, *Samayadant*

Martand (1850–51), *Banaras Akhbar* (1845), *Shimla Akhbar* and *Malwa Akhbar*.

Calcutta was the birthplace not only of English, Bengali and Hindi journalism; the first Urdu newspaper, *Urdu-Akhbar*, was published there in the second decade of the 19th century. Moulavi Akram Ali was its editor. The first Persian newspaper, *Jam-i-Jahan-Nama*, was also published in Calcutta on 28 March 1812. Urdu and Persian newspapers thus preceded the missionary newspapers *Digdarshan* and *Samachar Darpan*, but they did not catch the attention of journalism historians for a long time. We will return to Urdu journalism later.

Newspapers in different languages were started in Calcutta because Calcutta was the seat of government until 1911, when the capital was shifted to New Delhi.

By the middle of the 19th century, there were Urdu and Hindi newspapers in many parts of northern India. The role of Hindi and Urdu papers in the northern provinces in forming public opinion against the East India Company during the Great Rebellion of 1857 has yet to be fully assessed. However, one can be certain that the impetus for journalism provided by the religious communicators and secular scholars paved the way for political rumblings among the English-educated elite of India. The fact that the British government imposed stringent measures against the Indian language press is clear evidence that there was a fear among the rulers of the growing political influence of newspapers.

Kannada

First published from Bellary and then from Mangalore, *Kannada Samachar* was the earliest Kannada journal, according to many scholars. But others think that the first Kannada journal was *Mangaloora Samachar*, the first issue of which came out on 1 July 1843 under the editorship of Herman Moegling of the Basel Mission. It was a fortnightly. Since metallic types and a letter press were available in Bellary, the publication was moved there from Mangalore in March 1844, at which point its name was changed to *Kannada Samachar*. However, it ceased publication on 15 November the same year, owing to financial reasons.

Subudhi Prakasha was the next regular Kannada publication. It was published during 1854–55 under the patronage of the ruler of Sangli near Dharwar. The editor was Khiru Sheshu of Belgaum. Some other Kannada newspapers during the 1850s and 1860s that were published from Mysore and Bangalore: *Kannada Vaartika* (1857), *Arunodaya* (1862), *Mahilaasakhi* and *Sarvamitra*. Some of these were printed on the letter press, although lithography was widely prevalent in all parts of India even at the end of the 19th century.

Malayalam

The first Malayalam newspaper was a lithographed one that came out in June 1847 under the editorship of Hermann Gundert, a German literary scholar, orientalist and religious worker of the Basel Mission. Named *Rajya Samacharam* (literally, News of the Kingdom), this lithographed monthly carried news pertaining to religious activities as well as news of general interest. It was published from Tellichery near Kannur. It was followed by another journal from the same mission, namely *Paschimodayam* (Dawn of the West), which was more secular than the first because it carried articles on science, geography, world history, sociology and other topics. Most of the contents were contributed by Gundert and Frederick Muller. The first newspaper lasted till November 1850 and the second till June 1857.

The third Malayalam journal, *Jnananikshepam* (Treasure of Knowledge), was started in Kottayam in 1848 and printed on the Church Missionary Society Press. Its first editor was the Reverend Benjamin Bailey. Many people consider this the first regular newspaper in Kerala as it was patterned after a regular news publication, with features, special articles and editorials. It is published even today as a religious publication of the Church of South India. None of these early ventures had any substantial circulation. But they deserve special attention as pioneering efforts in Malayalam journalism.

The first secular newspaper from Kerala was the *Western Star* (1860) published from Cochin. Charles Lawson, who later on became the editor of the famous newspaper, the *Mail* of Madras, started his journalistic career in the *Western Star*.

The oldest surviving newspaper in Malayalam is *Deepika*, which was started in 1887 as *Nasrani Deepika* at Kottayam as a voice of the Catholic community in Kerala. Today, the paper is run by Rashtra Deepika, a private company; it has several sister publications and six editions.

Malayala Manorama, the second-oldest newspaper in Malayalam, was started in 1890. It was the first newspaper to be published by a joint stock company, formed in 1888 solely for the purpose of publishing a newspaper. It has 13 editions and a circulation of over 1 million copies. The other major daily newspapers of Kerala, today are *Mathrubhumi*, *Deshabhimani*, *Kerala Kaumudi*, *Mangalam*, *Madhyamam* and *Chandrika* (Vilanilam 2003b).

Marathi

The first Marathi newspaper was a bilingual fortnightly (English and Marathi) which was started on 6 January 1832 by a young professor, Bal Gangadhar Shastri Jambhekar, of Elphinstone College in Bombay. Though it ceased publication in 1840, *Darpan* did remarkable service for the cause of disseminating Occidental knowledge among the Marathi-speaking people of Bombay. Through its English columns, it also brought people's grievances to the attention of the British authorities in Bombay.

But the first all-Marathi journal was *Mumbai Akhbar* (1840). *Jnanodaya* (Dawn of Wisdom), begun by American missionaries in 1842, was vocal in speaking out against social evils such as superstitious customs, child marriage and caste oppression. Historian Vasant Rao has said: '*Jnanodaya* did help the cause of social reform ... the back files of the paper are very useful as a source of social history of Maharashtra' (1964: 54–57).

Oriya

Orissa and Bihar were part of Bengal province till 1912. But the progress in printing and communication made in Bengal remained confined mostly to Calcutta; it did not flow either to Orissa or Bihar. However, the first Oriya magazine, *Jnanaruna*, was published by the Orissa Mission Press in 1849 under the editorship of Charles Lacey. Then came another publication from the same press, *Prabhatchandrika*, under the editorship of William Lacey.

Many people consider that real journalism in Orissa was started by *Utkal Deepika*, which lasted from 1865 to 1936. The paper raised its voice for the separation of the Oriya-speaking areas from Bengal, and criticized the British government for its inaction during the Orissa famine that resulted in the death of more than 20,000 people.

Utkal Sahitya, Bodhadayini and other papers of the 1860s served the cause of Oriya language and literature; they also registered strong protests against corruption and ineptitude among the administrators. *Baleshwar Sambad Bahika*, started in 1868, was a monthly magazine, which became a weekly in 1878. It made a similar contribution to language and literature and took a stand against official corruption and inefficiency.

Punjabi

Although Maharaja Ranjit Singh encouraged the development of Punjabi journalism, the earliest Punjabi newspaper was a missionary newspaper. And it was English missionaries who set up printing presses in Ludhiana and other areas of Punjab. The first printing press in Punjab was established in Ludhiana in 1809. Although the Punjabi Bible was brought out by William Carey, the first Gurmukhi grammar had come out in Ludhiana in 1838. By 1860, other Punjabi grammars and an English–Punjabi dictionary were published in Ludhiana.

Tamil

The earliest printed books in an Indian language were all produced at Tamil presses in Tarangampaadi, Kollam and Goa. Later on, Nagercoil, Madurai, Tanjavur and towns in Tamil Nadu became major centres of Tamil printing. There was printing in the 'Malabar language' as early as 1578. The first periodical, *Tamil Patrika*, a monthly, was brought out in 1831 by the Religious Tract Society in Madras; it lasted till 1833. The next Tamil periodical, a weekly, was the *Dina Vartamani*, published in Madras from 1856 by the Dravidian Press and edited by the Reverend P. Percival. It had a circulation of about 1,000 copies.

The first secular Tamil newspaper was *Swadeshamitran*, started by G. Subrahmania Aiyar in 1882. Aiyar was also the co-founder of the *Hindu* with Kasturi Ranga Iyengar. In 1898 Aiyar left the *Hindu* to devote all his time to *Swadeshamitran* which became a daily in 1892. This was the only Tamil daily until 1917, when *Deshabhaktan* came out. The very names of these early papers indicates how nationalism had influenced them. A great patriot and poet of Tamil Nadu, Subramania Bharati, joined *Swadeshamitran* in 1904 as a subeditor. Bharati was inspired by Tilak and started two week-lies, *India* in Tamil and *Bala Bharati* in English. Soon the British government began to persecute Bharati and he went into exile in French Pondicherry, from where he continued to edit his newspapers. However, as they were banned from Tamil Nadu, the papers soon became extinct. In 1910 Bharati returned to Madras and rejoined *Swadeshamitran*, where he worked until his death at the young age of 39. *Swadeshamitran* lasted till 1970.

The early newspapers and weeklies in Tamil campaigned against superstitions and evil social practices. A social reform movement called Dravida Kazhakam was founded by E.V. Ramasamy Naicker (known also as EVR and as Periyor), who also edited *Dravidan*, which strongly supported the Dravida movement and issued reinterpretations of the Ramayana as the story of colonialism practised on a southern king, Ravana, by a northern king, Rama. EVR also spearheaded the Justice Party, with its anti-

Brahminism and rationalism. *Dravidan* became the mouthpiece of this party. Another publication of the Dravida Kazhakam was *Vitutalai* (Emancipation) which also advocated rationalism and sponsored popular movements against casteism.

EVR's movement inspired later political movements such as Dravida Munnetra Kazhakam (DMK).

Telugu

Kandukuri Veeresalingam Pantulu, known as the father of the renaissance movement in Andhra and the founder of modern Telugu, sparked a social reform movement through his weekly *Vivekavardhini* (1874). He also founded separate journals for women: *Satihitabodhini* (Women's Advocate), *Haasiavardhini* and *Satiavaadini*, all of which strongly advocated ending child marriage, the caste system and prostitution. In addition, they promoted monotheism, popular Telugu, and the rehabilitation of fallen women.

The earliest publications in Telugu were all brought out by missionaries. *Satyodaya* (Dawn of Truth) and others like it were published by the Christian Association of Bellary in the early 1830s. Some of these Telugu publications came out from Madras as in those days parts of what is now Andhra Pradesh were in the Madras Presidency.

One outstanding publication from the Veda Samajam in Madras was *Tatvabodhini* which serialized the Rg Veda.

Urdu and Sir Sayyid Ahmed Khan

Some Urdu newspapers were published in the early part of the 19th century in Calcutta but real Urdu journalism took root in the mid-19th century. Sir Sayyid Ahmed Khan, a great educationist, judge and social reformer, did much for the development of Urdu journalism. Sir Sayyid worked especially for the progress of fellow Muslims but he wanted all Indians to be emancipated through modern education. With this aim in view, he founded the Muhammedan Anglo-Oriental College in Aligarh which later became the world-renowned Aligarh Muslim University.

His contributions to Urdu journalism were perhaps not well known until recent years. He used his own journals for two things—to modernize Muslims and all other Indians through scientific education, and to fight against irrational and superstitious customs and beliefs indulged in by fellow Muslims. A scientific attitude and temper, he believed, was most essential for any community that aimed at progress.

Sir Sayyid founded a social reform organization called the *Tahzib-ul-Akhlak* in 1870. Under the auspices of this organization he brought out a journal of the same name. It lasted for 25 years, and most of its work was done by Sir Sayyid himself. Of the 459 articles published in the journal, he wrote 208—and they were well-researched, erudite articles.

At times, Sir Sayyid's pen was acerbic: he criticized the 'spinelessness' of some religious leaders who chose to remain silent when confronted by serious social issues. He reacted vehemently against hypocrisy and sycophancy. He opposed the fanaticism and evil practices of some leaders who kept both male and female slaves and entertained polygamy, opposed mixed dining (of different castes or sexes) and arrogance based on caste or gender. He criticized the religious bigotry of some of his orthodox friends. His critics opposed his views and even labelled him an atheist.

Sir Sayyid's contribution to Urdu journalism was long-lasting. He made Urdu capable of handling writings in science and social science. He introduced Western literature to Urdu writers through his articles in *Tahzib-ul-Akhlak*, besides translating some English classics into Urdu. Since he had his own printing press, he modernized the Urdu types and reformed the Urdu printing process. Another contribution of his was an Urdu grammar, which was highly useful in standardizing usage, a factor essential for the growth of journalism. Many later young writers were indebted to him in all these matters. He exhorted the younger generation to eschew superstitious practices and embrace modern knowledge. He established a scientific society in Ghazipur with the sole aim of creating a scientific temper among young writers and through it undertook several major translation projects. The books this society brought out were useful in improving the farming practices of the time. Sir Sayyid spoke frequently about the usefulness of modernizing production systems in India along scientific and technical lines and advocated the use of Western instruments and tools wherever applicable in agriculture and industry.

Growth of Journalism in the 19th Century: An Overview

The growth and development of journalism depends a great deal on people's literacy and education, as well as the socioeconomic activities in a given cultural and geographical environment. It also depends on the political awareness of the people, especially the educated class.

Towards the close of the 19th century, several colleges imparting science and liberal arts education sprang up in major towns of India. A class of intelligentsia came up in the metropolitan cities and industrial towns. Many who belonged to this group felt that the British liberalism and democratic approach to life were confined to the British islands and that double standards were being followed in the administration of colonies.

The British model of education for the colonies, based on Lord Macaulay's Educational Minute of 1835, succeeded in making the Indian educated class aware of the essential hypocrisy and insincerity in the administration of social justice. Members of this class were also frustrated by the restrictive employment policy followed by the British government. In the princely states also, opportunities were denied to many deserving young people on account of their caste status. It is against this background that we should look at the sudden growth of newspapers and journals in the last quarter of the 19th century.

Between 1860 and 1899, hundreds of newspapers came up demanding freedom of expression and criticizing the repressive measures of the princes and the British administrators. Some liberal Englishmen settled in the British-Indian provinces and the princely states raised their voices against British officials who, with the support of Indian officials and princes, tried to suppress free expression. This motivated many patriots and radical thinkers to start journals demanding justice and fair play. The political unrest in different parts of India eventually led to the formation of organizations for safeguarding the interests of local people and advocating socioeconomic and political reform. Because of all this, journalism received a fillip and it played a significant role in making educated Indians more aware of their rights. The English newspapers such as the *Hindu*, started in Madras in 1878 and the *Amrita Bazar Patrika* started in a suburb of Calcutta during 1868 are examples for this.

In these journals were voiced demands for administrative reforms in recruitment, social justice and privileges for the lower castes. But it took many more decades for advocates of reform to become fully aware of the economic drain that was occurring in India as a result of colonialism.

Although the Indian National Congress was formed in 1885 under the leadership of an enlightened Englishmen, A.O. Hume, it continued as a memorandum-submitting, upper-middle class organization until the advent of Mahatma Gandhi. However, expression of discontent and demands for political reforms were made through the columns of many newspapers. These publications helped in making the literate Indians and through them a large number of illiterates aware of the need for change.

The Sociological Background of the Growth of Journalism

The biggest problem in the 19th century, as now, was illiteracy combined with poverty, both contributing to the lack of concern for human rights, social justice and economic equality. India has shown a religious and historical indifference down the ages to these questions and her failure to find a suitable solution has lasted far longer than in other comparable countries. With the Indian renaissance of the early 19th century and the attempts of enlightened sections to convey the essential injustices in society through various organizations of communication, the elite gradually became conscious of the role they could play in removing some of the inequalities. The Brahmo Samaj, Prarthana Samaj, Arya Samaj, Ramakrishna Mission and various Muslim and Christian organizations in different parts of the country did much to spread awareness of the social problems confronting the people.

Along with this community awareness grew a sense of nationalism among the elite. The fact that the Brahmo Samaj and Prarthana Samaj published 37 periodicals (mostly in English and Bengali, but a few in Marathi, Telugu, Urdu and Hindi) proves that these social reform movements gave great importance to print journalism as a means to reach the educated classes on an all-India level. They also inspired many later movements for further social reform.

The work of the various social reformers and their communication activities have been discussed elsewhere at greater length. However, certain social reformers and religious thinkers are referred to here inasmuch as their views and work have had a national impact.

Swami Vivekananda, for example, carried on the work of his spiritual master Ramakrishna Paramahamsa, but he did not lose his original fervour for improving the condition of the poor and the suffering in India. What he said in the late 19th century is still valid:

> I consider that the national sin is the neglect of the masses, and that is one of the causes of our downfall. No amount of politics would be of any avail until the masses in India are more well-educated, well-fed and well-cared for ... if we want to regenerate India, we must work for them. (Chatterji 1956: 635)

Aurobindo Ghosh, who was educated in Manchester, London and Cambridge, left his teaching post at a college in Baroda and joined a secret revolutionary movement at the time of the Bengal partition in 1905. He advocated radicalism through his journals *Bandemaataram*, *Karma Yogi* and

Dharma. In 1910 he moved to Pondicherry, in those days a French territory, established an ashram which eventually became world-famous, and retired from politics. He continued his journalistic efforts through his journal *Induprakash*, to propagate his religious and spiritual along with his nationalistic views, based on the four pillars of swaraj, swadeshi, boycott of foreign textiles and national education. He also used his journals to propagate his political philosophy based on democracy, socialism and pacifism, all of which, he believed, nourished humanism, the core of his philosophy.

The social reform movements in the 19th century were initiated mostly by enlightened men belonging to the upper castes: Rammohan Roy, K.C. Sen, Vidyasagar, Vivekananda, Dayanand Saraswati and others. But there were some reformers who belonged to the lower castes: Mahatma Jyotiba Phule in Maharashtra, Sreenarayana Guru and Sri Ayyankali of Kerala. All these social and religious reformers introduced an ideology of protest, upheld universal brotherhood, encouraged mixed dining and women's and girls' education. They stood for the human rights of the lower castes and worked against untouchability. Besides, they encouraged their caste groups to start industries and businesses that would give them economic security and liberation from monetary oppression practised by the higher castes. They encouraged their followers to opt for an English education. Many of their followers started journals to propagate their ideas (see Vilanilam 1987 for more details).

Despite the great work done by these social reformers in various parts of the country, they were not fully aware of the fact or the scale of the economic drain that was the effect of British rule in India. As we now know, the exclusion of economic realities from the purview of social reform means that lasting social change cannot be bought about. Those who controlled the means of agricultural and industrial production and distribution of material goods essential for sustenance, human dignity, self-esteem and freedom had a free hand in applying an economic philosophy that facilitated such control. Colonialism and colonial institutions succeeded in bringing about appropriate economic, political and military changes which further strengthened that control.

Colonialism and Its Economic Impact on India

International communication and the expansion of colonialism and imperialism proceeded simultaneously. England was gradually growing into a major imperial power not only in South Asia but throughout the world, but imperialism was not England's monopoly. Other Western powers were reaping the benefits of the new economic, political and technological order generally referred to as colonialism.

The new order had its beginnings in the trade and commercial links established in earlier centuries through the efforts of the explorers, adventurers and pirates who were all referred to in history as 'discoverers'. Successive waves of Portuguese, Spanish, Dutch, French and British navigators and sea adventurers established trade links in almost all parts of the world. They went to most parts of Asia, Africa and the Americas and won territories for their respective monarchs. In the 18th and 19th centuries, most major European countries competed with Britain in imperial expansion.

By the early 20th century, France had brought Indochina under its control and occupied Algeria and Tunisia, in addition to sharing Morocco with Spain. The entire continent of Africa had been divided up among European powers—Portugal, Spain, England, Holland, Germany, Belgium and Italy. China escaped total subjugation, but large parts of it came under foreign domination. Even Russia and Japan participated in the gluttony of colonialism. Russia expanded both east and west while Japan flexed her muscles and annexed Korea. But Britain surpassed all others because of her superior technology and systematic planning of military and economic invasions, diplomatic alliances and cultural institutions.

The Indian princes, plutocrats, socioreligious leaders and thinkers who missed what was really happening in the world could not detect the canker that was eating away at the economic vitals of the Indian polity. Internal exploitation of the weaker sections by the stronger ones had been going on for centuries under the very noses of religious leaders who perhaps did not take their eyes off their ancient epics and scriptures, rites and rituals to look around and see the misery of the millions. And the structure of colonialism got reinforced by the steel and concrete supplied by 600-odd native princes.

Britain's manifest destiny was to rule the waves and build an empire on which the sun never set. This idea was to be internalized by the elite of India who could keep the masses under control. For this, the foundation was laid by the East India Company's College at Haileybury, England, where the future officers of the Company (and later on those of the British Indian government) were trained.

More than any economist, it was Adam Smith who provided the colonial economic philosophy through his seminal work, An Inquiry into the Nature and Causes of the Wealth of Nations (1776). Adam Smith did not perhaps advocate rampant rapacity and mindless profit-making, but the imperial powers interpreted his economic theory to suit their course of action.

The Economic Drain from Clive onwards

The Battle of Plassey in 1757 opened the door wide for the East India Company's economic penetration. Its first phase lasted for a century. In 1857 the princely class realized, too late, its folly of permitting access to the Company and tried to make a last-ditch effort to save its honour. But that effort did not succeed and India came under the direct rule of the British government. The second phase of British imperialism in India lasted till 1947 when India gained political independence from Britain.

The economic impact of British rule in India was severe but it was revealed and discussed by the Indian media only in the second and third decades of the 20th century. Native industries were destroyed and thousands of people lost their livelihoods. Peter Worsely has described what happened in this way:

> The plunder under the East India Company and the Company's restrictive economic policies left native industry and commerce in a very feeble condition. Flourishing industries had been destroyed. The export of cotton piece-goods fell disastrously .... At the same time, imports of cotton went up sharply .... The de-industrialization of the economy, and the *drain* (the flow of capital into Great Britain) inhibited the development of local industry .... (1964: 11; emphasis added)[2]

Without the means of support in the villages, and faced with starvation as well as epidemics, men, along with their women and children, were forced to migrate to the cities to look for work. In doing so, they were giving up ancestral homes and lands, traditional social security and the support of the extended family. Many of the cities they went to were sea ports: Bombay, Calcutta and Madras. Former weavers who were lucky enough to find work discovered that they were loading ships bound for London with the raw material that had formerly sustained their own local industries.

While the quality of life for the average Indian deteriorated, British capital flourished. Almost every modern industrial activity originating in Europe had its counterpart or subsidiary in India, but all of it was geared to the quick transmission of instructions from the seat of government to the representatives of the British Raj in various cities and large towns, and for the transportation of military personnel to far-off places where British institutions had to be protected. Local princes and local capitalists also benefited by these new facilities.

---

[2] It was this series of economic events that later on persuaded Mahatma Gandhi to launch a nationwide campaign against British-manufactured textiles and clothes.

Modernization was limited to the metropolitan cities and large industrial towns. The small towns and villages were neglected. This made the migration of rural population to big cities in search of jobs inevitable. As early as 1850, there were jute mills, coal mines and other capital intensive, heavy machinery industries in India. Railway lines connected the big cities to areas where raw materials were available. However, this modernization was superficial; it was beneficial only to a tiny portion of the population. In fact, it contributed directly to a political and economic machinery that cheapened life and brought misery to the majority of the people living in rural areas. While the masses quietly submitted, the wealthy few participated in the increasing economic devastation wrought by British financiers, manufacturers and merchants, and their local agents and collaborators. Indian brokers and financiers did well from all this.

All liberal movements that threatened British control were suppressed. It was evident that the political and military machinery of the British did not view the 'natives' as worthy of freedom of thought, expression and dissent.

After India was formally declared part of the British Empire, English education in India was expanded further through English medium schools and colleges, widening the gap between city-bred and rural Indians. Modern education became the privilege of the upper classes and castes. Illiteracy was the norm in the countryside. Even as late as 1928, only 1.2 per cent of the rural population could read and write (Philip 1932: 75–76).[3]

The small group of English-educated Indians contributed much to the growth of nationalism, journalism and political awareness. The elite who directed the national movement for Independence were mostly products of British Indian institutions. Some of them had been educated in England. They became aware of the reluctance of the British authorities to uphold liberalism and freedom of expression in India. This created a good deal of resentment against British rule.

English education undoubtedly exercised a liberalizing influence on the elite. It communicated the Western rationalism, democratic ideas, scientific thinking and ideals of equality and equal opportunity for all citizens that were enshrined in many English textbooks. Technological changes in production and style of living modernized the creamy layer of Indian society. But, as indicated before, any modernization effort carries within it two kinds of seeds: one kind generative and the other destructive. While most of the newly Anglicized Indians were satisfied with British rule, a substantial

---

[3] The percentage of literacy varied greatly from 30, the highest, in Travancore (south Kerala) to 0.15 in the United Provinces.

number became conscious of certain unjust practices of British administrators, particularly of the blatant inequalities in the administration of justice. Several of them wanted to know why educated Indians had to go to London to take the Civil Services examinations. A few wanted to know why Europeans in India could not be tried by Indian judges however serious their crime might be; or why Indians who were equal to Europeans in educational qualifications should be content with lower government jobs. Were Indians not intelligent enough to take up higher posts? Why were the top jobs always reserved for the British all the time? Even those wealthy Indians from the British Provinces who could afford to go to England and secure high ranks in the examinations were by and large denied the top jobs.

This purely middle- and upper-middle class discontent was aggravated by British writers and Anglo-Indian newspapers that gave uninhibited expression to their sense of racial superiority and divine destiny as rulers of the world. Rudyard Kipling, the British writer and journalist (he worked for the *Lahore Civil & Military Gazette*) said, for example, that 'the responsibility for governing India has been placed by the inscrutable decree of Providence upon the shoulders of the British race'. The same racial conceit came out through his now notorious phrase, 'the White Man's burden'. Years later, two famous journalists noted how Britain had cultivated a conviction in every Indian Civil Service (ICS) officer that he belonged 'to a race which God had destined to govern and subdue' (Collins and Lapierre 1978: 17).

Neither the Congress leadership in the early years nor social reformers of the same era were aware of the colonial economic exploitation that was going on in the country, although the latter organized philanthropic movements to fight poverty. However, two scholars who were aware of the economic ills advanced theories on poverty and its causes. They were Gopalkrishna Gokhale, whom Mahatma Gandhi considered his guru in the earlier years, and Mahadev Govind Ranade.

Gokhale was an eminent social worker and moderate political leader. His Servants of India Society inspired service-minded youth in many parts of the country. Ranade, a founder member of the Indian National Congress, was a judge of the Bombay High Court. He was also a distinguished thinker and economist. Since he had access to government records on farmers, he proposed schemes to establish of agricultural banks so that they could escape the moneylenders.

Both Gokhale and Ranade realized the ills of the economic system followed by the imperialists. They identified the system as the main cause of widespread poverty, especially in rural areas and among small farmers and agricultural labourers. The Indian language newspapers (Marathi, Gujarati and Hindi mainly) and some English newspapers published by nationalists of the time carried their articles. However, the British economic system, propped up by Indian businessmen of the metropolitan cities, was too entrenched to yield to the moderate pressures exerted by Gokhale and others.

Meanwhile, the nationalism of the upper class, English-educated people who were stung by certain job-policies of the British, and the upper-middle class, who were dissatisfied with the British attitude towards some of their religious rituals, came together to show their solidarity against the British. The partition of Bengal in 1905 and the shifting of the capital from Calcutta to Delhi in 1911 were other causes over which both moderates and so-called extremists rallied against the rulers. Gokhale, Ranade, Annie Besant, Motilal Nehru, Pherozeshah Mehta and Dinshaw Waccha were considered moderates. Bal Gangadhar Tilak, Bipin Chandra Pal, Lala Lajpat Rai and Aurobindo Ghosh were called extremists and radicals.

What is important for us here is that some of the moderates and extremists tried to spread their respective economic and political views among the educated sections through pamphlets, journals and newspapers. Others appealed to the lower sections of society through public orations and religious discourses.

Several of these leaders were outstanding writers and editors. They inspired the next generation of freedom fighters who were also writers and journalists in their own right. Jawaharlal Nehru and his father Motilal Nehru started The Independent in Allahabad; later on, Jawaharlal Nehru started the National Herald in Lucknow. Maulana Abul Kalam Azad, patriot and freedom fighter, founded the famous Urdu newspaper Al Hilal. Subhash Chandra Bose, C. Rajagopalachari, and above all Mahatma Gandhi were connected with several newspapers.

Tilak's radical slogan, 'Swaraj is my birthright' and Gandhi's 'Swaraj', 'Swadeshi', 'Ahimsa' and other ideas got wide publicity and acceptance among the elite and the masses because of the journals they edited. Tilak's journals, Kesari and Maratta criticized the British rule in very strong terms. The people living in the rural areas of India learnt about their national leaders' arrests and imprisonments through the newspapers read aloud by the literate to their illiterate compatriots. In those days, radio and other broadcast media were not available in India.

The greatest of all national leaders (and journalists) of the independence movement was Mahatma Gandhi. The basic ideas of Gandhian journalism and philosophy will be examined in a separate chapter along with the new developments in the field of journalism in post-Independence India. But before that, let us learn something about the role of news agencies in national and international communication.

3

national and international news agencies— the backbone of modern communication

*m*odern communication, whether national or international, depends on news agencies. Nationally and globally, the working of the media is influenced by them. If we recognize that the world is at the threshold of another revolution now, we will see that telecommunication (TC) is at the centre of that communications revolution. All aspects of our lives are being influenced by what is happening in the world of TC.

The process of bringing first words, and then words and pictures, from the far corners of the world to the centre of information processing and dissemination started in the 19th century. We mistakenly tend to associate this phenomenon with the 21st century because of the development of e-mail and the Internet in recent years.

Communication through the media has always had an international dimension, which is now strengthened further by satellite communication, cable TV, dish antennae, electronic mail and the Internet—all visible and practical manifestations of global communication.

Historically, the evolution of telegraphic transmission of messages in the mid-19th century can be said to have inaugurated the era of electronic communications. Imperial expansion and colonial subjugation were indirect results of the application of superior communication technology during the closing decades of the 19th century. As Headrick says, communication technologies were crucial in the establishment of European domination of the world during the era of colonial empires. The new communication technologies of the 19th century 'shattered traditional trade, technology and political relationships, and in their place they laid the foundations for a new global civilization based on Western technology' (1981: 177).

Telegraph, telephone, wireless and radio transmission on the one hand, and trains, ships, planes and other means of transportation on the other, facilitated the intercontinental movement of ideas, manufactured goods and raw materials. The very face of international communication was changed by the new technologies of information transmission and transportation of humans and materials. The inventions and the industrial or business enterprises that put them to commercial use opened a new era in communication globally. All the scientific and technological developments moved in the direction of globalization, an economic process greatly aided by the political process of colonialism and imperialism.

The work of hundreds of outstanding people in the world contributed substantially to international communication. Samuel Morse, Alexander Graham Bell, Guglielmo Marconi, Heinrich Hertz, J.C. Bose, Joseph Nicéphore Niépce, Louis Daguerre, George Eastman, Auguste and Louis Lumière, Lee de Forest, Reginald Fessenden, Vladimir Zworykin, John L. Baird, Philo T. Farnsworth, David Sarnoff—all these great men contributed to the growth and development of the various means of internationalization and globalization of communication. Add to this list great mathematicians and engineers such as Charles Babbage, George Boole, William S. Jevons, John W. Mauchly, J.P. Ekert, Claude Shannon and Warren Weaver, and we get an almost complete list of the prime movers in electronic and computerized information and communication technology (ICT).

There are four major technical operations in ICT: photophonics, microelectronics, digital systems and software. Of these, the first three are hardware and the fourth is what 'orders' them to perform certain tasks. In recent years, the division between one medium and another has become artificial or even meaningless. All media have become electronic and hence we live in an era of *media convergence*. Against this background, let us look at the evolution of international news agencies, which have been functioning right from the middle of the 19th century. Some news agencies today are more powerful than media corporations and even national governments!

The oldest agency is the Havas Agency of France founded in 1835, followed by the German agency Wolff, set up in 1849. Although the American agency Associated Press (AP) was established in 1848, it was not an international agency for many years. In fact, only the European agencies worked internationally in the initial years. The first European agency to grow into a network spanning several continents was Reuters, the British news agency.

Reuters

Named after its founder Julius Reuter, who started it in London in 1851, Reuters has specialized in financial and commercial information from the very beginning.

Reuters got together with Havas and Wolff in 1870 and the three agencies signed a treaty to divide the world market among themselves. Eventually, subsidiary agencies joined them, but accepted the leadership of the three. This altered the process of news dissemination throughout the Europe and its colonies in Asia and Africa.

As Thussu has said, 'British control of cable lines made London an uncontrolled centre for world news, enhanced by Britain's wide-ranging commercial, financial and imperial activities' (2000: 21).

Like all news agencies of the world, Reuters' first loyalty is to the country of its origin. All agencies have special obligations to their respective governments; in many cases, the agencies were initially subsidized by their governments.

By the early 1960s, when European influence in the world was on the wane, the European news cartel's hold on the world's nations weakened too. AP and UPI (United Press International) of the US began to spread internationally. Reuters continued to flourish since it had already expanded its activities to all corners of the world. Though it claimed to be independent, Reuters was the unofficial voice of the British Empire first, and then of the United Kingdom and the Commonwealth. In fact, George Jones, Managing Director of Reuters during World War II, was also in charge of cable and wireless propaganda for the British Department of Information. In 1999, Reuters was one of the world's biggest multimedia corporations dealing in the 'business of information'. Reuters is still the leading commercial and financial intelligence source for the British government, according to Thussu (ibid.).

Reuters' main business is not simply transmitting news of daily political events, it also supplies the media with news of financial transactions worldwide, including investment data and commercial rates of commodities, in 23 languages. In short, the world's financial transactions and their impact on the immediate and long-term interests of Britain and its allies are of primary concern to Reuters. Facts and figures are presented with historical and graphic databases, relevant news pictures and news video for television channels and newspapers. Thussu says that such financial information accounts for three-fifths of Reuters' total annual revenue. One may even say that Reuters is now the primary supplier of financial and commercial data rather than of ordinary news.

Reuters is the second-largest news and television agency after AP, with about 2,000 journalists and a total of 26,000 employees in 185 bureaus. The ownership of the agency now rests with the Reuters Holding Company. There is some Indian representation on its board of directors.

The 1999 Annual Report of Reuters (quoted by Thussu) recorded its revenue as £3,032 million. It had regional headquarters in London, New York, Geneva and Hong Kong, and offices in 217 cities. Its website generated 130 million page-views on the Internet in 1999. Today, it provides news and information to 220 or more Internet sites reaching about 12 million users every month. It has a joint venture with Dow Jones of New York, another financial and stock exchange news provider, and the backbone of the Wall Street Journal. This mega agency, in its early phase, used pigeons for carrying news to different regions of Western Europe!

As Boyd-Barrett says, news agencies not only set the international news agenda but also contribute greatly towards the 'globalization and commodification of international information' (Boyd-Barrett and Rantanen 1998). National news agencies are in plenty, but the trend in news values, priorities and judgements is set by the few international news agencies owned by British, American and French media companies. There are Russian, German and Chinese agencies which supply news to other countries but their share is very small compared to the top three (see Table 3.1).

Table 3.1
Working Details of the Three Major Global Agencies: AP, Reuters and AFP

	AP	Reuters	AFP
Worldwide bureaus	237	185	140
Countries covered	112	157	165
Number of languages used	6	23	6
Number of journalists employed	3,421	2,072	1,200
News output in words/day	20 million	3 million	2 million

Source: Thussu (2000: 151).

The Associated Press (AP)

The Associated Press serves more than 15,000 news organizations worldwide with news, photographs, graphics, audio and video materials. It claims that more than a billion people read, hear or see AP-supplied news every day.

AP has a digital photo-network that supplies 1,000 photos a day worldwide to 8,500 international subscribers and, since 1995, a 24-hour continuously updated online news service called the Wire. There are, in addition, a television news service (APTN) and AP Network News, the largest single radio network in the US. AP's various services are available in German, Swedish, Dutch, French and Spanish. Subscribers in other language areas translate AP stories into their own languages.

Many newspapers and radio and television stations have either reduced their intake of news or closed down their news-reporting operations worldwide. AP has filled the gap, selling packaged news to media, and nowadays even to non-members such as governments, non-government organizations, private corporations and industrial or financial institutions.

TV News Supply

The role of Reuters and AP in TV news worldwide is substantial, proving that Anglo-American predominance over global communication is overwhelming in the audiovisual media too. Table 3.2 gives details.

Table 3.2
A Look at Global TV News Dissemination

Global Channels and Ownership	Viewership	Number of Bureaus/ Countries	Number of Correspondents
APTN, Associated Press USA	330 subscribers	110	dna
Reuters TV channel, Reuters Holdings, UK	310 subscribers	93	dna
Cable News Network (CNN), owned by AOL-Time Warner, Inc. USA	221 million homes	32	150
BBC World, British Broadcasting Corporation, UK	135 million homes	42	250

Source: Thussu (2000).
Note: dna=data not available.

Agence France-Presse (AFP)

The Paris-based Agence France-Presse, the third largest news agency in the world, is not far behind AP and Reuters. It originated as the Havas Agency in the 19th century. AFP also supplies news to the media and corporations including banks and governments.

Subsidized by the French government, AFP distributes 2 million words a day (see Table 3.1), 250 news photographs and 80 graphics in English, Spanish, French, German, Arabic and Portuguese. AFP is especially strong in the coverage of the Middle East and Africa. It has regional centres in Washington, Hong Kong, Nicosia and Montevideo.

According to UNESCO, the three main news agencies are the source of news and picture data for about 80 per cent of the world's media users. All three operate in commercial environments. Speed, accuracy and the Western viewpoint characterize of all these agencies (Thussu 2000: 152–53).

Other Major Agencies

UPI

United Press International (UPI), the world's largest privately-owned news source, was part of the American newspaper tycoon Edward W. Scripps' media empire. He founded the United Press (UP) Association in 1907 from earlier regional agencies. William Randolph Hearst, another newspaper magnate, whose newspapers were denied membership in the Associated Press, started his own news agency, International News Service (INS) in 1909. Other news agencies did not last, but AP, UP and INS thrived until 1958, when UP and INS merged into United Press International or UPI (Agee et al. 1979: 75–76).

UPI functioned internationally till 1980. During the 1990s a majority of its shares were taken over by Saudi Arabian royal media interests. Then, in 2000, UPI was bought by the Reverend Sun Myung Moon's Unification Church (members of which are sometimes known as Moonies). In 1999, UPI had 600 correspondents worldwide, distributing nearly a thousand stories daily. Now, UPI's major business is confined to the US.

DPA

Deutsche Presse Agentur is a German news agency, mainly serving the German market. Occasionally, we find stories supplied by it in the Indian newspapers.

EFE

This Spanish agency has its headquarters in Madrid, and has close links with Latin America where Spanish is the major language.

NCNA

China's Xinhua News Agency is also known as the New China News Agency (NCNA). It was founded in 1931. Ever since China opened its doors in 1978, the NCNA has expanded considerably. It has four regional offices, in the Pacific region, Latin America, Africa and West Asia. It has branches in 100 countries and its average daily output is 250 stories.

TASS

This was the official Soviet news agency until the fall of the Soviet Union in 1989–90. The Telegrafnoe Agentsvo Sovetskogo Soiuza (TASS) was re-named ITAR-TASS in 1992. ITAR stands for Informatsionnoe Telegrafnoe Agentsvo Rossii.

ITAR-TASS has 74 bureaus in 62 countries, distributing an average of 105 stories daily. It cooperates with 80 foreign news agencies and also operates a photo service. Under the changed economic philosophy of Russia, ITAR-TASS has entered into joint ventures in operating corporate telecommunication networks based on satellites, microwave and radio transmission, and fibre-optic and cable lines. It also produces multimedia products for subscribers within and outside Russia.

Kyodo

Japan's main agency, Kyodo, has had an English-language service for the past five decades. It produces 200 stories or thereabout daily in nearly 100,000 words.

Other Agencies

Other major agencies include the Islamic Republic News Agency (IRNA) of Iran, Agenzia Nazionale Stampa Associata (ANSA) of Italy, Pertubuhan Berita Nasional Malaysia (BERNAMA), Caribbean News Agency (CANA), Ghana News Agency (GNA), Inter Press Services (IPS) of South America, Middle East News Agency (MENA) and the Panafrican News Agency (PANA) of Senegal.

Indian News Agencies

India has four agencies, the Press Trust of India (PTI), United News of India (UNI), Samachar Bharati and Hindustan Samachar. The first two are

76   mass communication in india

English news agencies and the other two offer news in Hindi and other Indian languages. In 1976, during the Emergency the Indian government amalgamated all the agencies into one umbrella agency called Samachar. After the change in government, the four agencies started functioning separately once again, in 1978.

The Press Trust of India (PTI)

The Press Trust of India was formed in 1949 by the merger of two agencies in operation at that time, namely Reuters and Associated Press of India (API). About 1,300 persons (including editorial, technical and other staff) work in the PTI today. The PTI teleprinter network has a total length of 60,000 kilometres. It has correspondents and bureaus in some important cities of the world, including London, Paris and Washington, DC.

More than 200 newspapers subscribe to the PTI. All India Radio (AIR) and some university departments of journalism as well as certain journalism training centres are among PTI's subscribers.

United News of India (UNI)

The United News of India was started in 1961. It gathers news, pictures and articles, and also has 'exchange' or reciprocal arrangements with foreign news agencies.

Samachar Bharati and Samachar

These two agencies mainly serve the newspapers in the Indian languages. About 80 newspapers in eight Indian languages subscribe to these two news agencies.

Financial News Agencies

Certain news agencies now provide financial services. In the changed globalized and liberalized economic scenario of the new millennium, there is a huge market for financial intelligence. According to UNESCO estimates, the global worth of this market in 1996 stood at $5 billion. Today, that figure must have increased to at least $10 billion.

Besides AP, Reuters and AFP, the new global players in financial journalism are the AP-DJ (Associated Press–Dow Jones) economic news service and AFX News, with a European focus provided by AFP and the *Financial Times* of London.

Knight-Ridder Financial

Knight-Ridder Financial is an international news service that reports on business, finance and economics from around the world, besides supplying regular news to some 80 newspapers belonging to the Knight-Ridder chain.

Asian Info Services

Asian Info Services, a joint venture of the US-based BDI Group and Wanfang Data Inc., China's largest database company, provides daily abstracts of business news from China.

Asia Pulse

Asia Pulse is a joint venture formed in 1996 by major news and information organizations, including Xinhua (NCNA), PTI and Antara of Indonesia, to distribute business intelligence on Asian markets.

Bloomberg News

The most important new player in the financial news business is Bloomberg, which has grown into a major rival of Reuters. Started in the early 1980s by Mike Bloomberg, this agency offers a 24-hour worldwide financial network of news, data and market analysis. By 1999, it had 140,000 users in 91 countries. Bloomberg News is available in English, French, Spanish, German and Japanese. It is syndicated in over 250 newspapers around the world.

Bloomberg Radio and Television Syndicated through more than a hundred affiliates worldwide, Bloomberg Radio reports market news every hour. Bloomberg Television is a 24-hour news channel reporting market news in seven languages. Besides its own programmes, it provides syndicated reports to TV stations.

The Bloomberg Press The Bloomberg Press publishes business books and two monthlies, *Bloomberg Personal Finance* and *Bloomberg Money*. It has a website providing selected content from its own financial service and information gathered from other sources.

News agencies are no longer mere purveyors of information but active participants in the selling and buying of shares and currencies with the added advantage of inside information of vital importance. Before providing financial intelligence, many news services earn substantial income from large-scale trading in shares and currencies. This naturally raises ethical questions based on conflict of interests; the possibility of corrupt practices cannot be ruled out.

We shall now turn to the most familiar news channel these days, namely, CNN, which supplies news and market information worldwide 24 hours.

Cable News Network (CNN)

Among international news channels, the Atlanta-based CNN is the world leader. It is perhaps the world's only 24-hour global news network as it describes itself, but the BBC is still the most influential in Western Europe and the former British colonies.

According to Thussu, 'CNN symbolizes globalization of television journalism, influencing news agendas across the world and shaping international communication.' One reason for CNN's rapid expansion was the use of satellite technology, which helped its founder, Ted Turner, to 'blanket the globe' using a combination of Intelsat, Intersputnik, PanAm Sat and regional satellite signals, within five years of its launch in 1980.[1]

CNN has news exchange programmes with about 100 broadcasting organizations across the globe.

CNN World Report was started in 1987. It was the first Gulf war in 1991 that made CNN a household word throughout the televised world. Its coverage during the second US–Iraq war in April 2003 raised its prestige and influence everywhere.[2]

The role of CNN in integrating the media systems of the former socialist countries into the Western fold is considered very significant. CNN was involved in the 1993 launch of TV6, the first private television network in Russia. And it created history by entering into agreements with China and

---

[1] For details, see Volker 1999. See also Fournoy and Stewart 1997.

[2] The United Nations Television Unit (UNTV), according to Thussu, was one of the most prolific contributors to the CNN World Report 'perhaps because it was related to Ted Turner's 1997 contribution of $1 billion gift to the UN. This gift was the largest such award ever received by the UN in its 55-year-long history.'

Cuba to beam its programmes there. No wonder it received high praise from eminent people such as Jimmy Carter, former president of the US.

But in 1991, CNN 'sanitized' a bloody war by televising just the 'doctored' news in soundbites, news conferences and videos of the war in Iraq. The gruesomeness, cruelty and misery of war, the plight of ordinary Iraqi citizens, especially children, and other such aspects of the war were successfully hidden from viewers in both 1991 and 2003. The 2003 reports were, however, more truthful, perhaps because of the allegations and consequent scandal in the US Congress and British Parliament about officials 'sexing up' reports on weapons of mass destruction (WMD), to convince citizens to support the Iraq war plans.

Although CNN has become the most-sought wartime channel, it has major services other than news of war and catastrophe, including a 24-hour sports news service named CNN/SI (Sports Illustrated) and CNNfn (a financial news service started in 1995).

By the late 1990s, CNN had regional versions for audiences and advertisers in Europe, the Middle East, the Asia-Pacific, Latin America and the US. It also has collaborations or regional units in Germany (CNN Deutschland), Japan (an arrangement with JCTV), Spain (CNN Plus in collaboration with SogeCable), Turkey (CNN Türk), etc. According to Thussu, CNN is now aiming at further expansion in major non-English markets (Thussu 2000: 156–57).

Other 24-hour channels were started by the end of the 1990s, such as BBC World, CNBC Worldwide and MBC (Middle East Broadcasting Centre), a channel aspiring to be the Arabic CNN. There is no doubt that the major broadcasting networks of the world have tried, and will continue trying, to imitate the CNN pattern.

Big national and international news agencies are here to stay, because they effectively serve big and small media of all kinds. But has communication between human beings, between nations and cultures, improved during the past 150 years? Can big media and big technologies bring about a revolutionary change in the minds of human beings? Is there a need to rethink the goals and instruments of communication? Do we have to de-emphasize mass communication and re-emphasize intrapersonal and interpersonal communication? Against this background, we shall now examine the salient features of Gandhian journalism and techniques of communication and also contrast it with the new and 'hi-tech' journalism of the 21st century, which, according to some, has lost its soul. The body of journalism is getting fat but its soul is famished.

4

gandhian journalism and the journalism of the 21st century

$g$andhian journalism was the product of Gandhi's approach to life, his concern for humanity and his deep commitment to the poor, for whose sake he fought for national independence. It was essentially the journalism of communitarianism and humanitarianism. He had certain noble goals that were based on his philosophy of non-violence (ahimsa), self-reliance (swadeshi), self-rule (swaraj) and truth-force (satyagraha). All these were reflected in his journalistic writings and oral communications, and his non-verbal communications (such as his innumerable journeys on foot, *padayatras*, within India, meditation, fasting and prayer meetings).

Realizing the potential of newspapers in moulding public opinion when he was in South Africa, Gandhi started using the columns of the *Indian Opinion* in 1903 to mobilize and educate Indians there. Commenting on the power of the press years later, he described how *Indian Opinion*, his first newspaper, helped him in his political career:

> I believe that a struggle which chiefly relies upon internal strength cannot be wholly carried on without a newspaper. It is also my experience that we could not perhaps have educated the local Indian community, nor kept Indians all over the world in touch with the course of events in South Africa in any other way, with the same ease and success as through the *Indian Opinion* which therefore was certainly a most useful and potent weapon in our struggle. (1950: 142)

A weekly published in four languages—English, Hindi, Tamil and Gujarati—to serve all Indians in South Africa, *Indian Opinion* drew the attention of the authorities to the legal and political disabilities suffered by the Indian community in that country. It, however, made no attempt to mobilize the Indians to work against the British government since in those days Gandhi still had faith in the fairness of the British system and never advocated disloyalty to the British monarch.

Indian Opinion is important from another perspective: it serialized Gandhi's booklet, *Hind Swaraj*, which contained the essential tenets of his political and socioeconomic views as held by him in the initial years of the 20th century. Of course he changed his stance on many issues as the years went by and as the political situation changed. Although he did not write many books, except his autobiography and *Hind Swaraj*, his complete writings and speeches, collected and edited by later compilers, run into more than 100 volumes. The Gandhiana section in many of the world's most important libraries is expanding every year.

After his return from South Africa in 1915, Gandhi began his political life in India. He started three newspapers, all during 1919–20, in defiance of the Indian Press Act. They were the *Satyagrahi* (in Hindi and Gujarati), *Navjeevan* (Gujarati) and *Young India* (English). Later, in 1938, he started *Harijan*, an English weekly. Although all these newspapers essentially reflected his political and socioeconomic views, *Harijan* more than the others, was his mouthpiece.

Harijan contained Gandhi's views on untouchability, village sanitation, rural reconstruction through village industries, women's education, women's rehabilitation, basic education, and the upliftment of all (*sarvodaya*) through employment for every able-bodied person. Therefore, Gandhi himself described it as a 'viewspaper' rather than a newspaper.

None of these newspapers had high circulations except *Young India*, which at one time printed close to 50,000 copies daily, but it was common practice among patriotic editors and Congress workers to copy many Gandhian newspapers (which had not more than 8 or 12 pages) totally or partially and circulate these among the people. In fact, Gandhi himself advised readers to copy and circulate his papers among their friends.

This way of circulating newspapers may perhaps look too low-tech in this age of Internet, fax and copying machines, but one should not forget that even now there are areas in India where there is no circulation of standard newspapers at all.

Gandhi, as editor, was faced with several practical problems besides illiteracy (although those who could read aloud to the rest) and lack of purchasing power among villagers. The repression he suffered was tremendous. A notice to the subscribers of *Young India* (started on 8 October 1919) is revealing indeed:

This paper has not been registered according to the law. So, there can be no annual subscription. Nor can it be guaranteed that the paper will be published without interruption. The editor is liable at any moment to be arrested by the government and it is impossible to ensure continuity of publication until India is in the happy position of supplying editors enough to take the place of those arrested. We shall leave no stone unturned to secure a ceaseless succession of editors. (quoted in Bhattacharya 1965: 34)

Readers of newspapers in the 21st century who are constantly bombarded by commercials about the big prizes in gold ornaments, cars and even flats that can be won through subscription may not be impressed by the Gandhian warning about discontinuity and government harassment, but they cannot ignore the Himalayan obstacles faced by Indian editors during the Gandhian era. Many an editor had to edit and be imprisoned; many publishers had to publish and perish! But phoenix-like, they came back to life, not necessarily in the same place or through the same press. Many freedom fighters and editors had to receive the hospitality of 'His Majesty's hotels', a phrase Gandhi used to describe British-Indian prisons.

The big difference between Gandhi and modern-day journalists is that he considered journalism primarily as service to society and a vehicle for his views on religion, ethics, morality, politics and economics.

Modern-day publishers and editors look upon their work primarily as a business—like any other business, motivated by considerations of profit, economic advantage and social prestige. In his autobiography, Gandhi wrote:

> The sole aim of journalism should be service. The newspaper is a great power, but just as an unchained torrent of water submerges whole countryside and devastates crops, even so an uncontrolled pen serves but to destroy. If the control is from without, it proves more poisonous than want of control. It can be profitable only when exercised from within. (1958: 99)

It is doubtful if this philosophy of journalism will be fully acceptable to press barons of today, especially the first sentence, although his pronouncement on freedom of the press will be totally acceptable to them. In principle, they may accept that freedom of the press is basically freedom of speech and expression for the citizens. In practice, they look upon freedom solely as their freedom to publish anything they want. They guard it jealously, and rightly so. Gandhi, the journalist, was in full agreement with the Jeffersonian and Nehruvian view that if there was a choice between a government without the press and a press without government, he would certainly opt for the latter.

However, service to the people as the sole aim of journalism will not be acceptable to the media moguls of the 21st century who build their media empires in conglomerate or cross media ownership style (see Chapter 1) or in collaboration with foreign media firms primarily for profit. Service to people based on national priorities is secondary or even incidental. Lord Thomson, a 20th-century press baron who is the model for modern newspaper and media magnates such as Rupert Murdoch, openly declared his purpose: he ran his newspapers to make profit and buy up more newspapers to make more profit. 'The bigger the better' is the principle of these businessmen-journalists or journalist-businessmen, whereas 'small is beautiful' inspired Gandhi.

Gandhi was totally committed to the cause of the freedom of India, but he wanted an India free of inequality and exploitation.

My ambition is much higher than independence. Through the deliverance of India, I seek to deliver the so-called weaker races of the earth from the crushing heels of Western exploitation in which England is the greatest partner. (quoted in Bhattacharya 1965: 43)

Towards the end of his life Gandhi was a disillusioned man. One of the causes was his misreading of the essential nature of human beings—who went after positions of power at a time when the country was divided on communal lines, and whose nature was revealed by the inhuman carnage that took place. But a second significant cause of his disappointment was the performance of the press. He did not like the imposition of control on news about Hindu–Muslim conflicts. He wanted the media to uphold the truth about every event. Not long before closing down *Harijan*, he wrote: 'The superficiality, one-sidedness, inaccuracy, and even dishonesty that have crept into modern journalism, continuously mislead honest men who want to see nothing but justice done' (Harijan, 24 October 1942; see also Munshi 1948: 52–53). What a prophetic statement! Gandhi could not have anticipated that what he said about the journalism of the early 1940s would apply to much of the journalism of the world six decades later.

We shall conclude this section on Gandhian journalism by examining his views on advertising, the prop that supports all media in the modern world.

Modern media lean heavily on advertisements. In fact, some sociologists think that the media exist mainly for the advertisers' and their own monetary benefit, not for the betterment of society.

It is debatable whether heavy dependence on advertising can influence editorial functioning, independence, honesty and impartiality; but it is clear that if more time and space are given to advertising, less will be left for news and general information. What we find in the Indian media, particularly the cable channels, is that there is a plethora of advertising and that the quality of the programming suffers.

Newspapers must not turn into 'adspapers'. Broadcast media should not become 'adscast media'. The media should, on their own, limit the time and space for advertisements. Will this be practical in a highly competitive, free enterprise system? Gandhi's *Young India* accepted advertising. However, Gandhi believed that it was undesirable to depend on advertisements if editorial freedom had to be maintained. The limited space given for advertisements in his papers was devoted to such advertisements that were educational and in conformity with the essential needs of the average reader. If a new and useful product came to the market, the editors should write about it and make people aware of its usefulness to society. This may sound naïve to modern media users, but if they think about the problem, they will agree with Gandhi.

This view of advertising was in consonance with the Gandhian view of limiting wants. A society that believed in acquiring goods or saw goods as status symbols was not, in his view, an ideal society. In India's economic condition then (and to a great extent even now, as revealed by the tragic event in Lucknow in April 2004, in which dozens of poor women were crushed to death in a stampede during a distribution of free saris) such a view of acquisition of goods and their subsequent discarding for newer products was a curse rather than a blessing in Gandhi's view. We may see other incidents like this one in Lucknow, because its root cause, poverty, is not being successfully tackled in India.

The advertisements in Gandhian newspapers were not part of any sustained campaign for the promotion of products that had already got public attention. Gandhi maintained that editors of newspapers whose aim was service to the community should never yield to the pressure of advertisement support since it was his firm conviction that this would tie their hands and make them subservient to big business. He argued that most advertisements resulted from unhealthy competition to win customer preference for luxury items which the large majority of the population could not afford to buy.

Gandhi believed that advertising increased the purchase price of products and services and thus became a burden to the average citizen. Gandhi thus anticipated John K. Galbraith, who raised questions about the wastefulness of advertising in his 1958 book, *The Affluent Society*, and suggested that money spent on advertising could be diverted to the betterment of poorer sections of the community.

Gandhi's objection to advertising also had moral and ethical grounds. In their greed for money, media owners sometimes accepted advertisements that were improper, harmful and deceitful. This, according to him, was not only 'not the objective of journalism, but also a destroyer of good journalism.

Through heavy dependence on advertisement support, are not the news-papers willingly subjecting themselves to the evil influence of money', he asked. During Gandhi's time, media in India (mainly newspapers and periodicals) had not become huge businesses. Today, the media and editors are evaluated based on the nature and volume of advertisements and commercials they bring in.

Barring his views on advertising, Gandhi's views on the press are in conformity with libertarianism and social responsibility as advanced by Siebert et al. (1956), in their theories of the press. Gandhi would defend the freedom of the press at any cost, but he was wedded to social responsibility. This can be seen from what he said about the decline that had set in in the press of his time. He did not want any curb on people's freedom to express their opinions, however wrong they were. The remedy against abuse of freedom, he said, was the creation of healthy public opinion that would refuse to patronize poisonous journals. He wrote in the *Young India* of 12 May 1920:

> Freedom of the press is a precious privilege that no country can forgo. But if there is, as there should be, no check save that of the mildest character, an internal check should not be impossible and ought not to be resisted.

The Indian Press at Independence and Today

In 1947, the major English newspapers in India were the *Times of India* (Bombay), *Statesman* (Calcutta), *Hindu* (Madras), *Hindustan Times* (New Delhi), *Pioneer* (Lucknow), *Indian Express* (Bombay and Madras), *Amrita Bazar Patrika* (Calcutta), *National Herald* (Lucknow), *Mail* (Madras) and *Hitavada* (Nagpur). Of these, the *Times of India*, *Statesman* and *Pioneer* were under British ownership. Soon the ownership of two changed to Indian hands. The *Statesman* continued under British ownership till 1964, when it came under a group of Indian businesses.

During the long struggle for India's Independence, the major English newspapers that served the national cause were the *Hindu* (established in 1878), *Amrita Bazar Patrika* (1868), *Bombay Chronicle* (1913), *Free Press Journal* (1930; it later became the *Indian Express*) and *Hindustan Times* (1924). Among the Indian language newspapers, the prominent ones were *Aaj* (1920), *Anandabazar Patrika* (1922), *Sakal* (1931), *Swadeshamitran* (1882), *Mumbai Samachar* (1822), *Malayala Manorama* (1890) and *Mathrubhumi* (1930).

Generally speaking, journalism is flourishing in India today. The Indian language newspapers have overtaken the English newspapers in number and circulation (see Tables 4.1 and 4.2). The highest circulation till the 1990s was enjoyed by the English newspapers despite the fact that less than 5 per cent of the population of India claim English as their mother tongue. English is still the medium of instruction in colleges and many prominent schools. It is also the language of administration, although state governments have introduced legislation in favour of local languages.

Table 4.1

The National Readership Survey (NRS)—Dailies, 2003

Rank	Name of the Publication	Readership in Million
1	Dainik Bhaskar (H)	15.709
2	Dainik Jagran (H)	14.985
3	Daily Thanthi (T)	10.094
4	Eenadu (Tel.)	9.458
5	Malayala Manorama (M)	8.798
6	Amar Ujala (H)	8.640
7	Hindustan (H)	7.899
8	Lokmat (Mar.)	7.867
9	Mathrubhumi (M)	7.646
10	Times of India (E)	7.419

Table 4.2

National Readership Survey (NRS)—Magazines, 2003

Rank	Name of the Publication	Readership in Million
1	Saras Salil (H)	9.385
2	India Today (H)	5.900
3	Vanitha (M)	5.514
4	Grihasobha (H)	5.414
5	Malayala Manorama (M)	5.406
6	Meri Saheli (H)	4.266
7	India Today (E)	4.194
8	Balarama (M)	3.958
9	Mangalam (M)	3.578
10	Filmfare (E)	3.518

Source: The Hindu, 22 December 2003.

Notes: (a) E=English; H=Hindi; M=Malayalam; Mar.=Marathi; T=Tamil; Tel.=Telugu.

(b) The survey covered 2,300 rural villages and 837 towns. A total of 140,000 persons were surveyed, of whom 42,000 were from rural areas.

(c) Readership is calculated on the assumption that one copy of a publication is read by 10 persons. The above figures are for 2003.

Hindi newspapers have the largest total circulation in India. The progress made by Hindi dailies and periodicals is enviable. Hindi is the main language of 10 Indian states—Bihar, Chhattisgarh, Delhi, Haryana, Himachal Pradesh, Jharkhand, Madhya Pradesh, Rajasthan, Uttaranchal and Uttar Pradesh.

Moreover, it is understood by a sizeable section of Maharashtrians, Gujaratis, Punjabis and Kashmiris. It is also understood by a considerable proportion of people living in metropolitan cities and in large business and industrial towns, no matter where they come from. In fact, about 45 per cent of Indians have Hindi as their mother tongue and more than 5 per cent in non-Hindi areas can converse in Hindi and read and write it.

Although about 500 million Indians can understand Hindi, the literacy rate in the larger states such as Bihar, Uttar Pradesh, Madhya Pradesh, Rajasthan and Jharkhand is very low, particularly among women. These states have a combined population of nearly 200 million, but the total circulation of newspapers is under 10 million! This is a very pitiable situation. Rural newspapers are not available anywhere. This is a great challenge for journalism and communication in India.

The imbalance in circulation can be discerned more clearly when we look at the southern states where the literacy is higher. In Kerala alone, where about 93 per cent of the population of 32 million is literate, newspaper circulation is almost 10 million, whereas in the large states in the north, as stated above, there is a combined total of less than 10 million circulation. The states that have the highest circulation of newspapers are Delhi, Kerala, Tamil Nadu, Andhra Pradesh, West Bengal and Karnataka.

We have just seen some quantitative aspects of the new journalism that is thriving in India today. Let us examine its major characteristics from the perspective of Gandhi and also in the light of concerns expressed at the Salzburg Seminar on Journalism as a Public Trust. Certain trends in communication and journalism throughout the modern world prompted several sociologists and media experts to discuss the desirability of re-examining the trends in the light of basic issues. In other words, 'back to the basics', say the experts. This is where Gandhi becomes relevant. High technology is good, but if it does not enable us to solve basic problems confronting the majority of the world's population, it will only succeed in catering to the greed of a few to the exclusion of the need of the many—as it has done through the recent decades and in all countries that experienced colonial subjugation in the past.

Changes in Technology and the Advent of New Journalism

Like the 'new wave' in film, 'new journalism' is also open to different interpretations. Therefore let us first of all be clear about what we mean by new journalism.

In the late 1960s and early 1970s, writers (and also journalist-writers) such as Tom Wolfe, Truman Capote, Norman Mailer and Gay Talese wrote non-fiction novels based on actual events reported by other journalists according to the conventional '5 Ws and H' (who, what, where, when, why and how) sequence. These writers disregarded the conventional limitations of reportage as well as principles of journalistic objectivity in order to make their writing more appealing and colourful. They delved deep into the inner working of the minds of the main 'actors' in the news reports.

Although this new style gained wide currency in the early 1970s and earned the sobriquet of 'New Journalism', it faded away in the 1980s, especially after it was discredited by an American reporter named Janet Cooke. Cooke fabricated a heart-rending story about an 8-year-old drug addict and published it under the title *Jimmy's World*. Even the Pulitzer Prize committee was moved, and she won the prize (Dennis 1992: 104).

Perhaps all newspaper and television reports are not fictitious, but there seems to be an element of Janet Cooke in many reporters who present news in the form and style of fiction—overstating facts, using colourful adjectives and sensational expressions. Every story that can be told in a hundred words is bloated into a thousand and illustrated by photographs, drawings, and so on. Media magnates conveniently dismiss all criticism by saying that they are giving the public what it wants.

New publishing technology has made it possible to romanticize features so much that most news reports in general newspapers (not financial newspapers and special publications) are no longer straight reports but fictionalized versions containing certain elements of truth.

This sea change in the philosophy of mediated communication began in the early 1970s in many parts of the world, and perhaps in the early 1980s in India—the delay owing to the late arrival of new technologies of printing and media production in India. The new technologies have influenced not only production but also distribution or dissemination in broadcasting and film exhibition. Based on the observations of Anthony Smith almost 25 years ago, the changes in the print media world of the late 20th and early 21st centuries can be summarized as involving the following:

• The convergence of a series of changes in society and demographics.
• Changes in the economics of advertising.
• Basic changes in the technology of media production.
• The changed goals and purposes of editors and publishers (and hence all media workers), who look for new content and new ways to serve their dual market of media users and advertisers.
• Newspapers yielding space to electronic media in the devices of production and in basic character.

- Competition with other media which offer users more content in a more attractive form at much lower cost.
- The inconvenience in transportation and storage of the end product (until all newspapers are delivered electronically to readers). The print media are therefore less timely and slower than other media.
- Big changes in the ownership of the newspapers, particularly in cross-media ownership, conglomeration and vertical integration.

All these changes in technology of production, organization of distribution, etc., have resulted in the new journalism of today. The old journalism of the Gandhian era, of journalists with noble goals, motivated by the need for social change in India, has disappeared, yielding to the journalism of the pocket book, of the purse—in short, of pure greed.

Journalism as service to society has been replaced by journalism aimed at profit and affluence for media promoters and media workers. The very nature of the media has changed in India. To justify this change by saying that the same process is taking place throughout the developed world is a lame excuse often advanced by media tycoons.

During the Independence movement, the press in India (the Indo-Anglian and the Indian language press) stood for national ideals, the most important of which was the readiness to sacrifice everything for the sake of freedom from foreign domination. The press in those days gave literate and educated opinion leaders (the social and economic elite) the inspiration to work for social change. Unfortunately, those ideals have almost wholly vanished from the mainstream media. A certain smugness or false complacency, if not greed, fills the media world these days. The purpose of the modern media seems to be to bring out a product that caters to the gossip interest of the literate and the well-to-do and protect the business and sociopolitical interests of the higher echelons.

The big changes in the Indian media world started in the late 1970s and culminated in the early 1990s, the period when the process of computerized and offset printing entered into widespread use in almost all leading newspapers, and other technological changes were introduced in the electronic media.

The competition between newspapers for maximum circulation (almost a circulation war) has now resulted in offers of gold and other valuable gifts to attract subscribers in all regions of India. The readers' greed is appealed to through television commercials and print advertisements. Similar efforts to increase the reach of radio and television programmes are also being made.

The media are no longer a channel for communicating news of significance to the users; they are utilizd increasingly for selling objects, particularly
gold ornaments, expensive perfumes and clothes, that are unaffordable to
common people.

Some leading newspapers have also become film and television programme-
producing companies, and makers of audio and video tapes.

The assumption among global media industries is that the 21st-century
citizen is a 'consumer-citizen'. This is true, no doubt, of a significant minority
in urban centres of both developing and developed countries. The 'new
media user' is catered to by the 'new media'. The 20th-century elite was a
'voting elite', but the 21st-century elite has less interest in politics and voting,
as evidenced by the steady decline in the percentage of citizens who vote in
the urban areas of India and the world.

Pandering to the elite mood became a habit of the media during the early
1990s. It could not be otherwise, because maximizing revenue from advertisements was the major goal of all successful media units. To swim with the
current was the easiest thing to do and questions of right and wrong, constitutional guarantees and directives among other things, had only secondary
importance. The media had only one goal: to deliver the maximum number
of readers, viewers and listeners to the advertiser. In this, they have succeeded and the media boom in India is continuing.

Cynicism and negativity have become notable characteristics of the modern media. Despite occasional tributes to nationalism, internationalism and a
global outlook, the media thrive on factionalism and social division. Unwary
sections of the public believe the myth that the media give every viewpoint
an opportunity to be heard. The public is misled by media's dictum of diversity of opinion and the superficial nobility of 'giving the public what it wants'.

Even the definition of news seems to have changed. News is interpreted
by some media producers as that which entertains the majority of the audience and the lucky-dip contestants, 'the gold miners'. The newspapers that
had different goals and ideals in the past century are now practising the
techniques of entertainers.

Using electronics technology, news about far-off disasters and natural
calamities is regularly presented as if it is the most important news for local
media users. All over the world, it is the tabloids, which focus on gossip,
scandal, crime and disaster, that have achieved the highest circulation. Regular newspapers, especially in the regional languages, are vying with one another to imitate the tabloids in content, without changing their size. The
Indian newspapers publish weekend supplements these days, devoted to
food, recreation, hobbies, sports and business affairs, each with complementary

advertising, in live and bright colours. With a few exceptions, commercially successful newspapers are becoming more trivial than serious.

As Anthony Smith avers, 'newspapers with a high content of sexual stories and pictures are becoming increasingly popular, as are papers that concentrate on financial and industrial news' (1980c: xi, xiii). Radio and television are doing the same, as evidenced by certain programmes such as the Howard Stern and Jerry Springer shows. Although the Indian media have not yet taken up similar shows and themes, there is every likelihood of such shows being taken up either by private TV channels or channels with foreign collaboration, thanks to foreign direct investment (FDI).

The Government of India has come in for severe criticism from the parliamentary opposition for having failed to implement the 1955 regulations in regard to the publication of foreign newspapers in India. Recently, the publication of the Indian edition of the *International Herald Tribune* (IHT) has started in Hyderabad 'in clear and blatant violation' of the policy decision announced by the government in Parliament in 1955 and the syndication guidelines issued by the information and broadcasting ministry. The critics point out that the paper was published without any approval and without a No Objection Certificate (NOC) from the government.

The new media such as the teletext and videotex in the West 'tend to unpack various categories of information from the regular press and repackage it in (their own) screen-delivered form direct to home' (Smith 1980c: xi, xiii). These, the fax (facsimile), and Internet-supplied news pages reach citizens in the advanced countries directly; home delivery routes and news stands are no longer necessary to reach them.

It is worth noting that these days the media, particularly the print media, have ceased to be labour-intensive—they have become technology-intensive electronic industries. Ownership patterns are also changing; chain ownership is still the most common form of ownership in India, but cross media ownership is gradually creeping in. The combination of the two trends has tempted newspaper companies to start lucrative new ventures, some connected to the media business and others not. Many newspaper companies are now television serial and music producers. Some have started FM radio stations. They are all engaged in serious competition to expand their media empires and social influence. Editionalization is part of this effort to maximize market penetration and hence revenue.

One serious consequence of conglomeration and the concentration of many media units in the hands of a few media businessmen is the likelihood that dissenting voices will be suppressed—thereby compromising the freedom of the press, which is essentially the freedom of citizens to express their opinion on matters affecting their lives. Mass communication will then become *communication from a select few to the many*. The purpose of communication in society will be defeated.

Analysing the relationship between technology and the media, many sociologists have raised a pertinent question: 'What happens to the fourth estate in the new IT environment?' And the answer, according to them, is: The newspaper industry is becoming just an information-providing device. This change started in 1973 when the Harris Corporation of the US put the first electronic editing terminal on the market; now the newspaper world can hardly function without computers.

Newspapers that used to stress universal primary education and universal access to education are now devoting full supplements to elitist education accessible to the tiny minority that can spend Rs 100,000 or more per year on tuition at the lower primary level alone, conveniently forgetting that India is a country of many millions who cannot afford to spend even Rs 100 for the education of their children. Newspapers may claim to be promoting quality education, but it is quite obvious that, in fact, they only wish to earn advertisement revenue from such institutions and augment their earnings from other schools in the future. In a country where there are tens of thousands of villages with one-room primary schools or no schools at all, concentrating on the kind of elitist primary education that only rich people—who want to send their children abroad to study at universities and ultimately settle down—can afford is almost a cruel game played by the media.

Economic and social realities are thus deliberately forgotten or casually sidelined. In their stead, the priorities highlighted by the media prove that the Indian media are of the elite, by the elite and for the elite.

The wrongdoings of certain politicians and their followers are given undue importance by the media. When the Babri Masjid was destroyed in December 1992 and innocent citizens were massacred in their hundreds during the Gujarat pogrom in March–May 2002, the events were reported widely in the various media as Hindu–Muslim confrontations, not as citizens versus citizens or as a failure of the national and state governments of the time that were responsible for maintaining law and order and protecting the lives of all citizens, whatever their religious faith. Some media units deserve praise for bringing out the horrors of these episodes, but the framework of all the reports remained 'Hindu versus Muslim'. With a few exceptions, the media were apathetic about discussing the deep significance of the 'anti-people' activities of a few unruly elements, perhaps with the connivance of members of the ruling parties, as noted by various impartial observers (such as the Citizens' Committee under the chairmanship of a former Judge of the Supreme Court, the National

Human Rights Commission under the chairmanship of a former Chief Justice of the Supreme Court and the Supreme Court itself). The Supreme Court's sanction of the request to retry the Best Bakery case outside Gujarat indicates the seriousness of the situation and the fear that justice would not be done if the retrial was conducted in Gujarat itself.

Were the media 'privy to an intense ideological struggle that the Indian society is currently witnessing between secularism on the one hand and communalism on the other', asks historian K.N. Panicker in the *Hindu*. 'Are the informed interventions by institutions like the media, exceptions rather than the rule, in contrast to the era of the national movement', he wonders (2004).

Although media directors and proprietors frequently draw attention to positive thinking and its importance in nation-building, they let their own media units indulge in negativism and cynicism because they consider it good for circulation. This hypocritical situation can be corrected only by the media proprietors themselves, as outside intervention is undesirable and unproductive, if not harmful in the long run for media freedom and citizens' rights.

There are other instances in the recent past which show the loss of idealism that characterizes media performance in India today. Every year hundreds of farmers commit suicide, crushed by debts they cannot clear. The tragedy is continuing across India, but especially in Andhra Pradesh, because of the wrong economic policies of state governments. Instead of thoroughly investigating the social and economic causes of the unprecedented waves of suicide, the media simply reported the deaths and published pictures of the bereaved families. Writing in the *Hindu* of 15 June 2004, well-known journalist P. Sainath commented as follows about the farmers' suicides in Andhra Pradesh:

> Álmost every sector of Indian democracy failed the Andhra farmer; the Government and the political class; the tame intellectuals and planners; the human rights groups and a once activist judiciary. And a media that failed in their simplest, yet vital duty in a democracy to signal the weaknesses in society.

Editionalization

Good use of technology is made by them to 'editionalize' the newspapers these days. All the big newspapers of India are doing this and they have a minimum of six editions and a maximum of 22 editions each. These are false editions because the same product is published with a page or two of local news to make it appear different. The proliferation of editions has been made possible by the facsimile reproduction of most pages from headquarters and the addition of one or two local pages from each edition-location. And this is certainly in the interests of the publishers themselves as it gives them the advantage of securing advertisements from the local (edition-town) businesses and manufacturing firms.

Rural newspapers are absolutely essential for India if we are serious about improving communication through the media for the benefit of people living in rural areas. A study done by this writer in the 1980s showed that there were practically no rural media in those days (Vilanilam 1984, 1989). The situation has not changed much even now, though occasionally some noise is made about the spread of television in the rural areas. The fact is that there are no rural television stations where programmes based on rural social and economic issues are produced and in which rural people participate; programmes are produced in the metropolitan cities and telecast to rural areas. Only the radio in India gives some attention to rural issues, but there are only a few rural radio stations.

In short, very little attention is paid by the media and by the state and central governments to the question of rural communication. There are practically no media units that give a voice to the voiceless—the landless, unemployed, unhoused, hungry and unskilled. Very little is heard from and about the 315 million or so very poor people in India these days except at the time of general elections. This trend started soon after the high-tech era set in. Perhaps the 'poor are always with us' attitude characterizes the mindset of the elite, commercial media. This is not a sign of healthy or responsible journalism, nor is it a sign of ethical journalism. It is totally different from the journalism of the Gandhian era. Established commercial newspapers however, continue remind readers about their revolutionary past and they do not miss any opportunity to celebrate important milestones in their own history. Readers are led to believe that the revolutionary and patriotic tradition of those newspapers continues despite their crass commercialism.

The existing media and their sophisticated technology can be used to bring the rural areas within the fold of communication and mass communication. There are financial reasons for them to ignore the rural areas, but there can be equally strong financial and sociological reasons for them to turn increasingly to the rural market. As has been pointed out by many experts, new technologies can be used profitably in enhancing rural communication through a combination of high-tech and low-tech media. If India was able to bring about a revolution in the use of telephonic communication in the rural areas during the past three decades, she can certainly revolutionize the systems of mediated and interpersonal communication in the countryside, provided more attention is given to the development of basic education and health care awareness and facilities in those areas.

In this connection, it is relevant to remember that even in the most advanced countries of the world, the new media technologies introduced in the late 1960s and early 1970s progressed in a modular fashion—first photo-composition, then the Video Display Terminals (VDTs) for editors, then VDTs for reporters, classified advertisement personnel and finally VDTs for display and composition.

To begin with, such technologies can be introduced in the 600-odd district headquarters in India and then gradually extended to rural newspapers and radio and television stations in the 1,000 or so villages under each district headquarters, with newspapers and broadcast stations for each cluster of 50 villages. This is not wishful thinking, provided some technology-oriented promoter of media inspired by Gandhian ideals of rural development takes up the project in each district. Full-pagination and transmission systems can be used at the district headquarters to produce village newspapers, even as the present system of editionalization introduced by the existing large-circulation newspapers continues. Perhaps the Gandhian institutions and Gandhians can take this up as a pilot project for a couple of districts and test the effectiveness of the system.

Almost all tasks including distribution, circulation and sales can be entrusted to the computer system installed in the district headquarters, provided there is an uninterrupted supply of electricity there. Village development in modern times certainly depends upon the supply of electricity, water and drainage systems. Gandhi was not against technology and sophisticated methods of production if those did not lead to the further exploitation of the villagers but instead led to a general improvement in the life of the village.

We live in exceedingly exciting times. Computerized information technology and communication systems are here to stay. They can be fully utilized to transform mediated, interpersonal and intrapersonal communication systems. But if the new technologies are used for conglomeration which results in monopolization of ICT by a handful of promoters, as is happening in rich countries today, where large media corporations gobble up smaller ones and ownership of all forms of mediated communication is concentrated in the hands of a few multinational corporations owning both the hardware and the software for national and international networks, it will not advance the cause of good, public-spirited journalism.

Journalism as a Public Trust (The Salzburg Declaration)

The Salzburg Declaration of Journalism as a Public Trust made by journalists from 32 countries in March 2002 is reproduced below.[1] It deals with many of the issues of great concern to thinking journalists and is relevant to our discussion.

In Defense of Journalism as a Public Trust
SALZBURG, AUSTRIA; MARCH 26, 2002

I. PREAMBLE

This statement expresses the concerns of international journalists and supporters of journalism attending the Salzburg Seminar Session 396, March 20–27, 2002, in Salzburg, Austria. The topic: The decline of the news media's role as a public trust and the effects of that phenomenon on its obligations to civil society. Our discussions revealed that journalists and their supporters from many countries share a strong conviction that market pressures are undermining the quality of journalism; specifically, as news organizations preserve high profit levels by reducing newsgathering resources and neglecting journalism in the public interest, the fundamental role of the press to inform and empower citizens is endangered.

These concerns are the motivation for this statement, which we hope will prompt further consideration, discussion and action around the world.

A free and independent press is essential to human liberty. No people can remain sovereign without a vigorous press that reports the news, examines critical issues and encourages a robust exchange of ideas. In recognition of the press's vital role in society, many countries extend it special legal protections under constitutions or legislatively-enacted statutes. These protections are unique, for they safeguard print, broadcast and online organizations against government interference and censorship.

Where this special status has been accorded the press, news organizations have been held to a high standard of public service and

---

[1] Text as reproduced on the website of the Poynter Institute (http://www.poynter.org/content/content_view.asp?id=4949).

public trust. Over time, this ideal has become a bedrock of journalism, an enduring tradition by which a free press has been a powerful force for progress and informed citizen participation in society.

Historically, threats to press freedoms have been political in nature. At the start of the 21st century, however, a new kind of threat emerges that, if continued, will endanger the freedoms guaranteed to the press and put at risk the sovereignty of the citizens.

The nature of the press as a commercial enterprise has changed significantly. The emergence of media conglomerates and intense market competition are creating new organizational priorities in which profit growth is replacing public service as the principal mission. Sustaining profit growth often requires reducing the resources for news gathering, thereby diminishing the role of the news media as a public trust.

Business priorities are encouraging the blending of news and entertainment as a strategy to build audiences and ratings. This trend, most noticeable in television, has led to a reduction in serious news coverage and may be responsible for a decline of public confidence in this medium as an essential source of information.

Finally, a shrinking commitment to both domestic and international news means that news organizations are missing opportunities to connect people and ideas globally at the very time technology has made such connections increasingly possible.

This international group of journalists and supporters of press freedom calls on the leaders of news organizations worldwide to recognize the need for a wiser balance between business goals and public-service responsibilities, and to reaffirm their commitment to journalism and the role of a free press in sustaining human liberty.

II. CONCERNS ABOUT JOURNALISM

We recognize that news organizations function in a competitive, multimedia environment, and that financial strength is essential for journalistic independence. However, an unbalanced priority on profits and financial growth weakens the foundation of journalism as a public trust. We are convinced that the growing imbalance in the priority given to journalism quality and profit growth ultimately impairs citizens' ability to participate fully in their communities. And we recognize that neglecting the public interest erodes public support for legal guarantees of the freedom of the press to report the news. We conclude that market forces and other pressures are causing the following problems:

1. On citizens and society

   ● Inadequate access to diverse sources of information.
   ● Decline in public understanding of current affairs.
   ● Decline in citizen participation in community life.
   ● Diminishment of citizens' political authority.
   ● Improper confluence of media ownership and political interests.

2. On journalism content and influence

   ● Decline of diverse and comprehensive news produced in the public interest.
   ● Neglect of audiences that are not valued by advertisers.
   ● Compromising editorial integrity for commercial purposes.
   ● Encroachment of entertainment into news coverage.
   ● The shrinking impact of news organizations as audiences dwindle.

3. On news media organizations

   ● Concentration of ownership and creation of monopolies.
   ● Vulnerability to the imperatives of stock markets and other financial interests.
   ● Increasing tendency of multimedia conglomerates to use news resources to promote commercial interests.

III. PROPOSALS FOR CONSIDERATION

To address these concerns, we encourage the press and the public to consider the following suggestions in communities and situations where they may apply:

1. Encourage diverse news media ownership and urge media companies to commit to providing quality journalism to all communities they serve.

2. Ensure that television networks and radio stations provide quality news programs as part of their societal obligation to the public airwaves.
3. Help citizens evaluate the quality of the news they receive and express their views so that their voices may be heard.
4. Use journalism to enhance citizens' ability to participate in community life.
5. Call on companies that own news organizations to:

   a. Adopt mission statements reflecting their journalistic values and the priority they attach to their role as a public trust.
   b. Adopt a long-term business strategy based on producing quality journalism.
   c. Include journalists on the boards of companies that own news organizations.
   d. Adopt professional standards that promote high-quality journalism.
   e. Compensate news executives based on the quality of their company's journalism rather than its financial performance.

6. Ensure that entertainment content does not compromise news coverage.
7. Keep a clear separation between advertising and news content. All advertising should be clearly labeled.
8. Reaffirm journalism values of accuracy, fairness and balance; and maintain the press's roles as watchdog and voice for citizens.
9. Promote professional standards of excellence in journalism education.
10. Foster media education of young people in schools and through media.

ENDORSED BY PARTICIPANTS FROM THESE NATIONS/REGIONS

Argentina, Armenia, Bosnia, China, Egypt, European Union, Colombia, Germany, Ghana, Hungary, India, Israel, Italy, Kosovo, Latvia, Pakistan, Palestine, Philippines, Saudi Arabia, South Africa, Spain, Thailand, Turkey, Ukraine, United Kingdom, United States of America, Yugoslavia.

Conglomeration and Concentration of Ownership

The threat from the concentration of ownership in fewer and fewer hands is an inevitable consequence of cut-throat competition in any business. The media business is no exception to this general rule, which governs all businesses in the West.

Columbia Broadcasting System (CBS) was taken over by Lawrence Tisch, the National Broadcasting Corporation (NBC) was taken over by General Electric (GE) and the American Broadcasting Corporation (ABC) was first taken over by Capital Cities and later by the Disney Corporation.

News Corporation Limited (NCL), the biggest media company in the world, is reaping the greatest revenue from advertising. Rupert Murdoch is the head of NCL, which owns media companies in the US, UK, Europe, Asia, Australia and the Pacific Rim. The 20th Century Fox Film Corporation, Fox Broadcasting Corporation, Fox Television stations, HarperCollins, TV Guide and News America Inc., are owned by NCL in the US.

NCL owns the top British newspapers such as the *Times* (London), the *Sunday Times*, the *Sun*, the *News of the World*, the *Times Literary Supplement*, the *Times Educational Supplement* and the *Times Higher Education Supplement*, besides BskyB (British Sky Broadcasting) and the UK Multichannel Pay-TV Service. It also owns a German TV channel named VoxFilm-und-Fernesch GMBH.

In Australia and the Pacific Rim, NCL is the largest newspaper publisher, owning nearly 100 daily, Sunday, weekly, bi-weekly and tri-weekly newspapers. In New Zealand, NCL owns 50 per cent of Independent Newspapers Ltd., which publishes 60 newspapers and 25 community newspapers in the US and five provincial newspapers in Australia, besides a magazine distribution business in Australia and New Zealand. The Seven Network Ltd., one of Australia's three major commercial TV networks, is also partly owned by NCL.

NCL owns a 50 per cent share in Cable Television Network a joint venture with Telstra Corporation Ltd., and a 42 per cent share of the Queensland Press Ltd.

NCL has almost three-fourths share in STAR Television Ltd., which beams television programming via satellite into China and India and 50 other countries from Israel to Japan and Turkey to Indonesia. STAR (Satellite Television Asia Range) programmes reach nearly 50 million households in Asia (Vanden Bergh and Katz 1999: 54).

The largest media chain is in the US, namely, the Gannett chain of two dozen television and radio stations and over 90 dailies, earning profits close to a billion dollars a year. As a company, its main objectives are to acquire more media units and increase its profit.

A trend in major media corporations in recent years is to appoint as chief executive someone from a non-media company, having little or no experience in journalism. People from big corporations such as General Motors, General Electric and General Mills come in as CEOs of major media companies. For example, the Times Mirror Company, parent of the *Los Angeles Times* and *Newsday*, appointed as its CEO a marketing manager from General Mills in 1995.

There is also a trend towards hiring MBAs as news and advertisement executives in media organizations. All this is a clear indication that the media corporations want to put the media business in the hands of non-media professionals who can raise profits. What matters is not political ideals or social goals, but reaping higher and higher profits every year. Media production is treated just like the manufacture of cereals, hamburger helpers, cake mixes, soap, cement, rubber or jute products. No wonder that the most successful publications in certain countries are magazines that publish pictures of beautiful women and handsome men in various stages of undress!

Conveniently for media conglomerates, they can easily switch executives from non-media units under their management to media units and vice versa.

Media companies and their training institutes and some so-called five-star colleges are exhorting their wards to be fit for the highly competitive news world before working as media executives. Those already working in the media but deficient according to proprietorial judgement are either graciously shown the door or sent for retraining (re tooling) and repackaging to make them competent for the changing economy.

The result of such retraining is subtle skewing of news and submission to market needs (particularly of advertising and the hunt for ratings), saleability of half-truths and too much flexibility. Truthful and comprehensive reporting is not considered important; reaping consumers through entertainment and keeping them hooked is all important. Those who want to make their audience forget the realities of their surroundings must themselves forget them and that can be achieved only through intensive psychological—even subliminal—training and of course through very high salaries and perks even at the training stage. No wonder the harsh realities of the country are not of any great concern to the major media. Virtual reality is perhaps of more concern to them and the new journalists they train. Marketing the media product is what really matters. And what is good for profits is good for the new marketplace of ideas, because that is no longer a place of many voices.

Before 1965 in the West and before 1995 in India, those who went for studies in journalism had certain ideals, but thereafter aspiring journalists have been motivated primarily by glamour and greed. Ideals have become the idiots' icons and *adarshas* (ideals) are anathema to the new breed of communicators and their trainers.

The phenomenon of concentration and multimedia ownership is not confined to the West. It exists in India as well, a fact which we can confirm on the basis of ownership of media in India. An issue of far-reaching consequence is the trend among certain major media groups to imitate or collaborate with foreign media groups, which they justify on the grounds that it is a global trend. The new technologies of production and distribution contribute to this trend because they require huge capital investment, sophisticated management and constant growth in profit.

Global media companies enter foreign markets with varying degrees of direct investment, with or without the intention of gobbling up local media, but certainly to make huge profits. Such a trend is deleterious to the public's freedom of expression for the following reasons:

1. Technologies that existed separately are now converging to create new media linkages. Their efficiency is a cause not only for integration but also for disintegration among different groups whose tastes and interests are not satisfied.
2. In previous decades, the newspaper gave information at a fixed time and many people absorbed it slowly, and steadily. But now all kinds of information are repeated over and over again which act as a trigger for undesirable reactions and harmful actions by a large number of people who do not get the leisure to ponder received information. Moreover, many people are likely to take media information as if it were the gospel truth.
3. Those who cannot afford to spend Rs 200–300 a month on cable channels are cut off from the information dissemination that is going on through the mass media. There is no attempt on the part of the sophisticated media to reach this section of the population. The Conditional Access System (CAS) is likely to increase the gap between the information 'haves' and 'have-nots'. Even though CAS has been introduced in Tamil Nadu, there have not been many takers. It will not take roots in other states as well, in the opinion of many people.
4. The media are now inextricably locked into patterns of advertising and distribution and it is a heavy burden on those who have no access to big capital to keep pace with the 'high and mighty'!

5. The newspaper is becoming a deliverer of specialized information to some groups. Most of the time, information from other sources, not the newspaper's own but of the global news agencies that dominate the financial world, is highlighted. The functions of the press as a fourth estate demand that the newspaper be a complete social presence, not just a channel for someone else's information or information that is of importance and benefit to someone else.

6. Since demand for individualized information among affluent sections that can easily afford the new technologies will increase, the conventional newspaper will disappear or cease to be of interest to the average reader, especially when it deals more and more with investments, profit returns, stock exchange rates, shareholders' rights, foreign direct investment, etc., which are all matters of great moment for the upper middle class engaged in financial speculation. The newspaper of the new era will turn out to be an information medium instead of a news medium and will be accessible more to the computer-savvy than to the non-computer-owning lower middle class and the literate poor.

7. Above all, the price of newsprint, which is what conventional newspapers are printed on, has gone up several-fold since the 1970s. Newsprint is no longer as cheap or plentiful as it used to be.

8. Both printed and Internet newspapers are now unavailable to the average person in India with the exception of a few city-dwellers. The situation is made acute by the high price of modern newspapers printed in colour and by the inaccessibility of newspapers on the Internet. A single copy of a printed newspaper costs not less than Rs 3 which works out to more than Rs 1,000 a year, an amount that is a sizeable proportion of the per capita income of an average Indian!

9. Illiteracy is an insurmountable obstacle now to the spread of newspapers in the majority of Indian states, particularly in the highly populated but severely backward regions of Bihar, Madhya Pradesh, Rajasthan and Uttar Pradesh, usually referred to as the B I MA R U states.

10. The economic factors of high cost of production, publication and distribution and the social factors of illiteracy, poverty, ignorance, lack of transport and communication facilities, especially in the rural areas, act as barriers against access to the media for millions of Indians, while the new technologies of production are further concentrated within the urban areas, making mass communication a highly elitist phenomenon. Rural news is given as an occasional sop to the 'mob' in the non-urban areas.

Freedom of the Press

What Anthony Smith observed about the Western press is relevant to the media of many regions of the world, including India.

> Given modern technological and industrial costs, freedom of the press can only be interpreted as freedom of the already existing organs of the press. Since these are for the most part, at the service of particular interests, they do not add up to the harmonic representation of the general interest preached by Adam Smith. (1980c: 157)

The US Commission on the Freedom of the Press, called the Hutchins Commission (Professor Robert M. Hutchins was President of the University of Chicago at that time), said in 1947:

> Protection against government is not sufficient to guarantee that a man who has something to say will have the opportunity to say it. The owners and business managers of the press determine what persons, what deeds, what versions of the said deeds will reach the public. (quoted in Agee et al. 1979: 142)

The Commission listed society's five requirements from the mass media. Although this list was advanced before television became a major medium in the US, it is still valid in the 21st century. Media must provide

- a truthful, comprehensive and intelligent account of the day's events in a context which gives them meaning;
- a forum for the exchange of comment and criticism;
- the projection of a representative picture of the constituent groups in the society;
- the presentation and clarification of the goals and values of the society; and
- full access to the day's intelligence.

As far as the citizens of the United States are concerned, a sizeable proportion have access to the Internet and they can exchange ideas with fellow citizens even without the help of the mass media. But it will take at least half a century more for such a situation to develop in India.

The Hutchins Commission's views on sensationalism are quite apt for many media units of the East and the West even today:

> To attract the maximum audience, the press (media) emphasizes the exceptional rather than the representative, the sensational rather than the

significant. Many activities of the utmost social consequence lie below the surface of what are conventionally regarded as reportable incidents. (quoted in Agee et al. 1979: 142)

In most news media, such matters are crowded out by stories of nightclub murders, race riots, strike violence (student agitations) and quarrels among public officials. The Commission did not object to the reporting of these incidents but to the preoccupation of the media with them to such an extent that the citizen is not supplied with the information and discussion he needs to discharge his responsibilities to the community (ibid.).

Even the lowest rungs of society must have the freedom to express their ideas and be heard. But often the dissenting individual's voice may not be heard at all or even if heard will not be presented in a clear manner. Big media are not the answer; only the small media can be effective in voicing dissenting views and the views of the least in society. There must be media affordable to the voiceless and the unempowered.

Conventional values associated with the fourth estate have been eroded in this high-tech era. This may be characterized as an exaggeration, but it is an exaggeration of a vital truth. Big media devour small ones whether it be in New York, London, Tokyo or New Delhi. Ownership changes hands overnight. The public may not have any inkling about the extent to which economic pressures are exerted on the environment of communication and about the pace of conglomerate growth, mergers and interlocking of directorships. The large sums of cash earned by publishers and media owners through the media–advertising collaboration are used for further investment in the acquisition of other media units and non-media industries at lightning speed.

Let us now turn our attention to the growth of the audiovisual media in the world of communication.

5

image up, word down: the rise of audiovisual media

*i*n the beginning, there was only voice for humans to express their thoughts; but voice remained mere noise for millions of years. Sounds arranged in a certain order to make sense is speech, but scientists say that human speech developed only some 35,000 years ago. Then came writing, although some form of pictorial representation through drawings on cave walls evolved in the centuries before writing through alphabets came into being in certain civilizations—Phoenician, Akkadian, Sumerian (all grouped under the Mesopotamian civilization), Egyptian, Chinese, Greek, Roman and Indian (Mohenjodaro and Harappa), to mention just a few.

The development of alphabets in different parts of the world occurred in the 4th or 5th millennium B.C. This was perhaps the second major revolution in communication, the first being the evolution of speech and the third the evolution of printing from movable type. We are concerned here with the evolution of visual communication; and its first step was the representation of sound through alphabets and pictures.

Words are but symbols and graphic records of sounds which, in turn, are but expressions of ideas. For many millennia, thoughts were expressed nonverbally. Then our ancestors sought means by which they could record their thoughts visually for fellow humans and future generations. They drew, and their drawings conveyed their thoughts in lines, circles, symbols and signs—in short, alphabets, and through alphabets, words.

The earliest form of writing was *pictographic*, with symbols or crude representations of objects familiar to the people of the same area. Not only objects but also ideas were thus represented; experts call them *pictograms* and *ideograms*.

Cuneiform script ('wedge-shaped' characters inscribed with a stylus on clay tablets) developed in the Mesopotamian region. Later on, cuneiform developed ideographic elements. the symbolic representations carried not only the object but ideas and qualities associated with the object. Gradually, vowel sounds were also represented by symbols.

Languages developed in different corners of the world during different eras and civilizations, first in speech and then in writing. There are now at least 3,000 languages and tens of thousands of dialects spoken in the world, but not all of them have scripts. Many of them do not have alphabets.

Illumination (Illustration) of Written Material

Early manuscripts were 'illuminated' with intricately drawn pictures. Wooden blocks were used for illustrations in the early printed books. By the end of the 18th century, lithography (writing on stone—that is, engraving the letters on blocks of stone) was replaced by printing from movable type made of wood or metal, first in China, then in Korea in the 9th or 10th century and in Europe after Johann Gutenberg started printing circa 1450. Gutenberg's invention revolutionized printing, because metallic movable types speeded up printing and led eventually to the democratization of communication throughout Europe and ultimately in various parts of the world. It also led to the quick and more permanent transmission of ideas and messages pertaining to business and manufacturing industries.

The generation of knowledge and the speedy dissemination of information throughout the world became easy because of the invention of various techniques and the improvement in technology during the long Industrial Revolution, that took place in the 17th, 18th and 19th centuries in Europe and the United States in full measure, and in other regions of the world in a partial manner. The end of this period saw the development of various media and processes of communication, including cinema (film), radio, telephone, telegraphy, wireless and television. The 20th century saw the fastest modes of telecommunication, namely, satellite communication, electronic mail and the Internet. All these branches of mass communication have received an immense boost from what we call visual communication. First let us deal with the print media in Europe.

Calligraphed manuscripts embellished with hand-printed figures, big initial letters and drawings and pictures in golden or silver paint are called illustrated or illuminated manuscripts and came into frequent use in the 15th century. The art of manuscript illumination, practised in Europe in the Middle Ages, declined during the Renaissance when lithography and wooden block printing came into vogue. With the widespread use of movable type printing, illumination became a minor art. This followed the widespread use of movable type printing of books, newspapers, magazines, pamphlets and leaflets. One good example of an illuminated manuscript that has survived the ravages of time is the Egyptian papyrus roll called the Book of the Dead. Even in modern times different varieties of illustration are used in all the print media.

In India, some of the manuscripts of famous epics, engraved by stylus on palm leaves, are illustrated. For example, the Ramayana recorded on palm leaves in 1483 and kept in the Manuscripts Library of the University of Kerala, is a good example of early illustration of popular and religious works.[1]

'Illustration' is visual material that explains and enhances the text with which it appears. An illustration could be a map, chart, diagram or graph, a decorative element, or a pictorial representation of a scene, person, animal, plant or object. As technology advanced, more visual elements entered the communication scene: photography, cinema, radiophotos, facsimile impressions, television and finally satellite pictures, multimedia and Internet.

This chapter deals mainly with the growth and development of the art and science of photography and photojournalism and the basic principles of digitalization that form the foundation of all forms of audiovisual communication in the 21st century.

Photography and Photojournalism

What is Photography?

The encyclopaedic definition of photography (before the digital revolution) is that it is 'the science and art of producing permanent images on sensitized surfaces by means of the photochemical action of light or other forms of radiant energy'.

But today, photographs can be taken on digital cameras capturing images on magnetic disks or solid-state storage like flash cards, and these images are transferable on the Internet. The whole concept of photography has undergone a sea change since the 1990s. However, we should know some historical facts about the development of photography and photojournalism, as they are essential components of communication in the modern world.

Modern photography started with different kinds of cameras using a light-sensitive emulsion-coated thin material called film. The emulsion is spread in a thin layer over the material that is fixed on a supporting base. Most modern photographic film utilizes a flexible, transparent material coated with a light-absorbent backing on one side and a light-sensitive emulsion on the other.

---

[1] For more details, see K. Vijayan (ed.) 1997, *Ramayana in Palm Leaf Pictures* (*Citraramayana*). This 15th-century work was completed in 1483.

With this background information, let us look at the evolution of photography. The earliest type of camera was a box-like device called the camera obscura. It was in use in the 17th century. Light reflected from an external object passed through a slit or hole in the front section of the camera. An image of the object was caught inside the box on a ground glass screen or translucent paper at the back.

Experiments conducted late in the 18th century by Sir Humphry Davy and Thomas Wedgewood of England led to the capturing of photographic images on plates coated with photosensitive silver nitrate or other silver compounds. But these images were not permanent because the silver-coated paper blackened after exposure to light.

By 1822, a French physicist, Joseph Nicéphore Niépce, produced a *resist* for the etching of metal plates. This helped in obtaining a more permanent photograph.

About 1831, a French painter, Louis J. Daguerre, made photographs on silver plates coated with silver iodide. After exposing the plate for several minutes, Daguerre used mercury vapour to develop a positive photographic image. But these photographs gradually darkened. Daguerre, therefore, used a strong sodium chloride solution. Using metallic plates, he could 'fix' the images more permanently. However, producing more than one single photograph for each exposure remained a major problem.

The British inventor, William Talbot, developed a method using a paper negative from which any number of prints could be made. Paper coated with silver iodide was used, which was more sensitive to light if it was dampened before exposure. The same solution could be used as a developer for the exposed paper. After development, the negative image was made permanent by immersion in sodium thiosulphate (called 'hypo').

Both Daguerre and Talbot announced their processes in 1839. Within three years, the exposure time in both processes could be reduced to a few seconds instead of several minutes. Images created by Daguerre's process were called *daguerreotypes* and those by Talbot's, *calotypes*.

In 1851, the British photographer Frederick Scott Archer introduced wet glass plates using *collodion* instead of other chemicals as coating material. Archer's method was called the 'wet collodion process'. Darkrooms became necessary. Using wet collodion negatives and horse-drawn mobile darkrooms, Mathew B. Brady took thousands of photographs on the battlefields of the American Civil War during 1861–63.

The next stage of development was to perfect a type of negative that could be exposed when dry; and the development of a method by which the exposed negative did not have to be developed immediately. By 1878, Charles Bennett perfected Richard Kennett's dry plate negatives by coating them with an immersion of gelatin and silver bromide. These speeded up the process of photography. Bennett's plates were very similar to the ones used in modern times.

Colour Photography and Eastman's Flexible Film

In 1861, the British physicist James Clerk Maxwell succeeded in making the first colour image. However, it was in 1883 that real success came with the American George Eastman's production of a film consisting of a long paper strip coated with a sensitive emulsion. In 1889, Eastman produced the first transparent, flexible film in the form of ribbons of cellulose nitrate. This was the beginning of roll film and it marked the end of the early photographic era.

With the availability of roll film, thousands of amateur photographers came onto the scene, with suitable portable cameras. Photography became a much easier process by the beginning of the 20th century.

Meanwhile, attempts had been made by many French and American photographers and inventors to give photographs the illusion of motion. In 1891, Thomas Alva Edison, the American inventor, patented the kinetoscope, a machine for projecting moving pictures; he had first demonstrated this machine in 1889.

In 1895, the French chemist and industrialist Louis J. Lumière and his brother Auguste N. Lumière, also a chemist, patented their *cinématographe*, through which they projected moving pictures. In the 1920s, sound was added to the motion picture.

Early in the 20th century, commercial photography grew rapidly and became simplified for popular use. In the 1960s, zoom lenses became popular. With a zoom lens there is no need to use interchangeable lenses with different focal lengths.

In the early years, artists and painters turned into photographers. Generally, their work reflected the characteristics of art, painting and drawing. In more recent times, photography depends almost wholly on the timing, shutter speed, camera quality, lens sensitivity and such other technical matters which play a very significant role, along with the photographer's own split-second decisions and reactions.

More than art photographers and portrait photographers, it is photojournalists who have made photography a vital aspect of journalism.

Photojournalism

There is an old saying that a picture is worth a thousand words. Many facts that cannot be described fully in words, many objects that are beyond words, can be presented with the help of pictures. Photographs add authenticity and realism to descriptions. Journalism supported by photographs, and photographs that can tell a story, are both essential ingredients of photojournalism.

Outstanding documentary photographers of the 19th century who can be called pioneers of photojournalism include Roger Fenton, an Englishman who took photographs of the Crimean War in 1855, and Mathew Brady and Alexander Gardner who documented the American Civil War nearly seven years later. Their work is the best record of those wars. Brady's work, consisting of about 3,500 pictures of war scenes, helped contemporary and later historians who worked on the history of one of the most important periods in American history.

Other photographers who earned national and international acclaim in the pre-World War II period were Erich Salomon of Germany, who described himself as the first photojournalist, and Henri Cartier-Bresson of France, who used a 35 mm Leica camera to capture the flow of life at 'decisive moments', as he described his technique. (This great photographer passed away in August 2004 at the age of 95.) Margaret Bourke White was perhaps the first woman to become famous as a photojournalist. She worked for *Life* magazine. Her celebrity subjects included Mahatma Gandhi. The list of other famous photographers and photojournalists who worked for internationally-known magazines such as *Life*, *Look* and *National Geographic* is too long to reproduce here.

Photojournalism is now an essential part of journalism. Every newspaper and magazine employs a team of photographers; the size of this team depends on the size of the establishment and the circulation and reach of its publications. Some publications employ full-time photographers while others hire part-timers or freelancers.

Photography plays an important role in modern systems of communication. Even on the Internet, we can transmit photographs and pictures to far-off destinations. What makes this possible is digitalization. We shall discuss the principle of digitalization later. But let us note here that digitalization helps not only in the transmission of pictures and photographs electronically but also in all computerized systems of communication, and that it is the very basis of information technology (IT). What is important for us here is that the digital pictures have very special qualities.

Pictures for television or film are handled using electronic circuits to analyse them into electronic signals. Computer programming will help deal with the numbers, but it is expensive to formulate electronic circuits for each need. There are fast electronic computer programmes that help achieve picture analysis of the desired quality within seconds using simple calculations. The pictures that are stored in the form of numbers are thus given more effectiveness and clarity.

Such image enhancement is being used not only for special effects in film or TV production but also for improving the clarity of satellite pictures sent from space or pictures of surgical procedures sent through terrestrial/space transmission mechanisms.

Using different computer techniques, pictures and certain desired portions of pictures can be enlarged and clarified. Through 'mosaic' technique, the faces of persons interviewed for television investigative reports who desire anonymity can be hidden, but their voices can still be heard, so that the viewers do not lose faith in the credibility of the persons thus presented.

Digital pictures are used most in news media. Events are photographed using digital cameras and transmitted to television channels for instant retransmission to the audiences. Such transmissions are done in newspapers too, especially for instant page transmissions to different editions.

Digital cameras take pictures using charge-coupled devices (CCDs) that are highly photosensitive. Attached to the CCDs are a microprocessor, memory devices and an energy source. This equipment will electronically convert the light that enters the camera into numbers stored in the camera's memory or on a floppy or a hard disc. The pictures thus stored temporarily can be modified, enhanced or decorated, using a computer suitably programmed for the purpose.

A thumb-size CCD has the capacity to detect or identify about 4,000 grey levels. Scientists, particularly space scientists, have made the maximum use of this capacity to record pictures of distant comets, planets and even galaxies digitally. Digital cameras are used on a continuous basis to track the course of artificial satellites and probes sent to distant planets such as Jupiter. They are also being used to detect from orbiting satellites those areas of the Earth where natural resources are available. Such explorations are useful in the study of weather and climate changes in different parts of the globe and in predicting earthquakes, floods and other natural calamities. We mention all this to stress the large-scale application of computerized visual communication which is what modern photography means.

None of this progress took place overnight. The development of science and technology, electronic and digital devices, satellite technology, rapid telecommunication and computer operations, etc., have led to modern photography and visual communication. In this march of science and technology, some milestones are:

- The successful transmission by wire of pictures of the San Francisco earthquake in 1907, which inaugurated the era of wire photos and radio photos.
- The development of new cameras such as the speedographic press camera in 1912.
- The advent of 35 mm Leica, Rolliflex, Konica, Yashica and Canon cameras, which helped in the worldwide expansion of photojournalism.
- The advent of colour photography and its expansion on a commercial scale following the Eastman Kodak Company's launch of their Kodachrome colour film in 1935 (Eastman enabled the common man to buy color film at affordable prices).
- The advent of the American technicolour in 1935 which led to the production of colour movies such as Gone With the Wind (1939) and other films at MGM, Universal, Paramount and other studios.
- The arrival of the Edwin H. Land Polaroid camera in 1947, which eliminated messy developing liquids, inconvenient darkrooms, dryers, etc., and reduced exposure time from 60 seconds to 10 seconds in 1950. From 1963 onwards, Land cameras became useful in taking fully developed colour pictures within a minute.
- The entry into widespread use of the magnetic videotape invented in 1953, a major landmark in the visual communication field.

The Magnetic Video Tape (MVT)

The MVT could record a movie even as the film was playing either on the Video Tape Recorder (VTR), also called Video Cassette Recorder (VCR) coupled with the TV system or on the large silver screen. The MVT electronic process was started in 1953, and during the next five decades (and perhaps in the early decades of the new millennium) continued to be used for shooting both serial and feature films. The big advantage is that after every hour or so, the filmed tape can be replayed and mistakes caught before further shooting. This helps the producer/director to save on film footage, time and the tedium of re-shooting the whole scene or film. A highly useful device, MVT was developed with the active participation and encouragement of a great communications expert, David Sarnoff of the US, who started his career as a Marconi wireless operator and eventually rose to preside over both the Radio Corporation of America (RCA) and its national radio–television network, the National Broadcasting Company (NBC). Sarnoff was president of until 1970.

We shall now turn to the special responsibilities of photo-editors and some essential attributes of photojournalists. By photojournalists we mean those who are in the field working with their cameras, whereas by photo-editors we mean the ones working at their desks in the media office. Photo-editors are photojournalists in a sense, because many of them may have started their media careers as the latter.

Photo-editors work with photojournalists and general editors in newspaper and magazine publishing units. Photojournalists work like videographers who use video equipment instead of cameras that produce still photographs. Both photographers and videographers record events, scenes, persons, animals, objects, and so on, but whereas videographers record both pictures and sound, photographers record only pictures.

Photo-editors have the following responsibilities:

- Select photographers for special news and feature assignments.
- Enlist the supporting services of freelancers, if needed.
- Maintain close contacts with photo-feature and clip syndicates so that requirements can be obtained from them at short notice.
- Select suitable pictures, figures or graphics from the daily supplies provided by staff assigned for the purpose.
- Adjust the size of photos according to space available on the newspaper or magazine page.
- Highlight or emphasize certain scenes or poses according to the needs of the accompanying writeup and the policy of the publication.
- Oversee the work of all photographers and supporting staff.
- Examine the captions for pictures written by subeditors.
- Keep in touch with the latest books and journals on photo-editing and photojournalism.

All current and future photojournalists and television or video camera staff can profit from the following information.

The visual content of all print and electronic media (except, of course, radio) is gaining increasing attention these days. Photojournalists and videographers are getting more and more prominence in the media world as the days go by. The modern media world is a world of visuals. Many scholars think that the importance of the word is declining and that of the image is ascending.

Mitchell Stephens, for example, argues that a culture that was dominated until recently by the printed word is disappearing fast with the advent of a new culture that is dominated by moving images.[2] Seeing (videre in Latin) is considered more important than hearing or reading as far as the modern television generation is concerned. The image, according to Stephens, is replacing the word as the predominant means of 'mental transport' (1998: 11).

Almost four decades ago, Marshall McLuhan declared in his characteristic way that human beings were returning to the pre-literate stage in human evolution! We may not go that far, yet we can concede that the visual aspect of the media is very much on the increase—the photographic and picture elements in the print media; the rise of film, television and the video; the proliferation of visual elements in the Internet and, above all, in advertisements and commercials. Perhaps human beings are readier to believe what is seen rather than what is heard or read without visuals. In the world of Indian television, even songs are 'seen' rather than heard these days!

There is no doubt that visual journalism is very powerful and visual journalists are coming across newer and newer opportunities every day. With imagination, originality and commitment to their profession, visual journalists can rise to unprecedented heights quickly, although certain risks are involved. Some of them take up adventurous challenges such as photographing or videographing the sudden and unexpected furies of nature—a flash flood, an avalanche, an earthquake or forest fire. On rare occasions, they become so engrossed in their work that they forget their own personal safety. A case in point is the tragic death of a well-known photographer of a prominent newspaper of Kerala in 2002.

Media organizations never grudge the high expenses in acquiring the best and the latest equipment for their visual journalists. Some digital cameras used to cost up to Rs 100,000 a decade ago, but the price has come down drastically these days.

Journalists in both print and electronic media who interview sobbing and sorrowing subjects who have just undergone a traumatic experience should never wound their subjects further by asking trite or inappropriate questions. Humanitarian considerations should be given the utmost importance in such situations. Here, the right to personal privacy of the affected individual should get priority over the media worker's right to get more information. In normal circumstances, there is not much information of public value here.

---

[2] Stephens 1998. See the Preface in particular.

Photography was introduced to India in the mid-19th century. Currently, media have first-rate photographers and photojournalists in all the metropolitan cities and in media production centres in the state capitals. Professional portrait studios are available in almost all towns, big and small. Most photographers have switched to the latest techniques and equipment. Even in the district towns of small states, there are now digital studios. The rapidity with which digitalization has spread in India is amazing.

Before we move on to the more important visual media of communication, namely, film and television, let us dwell briefly on the phenomenon of digitalization (also referred to as digitization) which has become the most important common element in all modern media.

Digitalization

Being digital and electronic—that is the most outstanding characteristic of all modern media. We shall try to understand the basic principles involved in being digital and electronic, so that our understanding of the latest developments in all branches of the media will be enhanced. As mentioned earlier, what reach us through the media are pieces of information in words and pictures.

Information can be gathered, processed, stored, retrieved and transmitted digitally. Every piece of information can be translated into a '1, 0' or 'yes, no' binary system. The word digital comes from the Latin root *digitus* which means 'finger'.

Theodore Mommsen, German historian and archaeologist, was struck by the visual similarity and significance of the lower Roman numerals such as I, II, III, IV, V, etc. (which represent 1, 2, 3, 4, 5, etc., of the Indo-Arabic system) to early counting using the fingers (digits). Two Vs (one V on an inverted V) gave 'X' or ten, now written 10 after the concepts of zero and place value of '0' were introduced by Indian mathematicians of yore.[3]

The Binary System

In addition to the digital system based on 10 and the vigesimal system based on 20 (10 digits and 10 toes) followed by the Eskimos, Native Americans and some African tribes, there is the binary system, which is the basis of the modern computerized systems of communication, including telecommunications.

---

[3] For more details about the origin of digital counting, see Jacker (1964: 31).

In this system, all five fingers of one hand are taken as one unit. The system has a base of two and it is physiologically logical: we have two hands, two feet, two eyes and two ears. Some Australian aborigines, African tribes, and the earliest inhabitants of South America used to count this way.

Blaise Pascal built the first known calculating machine in France in 1642, basically an adding and subtracting machine. The great German mathematician-philosopher Gottfried Wilhelm Leibnitz designed a calculating machine that could also multiply, divide and extract the roots of numbers, and demonstrated it before the Academy of Paris and the Royal Society of London. He actually improved upon Pascal's calculator.

Leibnitz was also interested in the transmission of information, but what is more important for us here is that he considered the binary system (that is, the two-element system, the very basis of all electronic computers) as quite useful for computing. As a philosopher, he considered the number '1' as representing God, and '0' as representing nothingness or the void out of which the entire universe was created.

Through the great contributions of scientists of the 19th century[4] and the production and process improvements achieved during the Industrial Revolution, which reached its peak during the closing decades of the same century, much of the electrophysiological and electronic basis of intrapersonal and interpersonal communication, including mechanical and electronic counting, was established. The foundations of radio broadcasting were also laid during the closing decades of the century.

A chronology of digital system application and its use in computers, after trying it in calculators, is given here to get a clearer picture of advanced systems of computerized communication (compunication) including digital photographic communication.

Briefly, Pascal's desktop calculator was improved upon by Leibnitz in 1673 and Galvani published a report of his research activities in electrophysiology in 1791. Jacquard introduced his punched card system in 1801 to control the production of fabric patterns. Within a decade and a half, Magendi introduced the concept of 'feedback and control' in the animal system. In 1833, Babbage abandoned the Difference Engine he had been working on for a decade and concentrated his attention on the Analytical Engine. In 1848 Helmholtz measured the speed at which a frog's nerve impulses were transmitted. In 1854, Boole published *An Investigation of the Laws of Thought* and initiated what later came to be called Boolean logic for binary systems operations. In 1868, Maxwell

---

[4] The list is long, but some outstanding contributors are Watt, Magendi, Galvani, Volta, Jacquard, Babbage, Maxwell and Pavlov.

published his famous paper, 'The Theory of Governors', which discussed control mechanisms, the basis of cybernetics. The word has come from the Greek word *kybernetes*, meaning the person who steers or governs the boat.

The American mathematician Norbert Wiener who wrote *Cybernetics: Or Control and Communication in the Animals and Machine* in 1948 is called the 'father of cybernetics'.

Two MIT professors, Claude Shannon and Warren Weaver, had already worked out a mathematical model of information. They published *A Mathematical Theory of Communications* in 1949.

ENIAC (Electronic Numerical Integrator and Computer), developed by Professors J.W. Mauchly and J.P. Eckert, Jr., was the first electronic digital computer. It was put into operation in 1944 at the University of Pennsylvania.

In the latter half of the 20th century, rapid strides were made in the miniaturization of computers and the development of advanced programming techniques. The biggest development was electronic mail and the Internet, two technological marvels that can be considered the basis of the globalization of communication and commerce, including the multinational transfer of photographs, pictures, graphics and data of all kinds.

As mentioned previously, the digits in computer and digital technology are confined to 1 and 0. The binary digit is called, in the language of electronics and computer science, a *bit*. Scientists refer to 'bits' of information, that is, the number of pieces of information that the computer stores in yes-no, 1, 0 or on-off fashion. Eight bits form a *byte*.

All photographs and pictures can be analysed into bits of different intensity—light, very light, dark, very dark, etc.—by a computer. The colour and intensity of each dot are put into numbers. Each number becomes a digital symbol. We call a picture analysed this way a *digital picture*.

The following is equipment for digitalizing a picture for a computer: digital camera, charge-coupled device (CCD) camera, scanner, digitizer, and so on.

The scanner is used very frequently in the publishing industry. It works like a copying machine attached to a computer, converting each picture into a series of numbers. The analysed or scanned picture can be displayed on a computer screen or copied through a laser printer. If necessary, the characteristics of the picture can be altered using appropriate computer programmes. The scanned picture is a template of a series of 0s and 1s in a certain order.

Instead of 0 and 1, different colour gradations can be the basis of scanning: black, deep black, light grey, grey, white, etc. This will yield a more realistic symbolization and each symbol is a *pixel* (picture element).

The Basics of Electronics

Everything in, on, above or below the earth—in fact, everything in the infinite universe—consists of atoms, and the structure of all atoms, including those of human beings, animals and objects, is the same, as all atoms consist basically of a nucleus which in turn consists of a positively charged proton and negatively charged electrons; there are also particles without any charge, therefore called neutrons.

Electrons help in moving information from one point to another in mediated forms of communication, and therefore modern media are called electronic, shortened to 'e'. There was a time when printing was mechanical and media involving printing were known as print media. But in recent times, especially after the 1960s when electronic processing of information started in most Western newspapers through the use of video display terminals (VDTs), all media can be called electronic. This type of processing and production in the print media was started in most major newspapers in India during the late 1970s and early 1980s.

The use of electronic and digital photography and transmission started in India more recently—say, in the late 1980s and early 1990s. Nowadays we use the terms *image processing* or *electronic imaging* for the processing of pictures and photographs, and it is all done digitally.

There are two systems of communication within electronic communication the analogue system and the digital system. There are analogue computers and digital computers just as there are analogue and digital cameras. A digital camera converts an image into digits or number 1, 0 pattern in the computer of the camera. Then the 1, 0 dots are electronically transmitted either to a distant point, where they are reconverted into the image, or to the storage mechanism of the camera, from which they are retrieved electronically and converted back into the image. The colours of the original picture are also converted to pixels of different shades or colour levels. All this is done within fractions of a second.

A pixel is defined as a tiny point of light or picture element displayed on a monitor. A typical colour monitor may consist of a 640 by 480 *pixel array*. Different clarities are also called *grey levels*.

A popular system of picture analysis is to divide the picture into about 62,500 cells (250 horizontal and 250 vertical lines will give these many cells). Pictures analysed into so many cells are usually considered of good quality and clarity, fit for laser printing. Colour pictures are analysed on the same basis. The only difference is that the basic colours are analysed one by one.

Visual communicators in India, particularly photographers who freelance or are assigned by their organizations to shoot pictures, must be aware of the great diversity in the socioeconomic and cultural lives of millions of people, especially in the rural areas. They can take up the mission of informing people of the different regions of the country about this diversity, through photo essays and video reports. They can do much for the advancement of social or alternative communication and bring into the open the suppression of human rights and oppression by powerful groups that make the dalits, women, children and other vulnerable and voiceless groups suffer all kinds of indignities for no greater reason than their birth and station in life. Visual journalists get hundreds of opportunities to tell the nation and the world similar significant but hitherto unknown truths.

Let us now turn to the most powerful audiovisual medium: film.

film: the further expansion of audiovisual wisdom

i f photography paved the footpath to the world of visual communication, film built the macadamized road and television and the new media constructed the 12-lane highway to audiovisual communication.

The progression from still photography to moving pictures was natural. Attempts to make pictures move were taking place in many parts of the world during the latter half of the 19th century. There is no single inventor of film; several inventors were working in the US, UK and France almost at the same time, unbeknownst to one another, and all of them were photographers of one kind or another.

Six eminent inventors contributed to the development of the movie camera and the projector: William K.L. Dickson and Thomas Alva Edison (both from the US), who worked together; Etienne Jules Marey (France) and Eadweard Muybridge (US), who tried to capture photographs of fast-moving animals and machines; and the Lumière brothers, Auguste and Louis, who were the sons of an industrialist and photographic plate manufacturer, Antoine Lumière, of Lyons, France.

Edison, who is also credited with the invention of the light bulb and the phonograph (gramophone), together with his assistant William Dickson developed the *kinetograph*, a movie camera, in 1891, in his laboratory in West Orange, New Jersey. Edison also succeeded in patenting the *kinetoscope*, a crude form of motion picture projector, in 1893. The kinetoscope arrived in Paris in 1894 but it was mainly a viewing machine rather than a screen projector.

Meanwhile, the Lumière brothers, who had expanded their father's factory in Lyons into a 3-million-franc company with 300 workers making 15 million photographic plates a year, succeeded in developing a machine for the projection of films. On 13 February 1895, they patented a camera for filming and viewing *chronophotographic proofs* which could project films in addition to recording and developing them. They also started to make their first film, *La sortie des usines Lumière* (*Leaving the Lumière Factory*), using the camera they had patented. This minute-and-a-half-long movie depicted workers coming out of the factory during their lunch break. The film was exhibited before an audience of about 200 scientists interested in film and photography on 22 March 1895. Despite the suggestions and recommendations of many friends and well-wishers including their father, the Lumière brothers named their invention the *cinematograph*. It is from this word that we get *cinema*, for moving pictures.

According to the *Chronicle of the Cinema*, the first Lumière production was exhibited after Louis Lumière presented his lecture, 'The Photography Industry', to a gathering at the National Society for Industrial Advancement at a hall on the Rue de Rennes in Paris. The 'dumbfounded' audience saw on the screen the still factory building coming alive in a second and workers walking out of the factory (Karney 1999). Though the film lasted for only one and a half minutes, crowds gathered in large numbers at shows organized in other parts of Paris and in other cities. The Lumière brothers shot and exhibited other short films such as *'Arrivée d'un train à la Ciotat (The Arrival of a Train at la Ciotat)*. People could not understand how objects could be shown as moving. 'It was an astonishing vision of reality—of life caught in full swing.' Those animated pictures would certainly have made the members of the audience wonder if they were hallucinating!

There was a Lumière show in Paris on 28 December 1895 at the Indian Exhibition at the Grand Café at 14 Boulevard des Capucines. These early short films, which were all silent depictions of routine activities of ordinary people, lasted at the most two minutes. For example, *Repas de bébé (Baby's Dinner)*, shows Auguste Lumière and his wife trying to feed their unwilling and non-cooperative baby! In the background is a cluster of swinging trees and in the distance an undulating sea. The impression is given that the feeding of the baby lasts for ever! Of course, the silence on the screen makes it seem longer-lasting than it actually is!

The small, easy-to-handle cinematograph produced excellent projections; even though the picture did jerk or oscillate from time to time, it was found to be better than Edison's kinetoscope. However, the movie industry became very strong in the US under Edison and other pioneers. Moving pictures were shown in the arcades of many big American cities. Edison had a monopoly on the movie industry in North America. There were 600 nickel odeons in the New York area itself in the early part of the 20th century. Nickel odeons got their name from the nickel (popular name for one-twentieth of a dollar or 5 cents); moviegoers had to pay a nickel as entrance fee.

An article, 'Edison's Vitascope Cheered', in the *New York Times* dated 24 April 1896 says:

The new thing at Koster and Bial's last night was Edison's Vitascope, exhibited for the first time. The ingenious inventor's latest toy is a projection of his kinetescope [sic] figures, in stereopticon fashion upon a white screen in a darkened hall.... So enthusiastic was the appreciation of the crowd ... that vociferous cheering was heard. There were loud calls for Mr Edison, but he made no response. (Ebert 1997: 340)

In London, the *kineopticon projector* of Birt Acres showed silent films in January 1896.

The Skladanowsky brothers, Emil and Max, projected films in Germany in November 1895, using their bioscope apparatus.

The first American projector was developed by Charles Francis Jenkins. This was before Thomas Armat and Edison developed the Vitascope, which used sprocket wheels to advance the film, and marketed it as an Edison product for the first time on 23 April 1896 at Koster & Bial's Music Hall in New York (Sklar 2002: 29-30).

Whether in the US, UK, France, Germany, Russia or India, to begin with, movies were a mere spectacle, and that spectacle was enough for the audience who were astonished to see movement on the screen. But there were sociological evaluations and criticisms about the new medium even within the very first decade of its existence. Ebert, for example, refers to an article in the *Saturday Evening Post* in 1907 in which the author, Joseph Meddle Patterson, deals with the incredible rise of the movies as a sociological phenomenon catering to the entertainment needs of over two million people— the average number that attended the shows at the nickel odeons every day of the year, a third of which were children (Ebert 1997: 349)!

Nickel odeons were not regular theatres but small storefront halls big enough to accommodate 200 people at the most on improvised seats, giving 12-18 shows of short film projections accomplished through the cinematograph (there were 70-odd names for the same machine in those days including vitascope, kinetoscope, vitagraph and biograph).

Boxing films were the most popular in the US between 1899 and 1907. Although young women were rarely seen at the film shows, many middle-aged and old women were steady patrons. Many movies were violent and some sensuous or even sensual as could be learnt from some of the titles: *The Pajama Girl, The Woman at the Bath, The Great Train Robbery,* etc.

Of these, *The Great Train Robbery* (1903) deserves special mention as it has certain technical qualities of great historical importance and was directed by one of the greatest directors of the early silent movie era, Edwin S. Porter. Although Porter's name is not mentioned in the write-up about the movie in the *Philadelphia Inquirer* of 26 June 1904, his greatness as a movie director is recognized by historians. However, this, his first movie, is full of violence.

> [The movie] has proved a thriller in nearly all the larger cities of the US. It has been a source of wonder as to how photographs of such a drama (of shooting, gagging and murder of innocent train passengers and railway staff and finally pursuit of the robbers by the Sheriff's men in the mountainous terrains and their elimination by the policemen's guns) could have been taken in the Rocky Mountains …. There is a great amount of shooting. The smoke of the pistols is plainly seen, and men drop dead right and left, but no sound is heard. Nevertheless, while witnessing the exhibition, women put their fingers in their ears to shut out the noise of firing! (Ebert 1997: 341)

Edwin S. Porter directed other films too. He filmed the famous novel, *Uncle Tom's Cabin*, drawing on dramatizations and stage techniques. *The Gay Shoe Clerk* was another of Porter's films, in which he explored sexuality by means of a brief vignette in which a shoe salesman fits an attractive young woman with a pair of slippers. Porter was a director with a difference. Perhaps he was too modern for his times. Edison, for whom Porter worked, fired him, despite his originality and talent. Porter was the first filmmaker to treat temporal continuity, introducing flashback techniques instead of linear narration.

Is it not amusing that even in those early years of the moving pictures, films were criticized for sex and violence by no less than Leo Tolstoy and Maxim Gorky? Gorky, for example, saw a Lumière show at a Russian fair and published an article on 4 July 1896 in which he speculated about the future of the new medium, particularly its moving in the direction of sex and violence! He wrote:

> Last night I was in the Kingdom of Shadows. If you only knew how strange it is to be there. It is a world without sound, without colour. Everything there—the earth, the trees, the people, the water and the air—is dipped in monotonous grey …. I was at Aumont's and saw Lumières cinematograph— moving photography …. Suddenly, a strange flicker passes through the screen and the picture stirs to life. Carriages are moving straight at you …. All this moves, teems with life …. Noiselessly, the ashen grey foliage of the trees sways in the wind, and the grey silhouettes of the people, as though condemned to eternal silence and cruelly punished by being deprived of all the colours of life, glide noiselessly along the grey ground.

After expressing his wonder at the new medium, Gorky criticizes the decision of the Lumière brothers to organize the exhibition of their movie at

Aumont's, 'where vice alone is being encouraged and popularized, a place where kisses are sold'. Gorky connects movie-making with love-making at a house of ill repute! He continues:

> I do not yet see the scientific importance of Lumière's invention, but, no doubt, it is there, and it could probably be applied to the general ends of science, that is, of bettering man's life and the development of his mind.... I am convinced that these pictures will soon be replaced by others of a genre more suited to the general tone of the 'Concert Parisian'. For example, they will show a picture entitled 'As She Undresses'.... They would also depict a sordid squabble between a husband and wife and serve it to the public under the heading of 'The Blessings of Family Life'.

Gorky continues his venomous criticism in this vein, as also his satire and gloomy ruminations about the future of the movies.

Tolstoy was not a vehement critic of the medium and he loved to see movies. (Some of his novels have been made into films, for example, *War and Peace* in at least two versions.) But he anticipated, by about half a century, the devouring of the artist by the businessman in the film world (Ebert 1997: 346–47).

How the movies contributed to the democratization of communication in society is evident from the fact that all over the world it is the most exciting, and perhaps the most common and economical, entertainment for ordinary people. As Alexander Walker, film critic for the London *Times* said in his foreword to the *Chronicle of the Cinema*, film is the most influential entertainment and art form. Although the power of the moving image has been blamed for all social evils, movies are the best indicator of the development of a country and they have moved millions of ordinary people to worthy and unworthy causes. Robyn Karney, Chief Editor of the *Chronicle*, has said that movies have something for everyone: they educate and inform us, teach us about other cultures and also entertain us (Karney 1999: 100).

What Patterson observed in 1907 about the democratizing quality of the movies is apt even now:

> Civilization, all through the history of mankind, has been chiefly the property of the upper classes, but during the past century, civilization has been permeating steadily downward .... Today, the moving picture machine cannot be overlooked as an effective protagonist of democracy .... (even for those who are below the reach of the yellow journals) .... The nickel odeons are merely an extension course in civilization. (Ebert 1997: 352–55)

The early Western movies, as observed before, were very short. Reels varied between 300 and 800 feet in length and lasted a couple of minutes each. Usually, the movies were shown along with other entertainment programmes such as live music, dance and other stage shows. This was not the case, however, when movies started to entertain people in India.

Cinema in India

Cinema was shown for the first time in India by the Lumière brothers on 7 July 1896 at Watson's Hotel in Mumbai, six months after their public exhibition of moving images in Paris. But cinema developed in India in an entirely different manner.

Since the equipment for shooting movies and projecting them were already available because of the efforts of talented inventors in the West, movie-making in India was comparatively easy, although there was a great deal of teething trouble. In the early years of India's movie history, the country was under colonial rule. Colonialism puts fetters on creativity; yet, as Robert Sklar has observed in his voluminous work, *A World History of Film*, 'India, though a colony of Britain until after World War II, became the third largest film producing country (behind the US and Japan) and laid the groundwork for later decades.' How did this come about, especially since up until the late 1920s, as in many other lands, Indian theatres screened mostly Hollywood films (Sklar 2002 : 32)?

Before the advent of moving pictures, people's imagination had led to the production of moving images through magic lantern and puppet shows. Inventors in the Netherlands in the mid-17th century used sunlight during the day and candlelight at night to project images painted on a reflective surface through a lens onto a whitewashed wall—that was essentially the technique used in pre-magic lantern projections. The next stage was the development of a projector carrying a light source within itself and a lens. This looked like a lantern with the power to project images on the wall and hence called 'magic lantern'.

Magic lantern shows were a combination of shadow plays and still pictures, enhanced with narratives and dialogues as well as running commentaries provided by skilled narrators behind the screen. Puppet shows, moving images on lighted screens and shadow plays were prevalent in many Asian countries including Indonesia, Thailand and India. Country fairs in several countries made good use of magic lantern shows to entertain the populace.

Multimedia screen entertainment began long before movies became a significant part of popular culture. In our audiovisual age, we are likely to miss the historical importance of magic lantern shows, although it remains a fact that they existed for almost two centuries. Even after the advent of regular movies, magic lantern shows continued in the initial years of the audiovisual age. The role of the magic lantern shows where scenes of skeletons, lifelike moving ghosts and other figures in the form and style of Fantasmagorie (Phantasmagoria) were staged by a Belgian named Etienne Gaspar Robert is significant in the themes of some early movies. The early 19th century magic lantern shows utilized contemporary science to make the shows more realistic.

Following the big success of their first film, the Lumière brothers shot at least half a dozen movies in 1896 and another dozen that have survived in the following years up to 1907. '*Arrivée d'un train* involved distant and close-up shots of a train arriving and passengers disembarking. It is an unstaged event, almost like a documentary of events that take place on a railway platform. Sklar observes that the Lumières were constructing 'a basic *mise-en-scène* of the totality of the film's visual style: placement and movement of camera and performers, décor, lighting—all that appears before the camera' (2002 : 32).

Another Lumière film of 1896 was *L' Arroseur arosé* (*The Waterer Watered*), a mischievous, comic representation of a trick played by a boy on a gardener. What is of historical importance is that it is the first inter-media portrayal, as it is a filmic treatment of a popular newspaper cartoon of the period.

There was stiff competition between the Lumière brothers and Edison. The Lumières were greatly interested in the American film industry and Edison was trying to monopolize that industry. Eventually the Lumières gave up, although Edison had an arch-rival in the Biograph Company, another American film producer. The Lumières withdrew not only from the US but from their entire film producing operations, for reasons best known to them— but not before completing the production of nearly 2,000 short films by 1907, of which only about 20 have survived.

Another important filmmaker of the initial years was Georges Méliès, a renowned magician who had made his mark on magic and magic lantern shows at a Paris theatre called Theatre Robert Houdin. His film, *Le Voyage dans la Lune* (*A Trip to the Moon*), is a futuristic science fiction portrayal of the flight of a rocket to the pock-marked face of the moon, an event that really happened only in July 1969.

A remarkable development during those early years was that of the 35-mm film strip in Edison's labs. Before long, 35 mm became the standard width for conventional film strip. Another standard set by the Edison labs which had lasting significance was the standard for frames per second (fps). The Edison–Dickson camera operated on an 18–22 fps range for silent films. Today, sound films operate on a standard 24 fps.

These technical developments were a great incentive for filmmakers in different parts of the world. However, there was nobody to take up the production of movies in India, following the first cinema show in Bombay on 7 July 1896.

Evolution of the Movie Industry in India

In 1912, two enterprising people from Bombay Province, R.G. Torney and N.G. Chitre, made a short documentary, *Pundalik*, based on the life of a Maharashtrian saint by that name. Although this was the first movie made in India, the credit for laying the foundation for the Indian movie industry goes to Dhandiraj Govind Phalke, who made the first feature film, *Raja Harishchandra*, in 1913. It was based on the Mahabharata story of King Harishchandra, a righteous ruler whose devotion to God was tested. Like Job in the Bible, this king underwent all kinds of adversities including the sacrifice of his family and being forced to take up the menial job of disposing of dead bodies, including that of his own son.

Whereas in Europe and the US no single individual is honoured as the 'father' of cinema, Phalke is honoured as the father of Indian cinema and the highest film award in India is known as the Dadasaheb Phalke Award. It is given annually to the best film personality, whether it be the best director, playback singer, producer, music director, composer, cinematographer, actor or actress of long standing who has contributed significantly to the art and science of Indian cinema.

Phalke is affectionately known as Dadasaheb (revered father-figure). It would be good to know this pioneer more intimately. Phalke came to the field of film rather late, as he was 40 years old when he saw a film for the first time: an English movie, *Life of Christ*, in a Bombay theatre. That experience gave him the motivation to take up cinematography as a career, and inspired him to make films based on epics such as the Mahabharata and Ramayana.

'Could we, the sons of India, ever be able to see Indian images on the screen?' This question bothered him every time he watched an English movie. Obsessed, Phalke requested monetary help from friends and well-wishers in Bombay and Poona and set out for England, where he met many filmographers and watched many movies, all the time nursing his secret ambition. After spending a few months in England, he returned to India with basic cinematographic equipment: a camera, a film perforator, film stock, and plenty of enthusiasm.

According to Sklar, Phalke met Cecil Hepworth, producer of *Rescued by Rover*, in England and shared technical information which helped him in the production of his films, starting with *Raja Harishchandra*. After his return from England in 1912, he advertised for 'good-looking men and women' to act in his films, but it was not easy to get women. Therefore, the stage practice of men taking up women's roles was adapted by Phalke for his silent films. This was not the situation in the West where the rise of the silent film was meteoric and actors and actresses were plentiful. Though no prints of Phalke's first film are available now, his practice of preserving some scenes for a later *compilation film* helped historians to get valuable information about it (Basinger 1999: 475).

When the era of films was inaugurated in the West, there were no immediate feature films, although various techniques including film tricks were tried out by the pioneers like Edison, the Lumière brothers, Dickson, Méliès and others, in their one- or two-minute-long films. Regular actors and actresses came to feature-length movies later, say in the first decade of the 20th century. The period of silent films in the West had no dearth of actors and actresses. Eminent actors such as Charlie Chaplin, Douglas Fairbanks, Gary Cooper, William S. Hart and Rudolph Valentino, and actresses such as Mary Pickford, Norma and Constance Talmadge, Gloria Swanson, Pola Negri, Greta Garbo, Janet Gaynor and Marion Davies made a mark in the film world. The career and fame of some of them lasted beyond the silent era as they earned global fame in the talkie era too.

What the great film director Cecil B. DeMille wrote about Mary Pickford in 1955, that 'There have been hundreds of stars', but 'only one Mary Pickford', could be applied to at least half a dozen other actresses and actors of the silent film era in the West—Gloria Swanson, Greta Garbo, Douglas Fairbanks and Charlie Chaplin. And as Jeanine Basinger, Chairperson of the Film Studies Program at Wesleyan University, has observed:

> The stars who survived the end of the silent film era retained everything they had learned from it, particularly their ability to use their bodies expressively. Unencumbered by the past, they embraced sound and never looked back. Most of the silent stars, however, either went out with a bang or slowly faded away. (ibid.)

We have very little information about Phalke's actors and 'boy actresses' or those of any other pioneering Indian film director. But we know that despite all odds, Phalke produced dozens of silent movies, mostly based on the epics and Puranas of India. He laid the foundation for the film industry in India, having established a film studio not far from Bombay where he trained actors, wrote the scenarios, did the cinematography and even the projection of his films. 'Nobody knew anything in India about the industry in 1911' Phalke wrote later. 'Shooting in the day, doing lab work and editing in the evenings', Phalke completed his first film in six months. It was a major success. He wrote:

> I am proud to say that if I had not possessed the artistic and technical faculties required for film-making and if I had not the courage and daring, the film industry would never have been established in India in 1912. (Sklar 2002: 79)

Phalke's first film was so successful that he took several prints of it and of later productions to makeshift halls and open fields in the rural areas, where thousands gathered to watch. It is said that he had to cart away the coins he collected as ticket charges from them (as paper currency was not popular there)!

Besides a hundred or so silent films, Phalke made a couple of sound films. Despite all his great achievements, however, it seems he died in despair, penniless and apprehensive that he would never get the recognition that he deserved. However, posterity has not ignored him.

During the early phase of the movie industry in the world, the United States produced the largest number of movies; Japan came second. But, surprisingly, even as early as 1940 India was third in the world in the number of movies produced. By that time, silent films had disappeared into the archives and research scholars' dens.

The Introduction of Sound

It is ironic that many cinéastes of the United States and Europe objected to sound films or talkies in the late 1920s. Their contention was that sound spoiled the artistic quality of the moving pictures. Movies had their own universal language, so to speak. An Italian could enjoy an Indian movie as much as an Indian could enjoy an Italian movie, so long as the two movies were silent. Once actors and actresses had dialogues that could be heard, the audience could follow them only if they spoke the same language. This was especially applicable to Indian movies. India, China and the Soviet Union (in the early years of its existence) each had several languages, so the silent movies were popular. When spoken language became a vital ingredient of movies, people could no longer as easily follow the cinematic language that can be universally recognized without verbal dialogue.

There was another objection to sound films which we can understand better when we look at film not as an art but as business. Producers objected to sound film because it would cost them most of their earnings from the foreign exhibition of silent films. The foreign film market was of considerable significance in the economics of American and French film production even in those days. Dubbing in foreign languages, however, was still 'an unsure and very expensive process'. The *synchroscope, cinematophone* and *cameraphone* were used for dubbing, but they did not perform well, which was another reason for producers to object to sound films (Bruccoli et al. 1996: 297).

Whatever the merit of silent movies, they are no longer acceptable to audiences around the world. In a way, the existence of 15 major linguistic regions in India became a vital reason for the sudden growth of film in India because there arose 15 different varieties of movies, those in Hindi accessible to almost 45 per cent of the population, and the ones in prominent languages such as Bengali, Tamil, Telugu, Malayalam, Kannada, Marathi, Gujarati and Assamese accessible to regional markets. Prominence here is measured in terms of the number of movies produced in each language. Connected with the movie industry were and are large numbers of artistes from different regions—musicians, lyricists, playback singers and others.

There are also certain uniting factors. Hindi movies have had great appeal from the late 1930s onwards throughout India, because of the concentration of Hindi-speaking people in the metropolitan cities and large towns where most of the cinema houses have always existed. Almost all Indian movies have more or less the same pattern, with an emphasis on lyrics, plenty of dialogue and dance numbers enjoyed by people in all linguistic regions. No wonder the number of movies made in India increased so rapidly. Today, India has the distinction of producing more movies annually than any other country in the whole world.

The Bombay Talkies

The establishment of the Bombay Talkies by Himansu Rai and Devika Rani in the 1940s greatly promoted the film industry. The two were not only eminent cinema and stage artistes but also good organizers. Hailing from a prominent family in Bengal, Rai went to England to study law. His meeting there with Devika Rani, a niece of Rabindranath Tagore who was studying architecture in London at that time, lessened his interest in law although it heightened both individuals' intense interest in acting and the arts; that shared interest brought them together in several theatrical productions. After attaining technical proficiency in acting, stage management, cinema production and allied fields, they returned to India, got married in 1933, and started working on the establishment of a full-fledged film studio. Thus came into existence the Bombay Talkies which produced a series of important films and an impressive list of actors and actresses. Ashok Kumar and Dilip Kumar, who became giant actors later, were protégés of the Bombay Talkies. Devika Rani was the first recipient of the Dadasaheb Phalke Award when the Award was instituted in 1969. Ashok Kumar won it in 1988 and Dilip Kumar in 1994.

Rai and Rani had a vision. Their Bombay Talkies was established in a sprawling campus with not only the facilities for producing films but excellent natural scenery—tree-lined avenues, cottages, ponds and gardens. An outstanding feature was the establishment of living quarters for artistes, technical staff and others connected with the production and editing of films. This was intended to build a strong team spirit in all those who were connected with the studio. Although everything went well for a few years, the death of Himansu Rai and some restrictions imposed by the British rulers of India at that time affected the working of the Bombay Talkies.

Coming back to the advent of sound films, the first talkie was Warner Brothers' *Don Juan* (1926), although it was not a feature-length movie and the actors did not talk. According to Bruccoli et al., the only sound was a synchronized musical score and sound effects (1996: 410–11).

But the first real talkie in the US was *The Jazz Singer*, a musical in which Al Jolson, a singer, was the hero. It ws first screened on 6 October 1927 at Warners' Theatre in New York's Times Square. As Al Jolson played the piano and sang in the movie; he uttered the words 'Wait a minute, wait a minute, you ain't heard nothing yet', and these are considered to be the first words ever spoken that became part of synchronous speech in a feature film (Sklar 2002: 168).

The sound system which the Warner Brothers used was the *Vitaphone*, invented by Hugh M. Stoller and Harry Pfannenstiel of AT&T Bell Labs, and utilized by the Warners in their Hollywood production, *The Jazz Singer*, in 1927.

According to Sklar, there were earlier sound productions, but they were 'inhibited by stationary microphones, constraining performers' movement, and an immobile camera, enclosed in a large sound-tight box so microphones would not pick up the noise of camera motors' (ibid.: 171).

The first talkie in India was Ardeshir Irani's *Alam Ara*; it came out in 1931.

Film directors in India found that despite the multiplicity of languages, there were certain common elements that appealed to audiences in different linguistic regions, such as religious themes based on the two great epics, the Mahabharata and the Ramayana, and on folk tales and legends. The three systems of music (Carnatic, Hindustani and folk music) appealed to English-educated, traditionally educated and illiterate village people in all regions of India.

Indian film themes, music and style of presentation are totally different from those of the West; in fact, there are basic sociological differences between Eastern and Western films. For example, the expression of love, a basic instinct in all cultures, is totally different. Intimate, sexual scenes are not encouraged in Eastern movies, which does not mean that sexuality is different in different cultures, but that filmic or stage portrayal of the man–woman relationship differs according to social norms prevalent in each region of the world. Public expression of sexual love or open display of affection in public places is rarely seen in real life in Eastern countries.

Indian films also put great emphasis on song lyrics. Quite often, the lyrics are a continuation of the dialogue or a poetic dramatization of the major theme. The words in the songs complement the story.

Besides Himansu Rai and Devika Rani, two other names are of great importance in the early history of Indian movies: those of V. Shantaram, director of a large number of Hindi and Marathi films, and P.C. Barua, actor and director of several outstanding Bengali and Hindi films. Shantaram established Prabhat Film Company in Pune and Barua had a large financial stake in the New Theatres of Calcutta. Shantaram's *Jhanak Jhanak Paayal Baaje* is an extravaganza in colour, dance, song and scenic beauty. His *Do Ankhein Barah Haath (Two Eyes and Twelve Hands)* is a strongly social reformist movie that advocated prison reforms in India. Among the several movies acted in and directed by P.C. Barua, the scion of a royal family in Assam who spent many years in Europe studying film direction, *Maya* (1936) is the most appealing.

The most outstanding Indian filmmaker is, however, Satyajit Ray. This all-round talent (director, scriptwriter, cinematographer, artist and visualizer, all rolled into one) made his first film, *Pather Panchali*, in the mid-1950s. It was a pathbreaker in Indian film history. Critics acclaim it as poetry and art in celluloid; some of them also point out that Ray was influenced by the neorealism of Italian film director Vittorio de Sica's *Ladri di Biciclette (The Bicycle Thief)*.

Ray's first neorealistic film was followed by two others, *Aparajito* and *Apur Sansar*, thematically connected with the first; his most lasting contribution to the Indian film world is this trilogy. However, he made more than a dozen outstanding movies, most of which are in Bengali but a couple of which are in Hindi. Ray's film art has been recognized all over the world. His films have won prestigious international awards and he himself won a special Oscar for lifetime achievement.

Before we close this section, let us take a quick look at the early movies of the world, as visual reports during the silent era and as audiovisual reports during the early sound film era.

According to Sklar, the realism of the early movies in the West had severe limitations as they were in black and white, whereas the real world is one of colour. They were silent, whereas the real world is full of sounds—and noise, if you will. (We should not, however, ignore the fact that most silent movies were accompanied by music, dance and other improvisations.) Films did not stand alone, they were exhibited with other shows in the same theatres either before or after the movie shows. However, the camera had a special advantage: several copies could be made of a single film and exhibited simultaneously in different places. This was one great reason for movies growing into a major mass medium. This is why movies were shown in different parts of Europe and in India in the very year that the earliest movies were shown in France and the US. By 1901, movies were screened in many areas of Asia, Australia and Africa (Egypt, for example). No wonder film became a global medium so soon.

Another important landmark in film history is the arrival of colour, following the introduction of photographic colour film by Eastman Kodak. One of the earliest colour movies in the US was *Gone with the Wind* (1939) starring Clark Gable and Vivian Leigh. Colour movies became common in India in the late 1950s. Today, new black and white movies are a rarity in most parts of the world.

There were many startling developments in other media, such as linotype machines and rotary presses that speeded up the production of newspapers. Although at the turn of the century the main media were printed newspapers and books, there was a very rapid shift thereafter to films, radio and television. By the middle of the 20th century, the media on the whole were audiovisual. With the advent of computerization in the media, all media can now be called audiovisual, because even newspapers on the Internet can easily be converted into audiovisual products.

Radio, movies, recorded music, television, video, computers, CDs, DVDs and various other media and formats of communication are audiovisual. We will look into this further when we discuss the new media of the 21st century. Before that, let us have a quick look at the evolution of radio broadcasting and its emergence as a mass medium in the early part of the 20th century.

radio: the first real electronic medium

*A*fter the telegraph, the telephone and the film, the most significant development in the field of communication was the radio. In 1873, British physicist James Clerk Maxwell said that messages could be transmitted without the use of wires. There had been some protests in big cities of the West against the indiscriminate wiring of buildings as it detracted from the beauty of the architecture. A reason for this protest may have been that the telephone was still an instrument of business and not a personal device for long-distance communication.

For this or other reasons, scientists were experimenting with wireless systems for sending messages, taking inspiration from Maxwell's theory of electromagnetic radiation. Maxwell theorized that electromagnetic waves existed and that their radiant energy could be harnessed for sending messages at the speed of light over long distances. In 1888, Heinrich Hertz of Germany provided support to Maxwell's theory through the actual creation of electromagnetic waves in his laboratory. He measured their wavelength and confirmed that they travelled at the speed of light.

Jagdish Chandra Bose of India conducted experiments on electric waves based on the theory of Maxwell. Independent of Hertz, he obtained waves of short length (5 mm) using his own device, the 'Electric Radiator'. In 1885, he succeeded in sending wireless signals, but did not pursue the matter further as he was more interested in the growth of plants, which is measured by the crescograph.

It was Guglielmo Marconi of Italy, a young inventor, who put Hertzian and Maxwellian findings to practical use. First he sent wireless telegraphic messages from his upper room to the kitchen in his house. Continued experiments showed that he could send wireless messages to points 9 miles away. He had a practical business sense, although he was still young. At the age of 23, he established the Marconi Wireless Telegraph Company with the help of some financiers in England, where he had migrated with his Irish mother.

Marconi's company started sending wireless coded messages (using Morse code) across the English Channel. Within three years, in 1901, the company succeeded in sending three dots (the Morse code designation for the letter S) across the Atlantic from the English coast to Newfoundland.

Marconi's invention was found most useful by shipping companies and other businesses, which could exchange business reports and data, arrival and departure details of ships, for instance, with unprecedented speed. This brought further success for Marconi. During a visit to the US, he set up an American subsidiary of his company. In less than 15 years, the young entrepreneur had established his monopoly over wireless communication in Europe and America.

Then Marconi found an unusual use for his wireless. The New York Herald started using Marconigram (the telegram) for news dissemination. Gradually, hundreds of newspapers came to depend on wirelessly transmitted news. When news agencies came into being, dependence on wireless news and radio photographs increased severalfold.

The four scientists who effectively made radio a magic medium for carrying human voice across the globe were Reginald Fessenden, Karl Braun, Lee De Forest and Edwin Armstrong. Fessenden sent out the first radio signals that carried human voice and music to a ship at sea. The crew, which was used to hearing mere Morse code beep signals over the wireless, were intrigued by the human voice and Handel's music. At least some of them thought that it was the voice of sea nymphs or some supernatural creatures such as the sirens of Greek mythology! This happened on 24 December 1906 and it was the first step towards radio broadcasting.

Meanwhile, the German physicist Karl Braun, who was working on radio receivers (in those days they were called *crystals*) that used the energy in radio waves for power, succeeded in adapting *diodes* for radio use in 1900. Until this time, crystal radio sets had not had loudspeakers, so only one or two people could listen to the radio at a time. However, the use of diodes was a major step in the development of the radio. For their work, Braun and Marconi shared a Nobel prize in 1909.

Diodes are electronic vacuum tubes with two electrodes. They were used in radio receivers to change alternating current (AC) to direct current (DC). *Triodes* are three-electrode electronic vacuum tubes that strengthen weak electrical signals in order to control much larger electrical currents.

The credit for inventing the *triode valve* goes to Lee De Forest, who is considered the father of modern radio broadcasting. His 'audion' was costlier but more efficient than the crystal detector. With the audion commercial broadcasting became easier, as it amplified radio signals several hundred times, which was necessary to broadcast (like the seeds in a farm) signals over a very wide range.

Lee De Forest took his invention to Paris in 1909 and transmitted voice from the top of the Eiffel Tower to receivers up to 500 miles away. The terms *radio telephony* and *radio telegraphy* gave way to *radio*, mainly because of him.

Incidentally, De Forest had developed a sound system called *phonofilm* for converting silent films into sound films, but Hollywood was not interested. He was such a brilliant inventor that producers in Sweden used his process in 1924 to make a talking picture called *Retribution* which was thus the first talkie, according to Vincent Tompkins (Bruccoli et al. 1996: 200).

Edwin Armstrong through his invention, the *superheterodyne circuit*, succeeded in introducing a system by which listeners could tune into different broadcasts very easily.

Two names stand out in the annals of the rapid development of commercial broadcasting in the US (which is today the media Mecca of the world with more than 10,000 radio stations and 12,000 television stations): David Sarnoff and Frank Conrad.

David Sarnoff started life as a wireless operator in Marconi Wireless Company and rose to the position of President of the Radio Corporation of America (RCA). While working in the Marconi Company, he wrote a memo to his superiors pointing out the possibility of reaching radio programmes to individual homes. His ideas and his recommendations were ignored by his superiors. However, when he became the Commercial Manager of the RCA, he was finally in a position to implement his ideas.

Sarnoff was also a pioneer in the use of magnetic video tape for film and television recording. The development and widespread use of the video cassette recorder (VCR) in film and television production and among media users owe much to him.

Dr Frank Conrad was an engineer in the Westinghouse Electric Company before he took charge of the KDKA radio station in Pittsburgh, an industrial town in Pennsylvania, on 2 November 1920. At KDKA he pioneered commercial radio broadcasting, heading perhaps the first commercial broadcasting station in the world.

In those early days, news was the staple of broadcasting, but the interesting fact is that the radio stations depended on the newspapers for news, whereas today the opposite is true. Soon the stations found that people were equally or perhaps more interested in sports, music and other programming. Today there are 24-hour stations devoted to news. There are all-music stations, within which are stations devoted to different branches of music—rap, classical, rock and blues. But music radio stations have yielded to Music

Television (MTV) these days. Even the radio broadcasting of sports has been affected by the rise of television. People are more interested in the visual than in the audio medium, although audio cassettes and compact discs of music have captured the imagination of a large number of young listeners. Television has affected film and radio to some extent.

The development of miniaturization and transistorization by Japanese inventors and commercial promoters was a major event in the history of the radio. Big, unwieldy radio sets were replaced by portable sets which people could carry with them anywhere they went—on travel, during picnics, while jogging, etc. Today, there are dozens of varieties of these miniaturized entertainment instruments.

Radio in India

Early forms of modern communication—the telegraph, telephone and wireless—were strictly under the control of the British government in India before 1947 and later even under the independent Government of India What the British government did in the media world during pre-Independence days was continued by the new government. Radio was no exception.

All public communication except through newspapers was under the thumb of British authority. Even the newspapers were under surveillance, especially those that were nationalist and hence supportive of the Gandhian movement for independence. Media of public communication, including the telegraph, telephone and wireless, were monopolized by the British government. There were no independent entrepreneurs to support the research activities of Jagdish Chandra Bose, who had done some remarkable work in the creation of short electromagnetic waves in the laboratory, and turn them to public benefit.

The telegraph was used as an aid to the Indian railways, which were introduced by the British in the mid-19th century for the express purpose of moving troops and provisions to far-off stations where there were rumblings from disgruntled native princes who were uniting against the British suzerainty, though belatedly. The telephone was a luxury enjoyed by the British and Indian civil servants. There was no effort from any quarter for the democratization of communication, as the entire system was dominated by an alien government. With Independence in 1947 matters were expected to improve, but there were tremendous problems for the new government and the infrastructure for modern communication remained undeveloped until the 1980s, when rural telephone expansion took place in a major way.

To continue with the story of radio's development in India, broadcasting started in 1927 under the auspices of the Indian Broadcasting Company, Bombay, with transmitters in both Bombay and Calcutta. But the company could not continue operations, despite the government's political support, because of severe financial constraints. However, some 10,000 people, all elite citizens of the four metropolises, had already bought radio sets, and their political and economic clout resulted in a revival of broadcasting (there were no radio set manufacturers in India at that time; all sets were imported, and licence fees were collected from set owners). The name of the new company was the Indian Broadcasting Service and it was started in 1930 as part of the Information Wing of the British Government of India.

Whereas in other parts of the world various types of economic and technical changes in society led to corresponding changes in the world of broadcasting, no such changes occurred in India. For example, an electronic media culture had developed in the US and UK during the 1920s, which resulted in major changes in the operation of the radio medium. The print media had reached a higher technological status with the sophistication bestowed on them by radio photos, teleprinter (teletype) machines, faster rotary presses, better photograph reproduction in print, more efficient distribution systems, and so on. The early decades of the 20th century thus saw major developments in printing and publishing. Speed in telecommunication was universally recognized among most sections of the people as an essential aspect of life because of the spread of literacy and education among the large majority of the Western population.

As we have seen, there was initially no great competition for print media from the new medium of radio because, for the most part, radio broadcasters depended on the newspapers for news. Soon things changed. People found the radio more engaging and fresh throughout the day and night because the radio stations in the West were under private ownership unlike in India where, until recently, the broadcast media were wholly under the control of the government; and private entrepreneurs did not have to depend on government or wait for bureaucratic sanction to introduce novelty in timing or content. There were some restrictions on the frequency, timing and content of the broadcast media in the US until President Reagan's time, when most restrictions were removed, except those relating to technical matters.

But the most important factor in the development of the radio was the introduction of *commercials*, a technical term for advertising on radio and television. The newspaper companies were making profits or breaking even not from subscriptions but from advertisements. Those who were running radio stations learnt this lesson from newspaper publishers—some of whom happened to be radio station owners too. Thus, from a very early period, radio turned commercial in the West. It is generally recognized that the first radio commercial was heard in New York in August 1922—that is, less than two years after KDKA pioneered commercial broadcasting in Pittsburgh. It was a commercial for an apartment building, and the advertiser, it seems, paid $100 to the radio station for network time. It is also believed that by the beginning of the 1930s, advertisers were spending almost $25 million on radio commercials.

Commercial advertising on the radio in India started in 1967, although many media experts and others had suggested introducing it much earlier, because they maintained that for the successful functioning of radio, turning commercial was essential. The decision-makers in the Information and Broadcasting (I&B) Ministry, under whom radio functioned, would not change their policy until they saw that Radio Ceylon was capturing the interest and imagination of the Indian listeners. Thousands of radio listeners in all parts of India had by then become ardent votaries of the attractive entertainment and music programmes from India's neighbour, which had already carved special niches in their radio programming specially for Indian listeners. Indian advertisers were buying commercial time on Radio Ceylon for Indian products and services. This opened the eyes of the I&B Ministry and radio turned commercial in India from 1967.

In 1947, India had 11 radio stations—six under the central government and five in the princely states. The rulers of Mysore and Hyderabad had started broadcasting stations in 1935 and 1939, respectively. Later on, when All India Radio (AIR) was formed, these two stations were taken over by it. Delhi, Madras and Lucknow also had radio stations before 1947.

In 1936, Lionel Fielden of the British Broadcasting Corporation (BBC) was brought to India to streamline the operations of AIR, which had come under the direct supervision of I&B Ministry.

The Indian terms used for 'broadcasting', such as *akashvaani* (Sanskrit and Hindi and therefore familiar to most linguistic regions), *vaanoli* (mainly Tamil), and *vaani* (Telugu) are also used when referring to AIR, in different regions of India. It is said that the Mysore ruler suggested the use of *akashvaani* for radio in the 1930s and that name has stuck.

By 1977, the number of radio stations in India had increased to 62, and the number of radio sets to 20 million. In 1982, there were 86 radio stations and 160 transmitters. Today, India has 118 regional centres or full-fledged stations and 82 district centres, for a total of 200 radio stations. There are plans to increase the number of stations, particularly *frequency modulation* (FM) stations in the metros and state capitals. The number of sets has increased to 200 million, which indicates that radio is the most popular medium in India.

Considering the size of India's population, however, there is scope for increasing the number to at least 300 million. India needs more radio stations, transmitters and sets.

Radio is affordable to a very large number of people, especially in the rural areas, because of the transistor revolution of the 1960s. Even regular sets are affordable to most people because of the low price. TV is definitely a more attractive medium, but it is not easily affordable to people in the rural areas. There is a direct link between people's prosperity and their media use.

Radio Programming

Radio programming, and for that matter all media programming, depends on what the organizers of the media consider to be the interests and tastes of the listeners or the public. This is especially true of privately owned broadcasting systems, where the owners and operators make it a point to survey public opinion from time to time and decide on the changes required in programming so as to attract the maximum number of listeners or viewers, proportional to the amount of advertising they can canvass. Sometimes certain national priorities, as seen by the political and social leaders of a nation, may not be seen as priorities at all by media directors; this can lead to conflicts between government and private media.

Broadcasting in India (both radio and television) has from the start been under the direct control of the government (British as well as Indian). In recent years, however, because of the liberalization, privatization and globalization trends in India, some changes have taken place in the media world. Since September 1997, both the broadcast media have been placed under an autonomous corporation, the Prasar Bharati Corporation (PBC), formed by an Act of Parliament.

It is almost a decade since the PBC has been formed but many critics point out that there has not been any major change in programming. But to expect the media to help a country to achieve development without altering the basic socioeconomic structure of that country is too unrealistic. The United States has a highly developed media system; but to say that it was the media that helped the United States to reach a high stage of economic development is like putting the cart before the horse.

There are important historical factors working on the development of a country and its media. For example, in the US, where radios were first marketed for home use in 1920, about 5 million radio sets were sold annually in the early years of radio's expansion in that country. The leading brands were battery-powered, but buyers could afford expensive batteries and antennae besides the $35–$40 for the sets. Better models such as the RCA, Atwater Kent and Zenith brands cost $150 –$350. As indicated in the encyclopaedic publication *American Decades, 1920–1929*, by Judith S. Baughman and others, 'Broadcasting began for the purpose of selling radio receivers. Before the later years of the 1920s, radio programming was unimaginative, offering mainly speeches, lectures and music' (1995: 311).

In 1925, more than 70 per cent of the airtime was given over to music, 0.1 per cent to drama, 0.7 per cent to news and 0.2 per cent to sports, and most programmes were sponsored by companies. And the medium was the message! Even before McLuhan, this statement was applicable to the media, because people were attracted to the novelty of the electronic media when they appeared on the horizon of public communication. They were as interested in the quality or relevance of the programme as in the novelty of the radio. Again, as mentioned by media experts of the US, 'The fact of radio was still so remarkable that people would listen to anything just for the sake of hearing sound coming out of the box—just as in 1947, people would watch anything on television, and still do' (ibid.).

The other important factor in the rapid growth of radio in the US was the unprecedented growth in the media use of the American people following the establishment of newspapers tailored for ordinary people, the penny press. Media habits were formed by newspaper reading. People who were frequent users of one medium would tend to use more media. Newspaper readers were the first users of the radio. Gradually, radio became the carrier of news, although in the initial years, as indicated before, it was a medium for music and other forms of entertainment.

Some outstanding commercial promoters of radio and television in the US, such as David Sarnoff and William S. Paley, were responsible for the major expansion of both the electronic media. Described as one of the architects of modern American society, Paley, with an unerring instinct for entertainment, was a programming genius. He brought about major changes in radio as well as television programming in the Columbia Broadcasting System (CBS) of which he was the president.

Sarnoff, who had seen the immense possibility of radio as a home entertainment medium, did all he could to develop the National Broadcasting Company (NBC) from its inception. As President of the Radio Corporation of America (RCA), he not only organized the first radio network, the NBC, in 1926, but also purchased the Victor Talking Machine Company in 1929 and put the phonograph and the radio in the same unit. He did not stop there. He acquired a major share of the RKO movie studio, and also formed a new company in a tie-up with General Motors, the largest car manufacturing firm in the world, to make car radios. Thus Sarnoff built up the radio broadcasting system and brought its benefits to home listeners, car drivers and others.

Even as early as 1923, Sarnoff had predicted the advent of television. He said: 'I believe that television, which is the technical name for seeing as well as hearing by radio, will come to pass in the future', 25 years before television appeared in the US as a medium in common use.

Thus we see how the scientific inventions of Marconi, Fessenden, De Forest and Armstrong were put to wide commercial use by votaries of free enterprise like Sarnoff and Paley, to name just two of many.

Music was at the top of the programming ladder even in the US in the 1920s; in fact, even as late as the 1960s, a former chairman of the Federal Communications Commission (FCC), Newton Minow, observed that despite the coverage of Vietnam, the Apollo space mission and the landing of Neil Armstrong and 'Buzz' Aldrin on the moon, race riots and other events, radio remained the 'publicly franchised jukebox' (Baughman et al. 1994: 347).

Advertising and public relations had very early on become essential ingredients of the media business. No medium could become a huge business without the help of advertising even as early as the 1920s, and a business needs a public relations promoter to project a favourable image of itself among the investing and consuming public.

After the end of World War I in 1919 a boom occurred in the West in the manufacture, sales and distribution of hundreds of light and heavy durables and consumables produced on the basis of the scientific and technical research and development that had occurred during the war years. Existing advertising agencies expanded and new agencies came up. J. Walter Thompson's billings went from $10.7 million in 1922 to $37.5 million in 1927. Similar increases occurred at other agencies too.

Commercial battles were waged through the columns of the widely circulated penny press, the 'slick' magazines (magazines printed on quality art paper) and the airwaves. Cigarette advertising precipitated a 'war' among competing brands like Lucky Strikes, Camel and Chesterfield. Special efforts were made to woo the untapped constituency of women and entice them into the world of men with advertisements suggesting gender equality through smoking and drinking!

Women and adolescents did not smoke in public as yet in the 1920s (except perhaps in the movies), until the barrage of advertising in the press and on the radio broke their inhibitions and 'social shackles'. 'Reach for a Lucky instead of a sweet' became a catchy and popular slogan among fashionable women. 'Everyone knows that heat purifies [referring to the secret heating process used by the cigarette manufacturer] and so 20,679 physicians say that LUCKIES are less irritating to your throat', claimed an advertisement! (It is to the credit of the *Reader's Digest*—started by DeWitt and Lila Wallace in 1922—that it was the earliest magazine to publish the connection between cigarettes and lung cancer.) (Baughman et al. 1994: 353).

By 1950, US advertising revenues from local radio itself had reached $273 million. This went up to $889 million in 1965. During the same period, TV advertising revenue went up from $171 million to $2.5 billion. This financial information is provided here to show the clout or role of advertising in media development and to indicate that media expansion cannot occur without economic development. Often researchers, media enthusiasts and development experts seem to argue that merely expanding the media in poor countries would cause development to ensue.

American broadcasting networks reorganized their programming according to the public taste, and even took up 'narrowcasting' instead of broadcasting for this purpose. It became clear that radio programmes should appeal to different sections of the public based on sociodemographic and psychographic characteristics. Thus developed all-news stations devoted solely to news, with commercial breaks; classical music stations; rock and roll stations; light and pop music stations; and so on. This type of programming is being tried now in the FM stations of India. However, to attain the objective of reaching all sections of the listening public in India, there is a need for many more stations. This is an immediate task for the PBC, but more private entrepreneurs are essential. There are some changes in the ownership pattern of radio in India, but complete privatization has certain disadvantages, as experienced in the US.

Radio's development in India has been totally different from its development in America. No private enterprise was allowed in Indian radio, and the government showed limited initiative. Research and development activities were unheard of and higher educational institutions were few. In short, radio did not have any scope for commercial growth in India. No wonder the growth in the number of stations was until recently extremely small and expansion quite slow. Programming remained confined to classical music and news for the most part.

When we analyse AIR's programming pattern, we realize that nearly 40 per cent of broadcast time is set apart for music and music-related programmes. In the initial years, music programmes broadcast on AIR were aimed at the learned audiences in royal palaces and *sangeet sabhas* (music concerts or music assemblies) but, from 1952 onwards, both Hindustani and Carnatic classical music was broadcast. As mentioned earlier, AIR turned commercial in 1967 and from then on film songs and light music were broadcast on AIR channels to win back the audience lost to Radio Ceylon. Western music is broadcast from stations located in metropolitan and large urban areas.

Other than music, there are weekly dramas, adaptations of popular short stories and novels, talks aimed at youth, women or particular social groups, humorous skits and so on. A sizeable chunk of broadcast time is devoted to news every morning, noon and evening.

The News Services Division of AIR collects news and opinions on current events as they occur and broadcasts them in news bulletins and features. The PBC has shown more initiative and independence from the I&B Ministry in recent years, but it is still not completely autonomous.

Perhaps people outside India do not know the gigantic nature of the Indian radio broadcasting system. AIR, for example, broadcasts 250 news bulletins in different languages, of which 68 are broadcast from the Delhi station. Other stations relay them. The regional stations broadcast 119 bulletins in 23 languages and 35 tribal dialects. Listeners abroad get 63 AIR bulletins in 25 languages. When Parliament is in session, English and Hindi news analyses are given from AIR Delhi. Similarly, stations in the state capitals bring out analytical features when the respective state assemblies are in session.

The External Services Division of AIR broadcasts in 17 Indian languages and eight foreign languages for 56 programme-hours every day, besides releasing 300 news bulletins in major languages of the world.

AIR maintains original recordings of the voice and speeches of great national leaders including Mahatma Gandhi, Jawaharlal Nehru and Indira Gandhi in its Sound Archives Library. The renderings of famous Hindustani and Carnatic musicians are also kept in the Archives. A special effort is made to collect historical material of lasting importance and preserve it in the Archives.

There are worthy educational efforts being made by AIR now. *Gyanvani* of the Indira Gandhi National Open University (IGNOU), for example, is an educational programme of AIR which is of great help to people of all ages who wish to pursue higher education during their spare time.

As for the future, AIR has to take full advantage of the transistor revolution that started in the world some 40 years ago, so that people living in far-off, mountainous or hilly regions of India can be reached with music and news. There is no doubt that in the current economic situation, the radio is the most affordable and effective medium of communication in India. Radio is already the most popular medium in the rural areas but we can do more to increase rural participation in the communications revolution already in progress in India.

Similarly, educational programmes broadcast on AIR channels can be made more attractive and useful, especially through a change in the scheduling so that more learners can take full advantage of the system and improve their knowledge, not only of conventional subjects but also of marketable skills through value-added, job-oriented educational programmes. Let there be a proliferation of radio stations using low-power transmitting systems in every educational and social institution so that more and more young people, women, workers and other social groups enter into the business of running their own lives instead of depending on mammoth and often corrupt systems that are beyond their control and totally alienated from them.

Radio is far less costly to produce than television and it can be more localized and specialized than any other mass medium. Even a couple of thousand listeners are enough to attract advertisers, especially those who are trying to spread commercial messages about products and services rural people may need in these changing times. From the 200 radio stations that exist today, the number can be increased to 2,000 if more attention is paid to rural communication over the air.

If there is any mass medium in India that is truly *mass* in character today, it is the radio. To make it more effective and listener-oriented, a more democratic approach on the part of planners and system organizers is most essential.

Now let us look at the evolution of the most popular and widespread medium of audiovisual communication in the world—namely, television— and its position in India.

8

television: an endless parade

*i*f the radio was an 'ethereal voice' to begin with, television was an 'ethereal spectacle'. Even the tip of a child's finger could bring about the magic of that spectacle with just a gentle touch on the remote control. A wonderful world of strange sounds, pictures, scenes and drama, appears, along with news from the other side of the globe presented with an apparently genuine fidelity to the truth and to reality.

What flits before our eyes can make us laugh, think, react, protest, sympathize or commiserate. But the next moment, we see an Urvashi, Rambha, Tilottama or Helen, if you will, proclaiming that the heavenly fragrance of an exotic perfume is the very secret of her beauty and her appeal to men, or that the soft drink or soap in her hand will make life more meaningful and successful.

Another scene: A beautiful young woman appears on the screen in a wheel chair. She is paralysed from her chest down, the result of a terrible accident. How did it happen? While driving at a high speed on the highway, she reached out for the cell phone kept in her pocket book kept on the passenger seat—and the next thing she could remember was that she was in a hospital bed. At least that's what she told the talk show host on day X after the accident; but the same young woman appears on the same show on day Y to confess that she was drunk beyond legal limits while she had the accident. She wanted to share her experience for the benefit of all drivers, young and old—never mix drinking and driving.

A woman who weighed 80 kilograms underwent an exercise and diet regimen combined with a particular medicinal pill and succeeded in bringing her weight down to 60 kilograms in two weeks—so claimed the testimonial advertisement, with 'before' and 'after' pictures.

A macho young man driving a sleek, sexy automobile along a mountain road suddenly screeches to a halt at the edge of a cliff in a dare-devil stunt—just to demonstrate the effectiveness of the car's brakes.

But nothing was more dramatic than the high-tech suicide mission accomplished by some young men from Saudi Arabia who hijacked planes in Boston and directed them to the twin towers of the World Trade Centre in New York. Television networks not only in the US but throughout the world endlessly repeated the clips showing this terrible destruction of human lives and high-rise buildings.[1] 9/11 is still a nightmare not only for Americans but for people all over the world.

All these scenes flash before the viewer in quick succession. What does the viewer retain in her memory? Are all the items in the parade before her of the same importance? The viewer is bombarded with a series of scenes and narrations; she has to make her choice on the basis of her intrapersonal orientation and mental make-up. That is the big challenge offered by the most influential medium of public communication, namely, television, sometimes called the 'idiot box' 'the chewing gum for the eye'.

Viewing of television and discussing programme contents with others are common habits prevalent among people living in the modern era. Television viewing has become entrenched among those living in most urban and some rural areas of almost all nations these days. We do have to recognize, however, that almost half the population of the world has never used a telephone, not to speak of a radio or television—such is the imbalance in people's media use. But we are concerned here with the spread of television as a medium of entertainment, information and education among half the world's population.

The Pioneers of Television

Television—seeing things from distant places, even as distant as the planets or objects in space—became a household word and a household appliance in the late 1940s or early 1950s in Europe and the US. In other parts of the world, it reached that status only in the late 1960s, although some crude form of the television was available in many parts of the world during the late 1950s.

The first practical device for transmitting the likeness of an image over a distance was invented by Paul Nipkow, a German inventor, who patented his 'Electric Telescope' in 1884. Nipkow used a rotating disc with small holes

---

[1] A similar treatment was given by the media in the coverage of the tsunami disaster of 26 December 2004, in which more than 200,000 people in a dozen countries lost their lives following a massive undersea quake off the Indonesian island of Sumatra.

drilled through it in a spiral pattern. The *Nipkow disc* was of the same size as a gramophone record and the holes on it were quite small. When light rays were sent through the holes and the disc rotated at high speed simultaneously, they could be resolved into light and dark dots that could be sent over the wires. Although many other scientists and inventors contributed to the development of television, everyone seems to agree that it was Nipkow's concept of sending images as light and dark dots over a distance that prompted them to take up their own inventing missions. Hence, Nipkow is considered the prime mover of the concept of television.

The word 'television' was first used by Constantin Perskyi in a scientific paper he presented at the International Electricity Congress held in Paris on 25 August 1900. Perskyi described an apparatus based on the magnetic properties of selenium, an element that helped in the transmission of pictures through electromagnetic radiation (Abramson 1995: 13–26). According to Shirley Biagi, the word first appeared in the United States in the June 1907 issue of *Scientific American*. It is interesting to note that before this word became widely accepted, inventors used 'telephoto', 'telectroscope', 'wireless pictures', 'visual wireless', 'visual radio', 'electric vision', 'electric telescope', and other terms to describe the precursors of the television.

The marvel of television lies in the near-instantaneous transfer of pictures and sounds from the place where a performance or event takes place to the receiver kept far away; the transmitter and the receiver could be thousands of miles apart. Televised pictures of the Apollo moon flight and the subsequent space missions are examples of satellite communication.

The recording of audio and visual material and their transmission and reception in the television system are very complex scientific and technical processes. Readers are referred to standard textbooks on electronic recording, transmission and reception of signals including the working of the television camera, electronic gun, and black-and-white versus colour television.

Stated succinctly, the television camera captures the image with sound and converts it into dots that travel at the speed of light to the receiving point. Although picture and sound are recorded together, picture signals are transmitted separately. By adjusting the time of despatch, the two signals which are of different velocities are made to reach the receiver at the same time. The signals are sent from a transmitting tower, usually made of steel and standing higher than the nearby buildings and hills to avoid obstruction to the electromagnetic waves, which travel in straight lines. The distance travelled by the waves depends on their power and on the height of the transmitting tower. Usually television signals sent by high power transmitters (HPT) can travel uninterruptedly for 80–160 kilometres and those sent by low power transmitters (LPT) for 25–50 kilometres.

After Nipkow there were many pioneers whose contributions to the development of the television system are quite important. For example, the invention of the *cathode ray tube* (CRT) was of great significance. Alan A.C. Swinton of England conducted several experiments that proved that 'distant electric vision' was possible with tubes using cathode rays at both the receiving as well as the transmitting stations. Light was converted to electricity and vice versa. Unknown to Swinton, Max Dieckmann in Germany and Boris Rozing of Russia were working on the same scientific problem. All these scientists came up with different devices during 1909–10.

The contributions already made by Marconi, and a little later by Fessenden, De Forest, Braun, Armstrong, Conrad and others (see Chapter 7) to radio and wireless communication indirectly helped in the development of the television system.

But the biggest invention was that of the *iconoscope*, which could send not only visual images in dots through the atmosphere to distant places but also help the receiver capture signals and convert them back to visual images. The scientist who was responsible for this was Vladimir Zworykin, a researcher in the Westinghouse Company in the US who had also patented his picture tube in 1923. Zworykin worked with a handsome grant from David Sarnoff, head of RCA.

Meanwhile, John Logie Baird of London, who was experimenting with television, filed for his patent in July 1923. In April 1925, he set up his television apparatus in a London department store and demonstrated the first crude functioning of television. With further improvements made in his apparatus, Baird demonstrated his system before the general public on 26 January 1926, which, according to Abramson, was the 'first public demonstration of television' (Abramson 1995).

Philo T. Farnsworth developed a CRT in his California lab and called it the 'dissector tube'. It could produce images that were 10 times clearer than the ones produced by his predecessors. Farnsworth patented his invention in 1930, when he was 24 years old. When Zworykin moved from Westinghouse to RCA in 1930, he visited Farnsworth. Both he and his boss Sarnoff were impressed by Farnsworth's invention, and they decided to make use of it.

In April 1935, Sarnoff decided that RCA would spend a million dollars to conduct television demonstrations at the 1939–40 New York World's Fair through NBC, the broadcasting company owned by RCA.

The Spread of Television

Soon after World War II, Sarnoff and Paley developed their networks, NBC and CBS. Hundreds of television channels appeared and television made a significant mark on the cultural lives of Americans. It was not difficult for the companies to expand the market for television, although it began to supplant radio, their parent business. In programming also, the television networks followed the radio networks, with music, drama, skits, talk shows, comedies, etc. Although early television programmes were broadcast live, most are now taped and presented, except news, sports and important cultural programmes of global significance, such as Live Aid, which are telecast live.

Early television channels had frequencies in the VHF (very high frequency) range (30–300 mHz). In the mid-1950s, the frequencies in the UHF (ultra high frequency) range, from 300 to 3,000 mHz, were allocated by the FCC (Federal Communications Commission) to broadcasters, in the US. Since higher frequency electromagnetic waves do not travel as far as lower frequency waves, the UHF stations usually have smaller audiences than VHF stations. With the growth of cable television, many UHF stations began to rely on cable technology to carry their signals to homes.

Cable television was the most important technical development in television in the 1970s. Originally, cable TV was known as Community Antenna Television (CATV), and it was started in the mountainous regions of the US and Europe where reception of signals was murky or inadequate. CATV had its humble beginnings in the late 1940s in a few areas, but with the arrival of fibre-optics the cable technology burgeoned in the 1970s.

From 1972 onwards, cable TV was utilized by Time, Inc.'s Home Box Office (HBO) for showing movies to subscribers who had to pay a fee every month for the service. Now, dozens of cable television networks offer a variety of programming through local channels to subscribers—children's programmes, women's programmes, special programmes for ethnic minorities in the US, such as Hispanics, Asians and others.

There are Music TV (MTV) and VH1, channels that are devoted entirely to music; there are the all-sports channel, ESPN (Entertainment and Sports Network), and the all-business Consumer and Business Channel; there is an all-religion Interfaith channel. There are variations of these channels in different countries. The cable giants of the world are TNT (Turner Network Television), ESPN, AOL Time-Warner's HBO and CNN (Cable News Network).

The coaxial cable in the cable TV system has no spectrum limitations, whereas the ordinary telecasting spectrum has limitations. Cable TV homes can have a TV–Internet–e-mail combination. With minor modifications, it can also be useful in telebanking and teleshopping.

For viewing cinemascope films, high-resolution wide-screen TV systems and flat-surface screens are used in high-definition TV (HDTV). Digital TV is likely to become popular in the near future. Digital systems have already become part of the telephone system. When they come to radio and television, media users will be able to 'talk back' to their radio and television sets; that is, use the digital system to query the broadcaster of a particular programme! This means that the media will become interactive.

The other major changes in technology introduced in recent years are: big screens up to 84 inches wide; flat screens; the combination of computerized systems with television sets that can access the Internet and e-mail; holograms and virtual reality (VR); and facilities for interactive communication, playing of videogames, video discs, etc. The television set is no longer merely for receiving programmes telecast on a particular channel, it is now a multimedia system and a personalized entertainment device. We shall revert to this when we discuss the new media and their applications.

With this background information about the development of television, let us now turn to Indian television. In Hindi it is called *doordarshan*, which literally means tele-vision, *door* (pronounced like 'poor') meaning 'far' and *darshan* meaning 'sight' or 'vision'.

Doordarshan

All India Radio (AIR) in collaboration with UNESCO set up a television centre in New Delhi on 15 September 1959, purely as an educational experiment. The Ford Foundation donated 250 television sets to selected schools in the Delhi area. In a few months, television was extended to another 250 schools. Gradually, some community sets were installed in the suburbs of Delhi. Teleclubs were established for viewers to discuss programme contents, effectiveness, etc. Programmes were telecast from a temporary studio in the AIR building, using a 500-Watt transmitter with a range of 25 kilometres.

Initially, all the programmes were meant for children. Then came some programmes for the general public in the suburbs of Delhi. A few weeks later, there were programmes for agriculturists in the suburban villages of Delhi.

In 1972, TV stations were opened in Bombay and Madras; in 1973, a relay station started operation in Poona, a hundred miles from Bombay.

On 1 April 1976, the television unit was separated from AIR and given the name Doordarshan (DD). The activities of television were increased. Today, almost a thousand transmitters send programmes to different stations located in all the metropolitan cities, large industrial towns, state capitals and a few rural areas.

The four metro centres of New Delhi, Mumbai, Kolkata and Chennai have the DD-1, DD-2 and DD-3 channels. There are 11 regional centres where DD-1 and DD-2 channels operate. There are also 21 local channels. In fact, the number of channels needs to be expanded, especially in the rural areas where low-power transmitters (LPTs) are set up expand only with improvement in living conditions and higher standards of income through steady employment and health care. Media use does not depend on technical capability. Existing technical facilities are capable of reaching 90 per cent or more of the population but, in actual practice, the bulk of media users are in the metropolitan areas, state capitals and a few very large industrial and business towns such as Jamshedpur and Kanpur.

PAS-1 and PAS-4 are satellites whose transponders help in the telecasting of DD programmes in half the regions of the world. An international channel called DD-International was started in 1995 and it telecasts programmes for 19 hours a day to foreign countries—via PAS-4 to Europe, Asia and Africa, and via PAS-1 to North America.

Satellite Instructional Television Experiment (SITE)

One of the most extensive educational and social research projects, perhaps the largest national television experiment in the world, has been SITE. The Indian National Satellite (INSAT) was put into orbit following the favourable results of SITE. The effectiveness of television as a medium for educating the masses in rural areas was underscored by this experiment.

It was with the help of NASA, UNDP, ITU and UNESCO that the Indian Space Research Organization (ISRO) succeeded in launching SITE on 1 August 1975 using the US-supplied Applications Technology Satellite, ATS-6.

Thousands of messages on topics generally considered development-oriented were telecast to community television sets kept in 2,400 villages in 20 districts spread across six Indian states: Andhra Pradesh, Bihar, Karnataka, Madhya Pradesh, Orissa and Rajasthan. The experiment ended on 31 July 1976. The programmes telecast dealt with high-yielding varieties of seeds, better farming methods and management, family planning, public health, social and educational improvement of women and children, better learning and teaching methods.

The one-year experiment led to the unprecedented expansion of television in India. SITE influenced the course of television in India; it led to the establishment of HPTs (high-power transmitters) in most urban areas and LPTs in some selected rural areas.

The Sociocultural and Economic Aspects of TV in India

There were some criticisms of the introduction of television in India and other developing countries, especially because of the heavy infrastructural expenditure involved, the poverty of the large majority of the population, and the lack of media literacy and general education prevailing in those countries. But critics could not resist the argument that in a technologically less advanced country like India the media, particularly television, could be a great educational resource and inspiration for the illiterate to participate in national development.

Eminent scientists such as Vikram Sarabhai and others saw in television a great scope for reaching the rural population with educational and scientific messages. If messages could be transmitted through images, conventional alphabet-based literacy would not act as a stumbling block, they argued. All-out efforts were made to provide the technical infrastructure in most parts of India for the spread of television.

Inspite of the best intentions, the medium has reached its ultimate, real goal, namely, the marketing of products mostly affordable to the rich sectors of the urban and rural population. To look at the programme content is a futile exercise, because the most significant content is advertising. And in that television has fared extremely well. Therefore, the social effects of television will depend on the philosophy of life, attitude to social objectives and views about what will interest the maximum number of viewers prevalent among programme producers and media users and, above all, the economic status of the audience. The major trends in television content in India will depend on the major content producers, who happen to be the leading media owners of the world, who also happen to be in the rich and technologically advanced countries.

In the 1960s, countries were categorized into three 'worlds': the First World of rich, technologically-advanced capitalist nations of Europe and North

America; the Second World of socialist countries of Europe, particularly the countries that were led by the Soviet Union; and the Third World of mostly poor, technologically less advanced former colonies of the First World in Asia, Africa and Latin America.

In the 1990s, with the fall of the Soviet Union, the Second World (mostly Eastern Europe) and even some big countries of the Third World such as China and India began to restructure their economic organization. Thus, the earlier categorization of countries into First, Second and Third World is no longer valid. Media everywhere now follow the trends in the rich, capitalist countries, particularly the US, which has always been a trendsetter. As indicated previously, the cultural products of a country depend on the political, economic and social philosophy followed in that country. Since most countries including Russia and the Commonwealth of Independent States (CIS) are now following the free enterprise model adopted by the former First World countries, their cultural products are by and large modelled after those of the United States, with regional variations necessitated by language and some deep-rooted cultural traits.

Cable TV has influenced local media formats, especially in the news and film entertainment provided by television and in advertising. Television in India is oriented totally towards entertainment; it has become a mini version of the cine screen. Television was introduced in India and other countries of the East with great expectations that it would become a channel for reaching their millions with highly useful and essential messages of social change. The objectives of Doordarshan, for example, are a testimony to this social purpose.

When television was introduced in India in the late 1950s, the noble goals set by the decision-makers were as follows:[2]

- To act as a catalyst for social change.
- To promote national integration.
- To stimulate a scientific temper in the minds of the people.
- To disseminate the message of family planning as a means of population control and family welfare.
- To provide essential information and knowledge in order to stimulate greater agricultural production.
- To promote and help preserve environment and ecological balance.
- To highlight the need for social welfare measures including welfare of women, children and the less privileged.

---

[2] Government of India 1997.

- To promote interest in games and sports.
- To create values of appraisal of art and cultural heritage

An analysis of the programmes on Doordarshan or any other channel operating in India will convince us that the above goals are not given due importance, particularly the goals of social change, creation of scientific temper and social welfare measures. Entertainment through serials, film-derived material, sports and games is given all the importance. Social change is not even of secondary importance to the media (Vilanilam 2003b: 118–21, 222). Instead, the main objective of every channel appears to be the advertising of goods and a few services, persuading viewers to buy them. The very raison d'être of television all over the world seems to be the selling of goods through persuasive and attractive commercial messages and converting viewers to certain political viewpoints. The latter is achieved through the repeated presentation of news and views, discussions, debates, and so on.

Although the semblance of objectivity and impartiality is created by presenting opposing viewpoints (in many instances an artificial search for opposing viewpoints is evident, since some events and issues require no opposing viewpoint whatsoever!), a total analysis of the number and frequency, nature and content of news and features will show that the goal of the various channels (whether national or international) is the same, namely, to promote certain viewpoints conducive to the propagation of crass commercialism, profiteering and political neutralism.

In the 1960s, communication scholars and media experts were quite sure that television and other media of mass communication would help national development. The media were considered the prime motivators of development. Stalwarts in communication and development studies such as Daniel Lerner, Wilbur Schramm and Everett M. Rogers, who based their theories of development and media efficacy on the important work of Walter Rostow, namely, *The Stages of Economic Growth*, stressed that the economic and technological development achieved by the Western nations were the result of increased media use. If only the people of the 'developing countries' could follow the path of modernization initiated by the West, they would leapfrog centuries of inaction and underdevelopment and reach the stage of mass consumption in which the modernized West was placed in the 20th century.

All these theorists treated social change and economic development purely on a cognitive basis, without taking into account centuries of colonialism and psychological subjugation imposed by the 'modernized' West on most of the countries of Asia and Africa and to some extent on those of South and Central America. They ignored, perhaps unwittingly, their own history and created an untenable view that the media of mass communication were instrumental in their unprecedented growth and development. The role of mighty weapons they had developed and of their military expeditions was also ignored. Instead, the poverty and backwardness of people in the rest of the world were attributed to the lack of information.

From decade to decade, old paradigms were packaged in new bottles under new labels and presented by the developed world for the consumption of the elite in poor countries, who made vital decisions on communication and media planning. In the 1950s, it was 'growth through psychic mobility'; in the 1960s, it was 'education for development'; in the 1970s, it was 'satellite communication for development'; and in the 1980s and 1990s it was 'computerized communication systems'. The process continues today, in the 21st century, under the banner of 'information technology' or IT, for streamlining administration and creating market-friendly economies through privatized micro and macro media. Today, liberalization, privatization and globalization are thriving everywhere, but the old problems of poverty, illiteracy, malnutrition and poor health persist.

The P.C. Joshi Committee, and the B.G. Verghese Committee before it, hoped that the formation of an autonomous broadcasting corporation, the Prasar Bharati Corporation (PBC), would result in more relevant localized programmes which would help even rural people to think globally and act locally. However, instead of making regional and local stations into really autonomous, self-sustaining production centres under certain overall technical and ethical guidelines from the PBC, the Government of India permitted foreign and indigenous private companies to compete with DD and AIR.

When we look at the issue historically, we see that the developed or rich countries spread the benefits of the Industrial Revolution to the majority of their people through distributive justice, underscoring the dictum that distribution of goods and services and economic and political opportunities among the majority is the prime desideratum of development. The West's development resulted from the changes (social, economic, political and, above all, technological) that they themselves had introduced in production, distribution and management systems. It did not result from increased media use.

An information revolution ushered into a largely poor society without appropriate changes in social structure will be just a storm in a tea cup; it will not benefit the large majority of the people. India may not be a poor country, but it is a country with millions of poor people.

The hope that the hardware of communication—satellites, cable networks, etc.—will save the millions from centuries of poverty and ignorance is unreal. But India has already let foreign media into the country. Will this lead to cultural imperialism once again?

TV and Cultural Imperialism

Almost three quarters of a century ago, on 1 June 1921, Mahatma Gandhi expressed his fear of cultural imperialism when he said:

> I do not want my house to be walled in on all sides and my windows to be stuffed. I want the cultures of all lands to be blown about my house as freely as possible but I refuse to be blown off my feet by any.[3]

Today,

> The media aim at cultural synchronization, promotion of a global village, internationalism, etc., mainly for commercial purposes. This is in keeping with the basic philosophy of the transnational advertising, entertainment, leisure and tourism industries avidly promoted by multinational corporations and international financial institutions with headquarters in ENAJ countries. (ENAJ stands for Europe, North America and Japan.) But their philosophy goes against the basic needs of the large majority of the world's population, whether it be of South Asia, Asia minus Japan and some oil-rich countries of West Asia, or of the other highly populated and poor regions of the world, especially in Africa and Latin America. (Vilanilam 1996: 62–90)

The ENAJ countries are in a position today to look at information and media fare as commercial products. The elite in poor countries also see the main function of the media as entertainment and, to some extent, providing news and information of a certain kind. Moreover, this elite believes that in a few decades their countries can catch up with the ENAJ countries by achieving everything that the latter had achieved either through colonial exploitation or imperialist and totalitarian systems during the past century.

Three strong forces influence global culture: finance capital, high technology and mass marketing or communication. Of these, the last mentioned is what we should examine in the context of cultural imperialism in India. Several cultural streams that originated at different periods in India's long history—Harappan (Indus Valley), Dravidian, Hindu, Buddhist, Jain, Ajivika, Christian, Islamic and variations of these—are still flowing as undercurrents, nurturing the intrapersonal base of communication there. All these cultural streams are now muddled by the polluted effluents of religious fundamentalism and Mammon-worship, made stronger by crass commercialism and greed engendered by cut-throat competition.

---

[3] See also Gandhi 1954.

The effulgence of the new spirit is reflected on the mini screen more than anywhere else. The process is facilitated by market-conquering expeditions from the West which actually started in the 15th century when the Portuguese landed in Calicut. The reverse flow is weak and has been quite late and sporadic. But internal colonialism is very much alive, with the result that several regions of the country are unable to withstand the onslaught of powerful forces from within the country and outside. The upshot of all this is further deepening of poverty and misery despite all statistical advancements. The historical cause of poverty and the obscene economic disparities in Indian society receive very little attention in the channels of communication.

Most media reports and features nowadays centre on the following basic marketing and communication concepts prevalent in advanced sectors of the country:

- The technological imperative and the idea of progress force the multinational media and their new technologies to flow into new regions; it is inevitable that the poor in those regions succumb to the rich and imbibe foreign cultural fare. The poor have no choice. They do not have the technological clout or the monetary capacity to reverse the flow. The flow has to be necessarily one-way.
- The role of the media is primarily to entertain and provide relaxation to its users.
- The elite in India occupy 10 per cent of its population of over a billion. They follow a Western lifestyle, so they need sophisticated products and services to maintain it. The media should cater to their needs primarily through advertising messages in the print media and commercials in the broadcast media.
- Dubbing of foreign programmes into various Indian languages is easier than producing original programmes in native languages. Moreover, the elite, particularly children of affluent families, enjoy foreign programmes more than local ones.
- The world is getting smaller and any attempt to shut out information that flows in is not only barbaric but a serious threat to human rights, particularly the right to be informed and entertained.

Television as it exists today suppresses the Indian reality. It creates a world of fantasy for the rich and the poor, but the rich have access to at least some of the ingredients that construct that fantasy. This world of fantasy does not deal with the pressing problems faced by the majority.

What is the culture portrayed on Indian TV? It is mostly the culture of the 'global shopping centre', mixed with some dead, old customs and practices. This incongruous mixture is hated by the elite, who want everything to be in the mould of the rich countries, with which they have cultural contacts either directly or through their relatives.

The structure of the media in India today cannot be separated from India's socioeconomic and political structures, which have thrown open their windows and doors so wide that the upper and middle classes can be thrown off their cultural base. At the same time the structure reinforces the negative aspects of India's cultural past, which facilitates disintegration and disunity. The dominant new values that are reiterated and reinforced through the media serve only to divide and create mutual mistrust among the masses. Both have deleterious cultural consequences. TV in India has already embarked upon such a cultural division of the population, without realizing that by doing so, it is adding to the process of the destruction of the intrapersonal religious base of culture in the country.

The media underscore the elements and symbols of supranational culture, which are identifiable and affordable only to rich and socially superior groups in India, which think alike and contribute to the jet-set culture sustained by the philosophy of over-consumption, consumerism and obsolescence. This transnational culture rests on cheap labour (which happens to be the basis of outsourcing from rich countries) and cheap raw materials available from different regions of the world. The workers in these regions cannot afford to own most of the consumer products and essential goods which they themselves make, something contrary to what has become the norm in the ENAJ countries.

In a country with millions of people who barely succeed in acquiring and keeping a television set, viewers pass through a cycle of rising expectations and frustrations and finally leave everything to fate or rise up in revolt as a last resort when they realize that most of the goods and the lifestyle presented on TV are beyond their reach. Brutal suppression of dissent is what keeps the lid on the cauldron of boiling frustration in many highly imbalanced societies. While the ruling elite in many large developing countries uses the media, particularly television, to keep the frustrated populace under check, media directors willingly keep the mob amused.

The cultural or social role of TV in the present structure of the world is to act as the commercial messenger of 500 or so multinational corporations. The message is couched in entertainment; individual nations do not stress their own priorities, but quietly conform to international, supranational standards set by global marketing managers.

One last point. Television has become an instrument to reinforce superstitious practices and to glorify the existence and might of supernatural beings such as *yakshis* and *yamas*, gods and goddesses, since the portrayal of such characters has been found profitable by the commercial-minded producers. Such themes and portrayals are popularized in the new cultural environment where old customs and practices are revived in the name of religion. Coupled with this, one should recognize the frequent refrain from some communal organizations parading as political parties that members of certain communities are proliferating like rabbits and hence threatening the very existence of other communities! The media do not examine the scientific basis of such pronouncements but publicize them verbatim. What matters in a commercial culture is whether the cultural product will sell to the maximum number of people. Other considerations—religious harmony, universal brotherhood, human rights peace and communitarianism—do not matter for those whose aim is profit and profit alone.

In India, the media of mass communication ought to give some serious attention to the real priorities of the country. According to George Gerbner,

> For the first time in human history, children are born into homes where mass mediated story tellers reach them on the average of more than seven hours a day .... These stories do not come from families, schools, churches, neighbourhoods, and not even from the native countries. They come from a small group of distant (business) conglomerates with something to sell.
>
> Giant industries discharge their messages into the mainstream common consciousness. Channels proliferate and new technologies pervade home and office while mergers and bottom-line pressures shrink creative alternatives and reduce diversity of content. These changes may appear to broaden and enrich our horizon, but they may also homogenize our viewpoints and limit our alternatives.

The top 100 advertisers pay for the programmes televised in almost all the Amercian networks, such as NBC, CBS, ABC and Fox TV; and although there are no advertisements as such on PBS, most programmes there are sponsored by big industrial and charitable corporations or foundations. The first three networks are owned by the multinational companies GE, Walt Disney and Time-Warner. Fox TV is owned by Rupert Murdoch, the biggest media mogul of the world, who also controls the most prolific channel in Asia, STAR (Satellite Television Asia Range). Gerbner is of the view that these networks, allied to giant corporations, act like a private Ministry of Culture. Even CNN is owned now by AOL Time-Warner.

Half a dozen corporations control the bulk of the production and distribution of television and film products not only in the US, but throughout the world. They can decide what the world should know, how much it should know, what possible action it should take to deal with a certain national or global issue and what cultural products and information it should have on a given day, as Ben H. Bagdikian, veteran media expert and former ombudsman of the *Washington Post* once said (Bagdikian 1997).

Anthony Smith, formerly of the BBC and the British Film Institute and later President of Magdalen College, has expressed his concern about the ill effects of the globalization of mass media firms (Smith 1991).

The concerns of these researchers and scholars about the concentration of ownership that is happening in all the media, but particularly in television, is certainly worthy of our serious attention. Consolidation of media ownership in recent years has been so rapid that a few media conglomerates such as Viacom, Walt Disney, AOL Time-Warner, BBC, News Corporation Ltd., Sony, TCI, Seagram, Westinghouse, Gannett and GE can control the flow of news and information, entertainment, sports and every other conceivable form of mediated communications in the world (Solomon 1999)!

It is not realistic to expect that this situation will not happen in India, in the present context of globalization, privatization and mindless imitation of whatever happens outside the country in total disregard of the realities existing in the country. Almost all channels of the world are brought to India via satellite, cable and terrestrial transmission. The Direct-to-Home (DTH) service and set-top boxes are already spreading in India. In the coming years the bulk of the programmes that the elite of the country receives will obviously be based on the viewpoints of the erstwhile colonizers and their business associates.

As Smith has said, it is 'American television which has shaped the context (if not the content) of popular culture throughout the world' in this television era of ours; but he is optimistic that older civilizations of the world will find new uses for the television set and television technology. The new technologies that are shaping the new media are likely to act as deterrents to monopolization that is very strong now. 'Television has, insistently, touched the audience at the most superficial levels but without seeming to accept responsibility for its own consequences' (1991: 8). It has, as Smith has observed, wantonly manipulated our wants and distorted our true needs, but it has also democratized and levelled, opening the eyes of millions to things of which they had been long deprived. 'It has reflected the ugliness of this century but taught hygiene and brought literacy to rural and urban poor.' (This is more true of countries that have a higher diffusion rate for TV and therefore not quite apt for India, where there are only 25 TV sets per 1,000 people.)

According to its present ownership pattern, television is certainly a convenient tool in the hands of the rich and powerful, but the technology of production of information is gradually reaching the millions of the middle and lower middle class. Eventually it can become a true instrument for the communication of ideas between and among large numbers of real people and not just moving images of no substance on the mini screen. Chapter 9 examines the future possibilities of the new media which combine the advantages of television, radio, satellite and digital communication.

9

the new media: multimedia born out of convergence

*t*here were three big changes in the media world during the last decades of the 20th century: The introduction of digital and computer systems; the merger of various media technologies under the rubric of electronics, resulting in convergence; and the merger of large media companies, an economic and sociological phenomenon that is still continuing under different names such as chain ownership, cross-media ownership, conglomeration, vertical integration and media monopolization and concentration. All these changes have eased the birth of trashy media fare as also some outstanding media programmes. We shall first examine the application of new technologies.

'Compunication', or Computerized Communication

Nothing has changed the media world in recent times like the application of computer technology to all the media, including photography, sound recording and reproduction, film, television and radio.

The basic principles of electronic communication, computer technology and digitalization have been discussed in earlier chapters. However, it is necessary to point out here that in the US, from the 1960s onwards, computerization was utilized in different media at different times and to a different degree by the early 1980s, it was utilized in all the media to a varying extent. In India, it took another couple of decades for all branches of the media to be computerized and digitalized, although electronic photo-composition, electronic editing and offset printing had started in select newspapers by the end of the 1970s.

With the help of the computer, it became easy for the media to manipulate not only images but words and text. Although it could not supplant all traditional art techniques, the computer could also manipulate shapes, colours and even sounds. Some great artist-designers, such as David Hockney of England, made set designs for movies and theatre productions, working with traditional paints, photographs and screen-printing. Others, such as Robert Rauschenberg, experimented by combining photography with screen-printing, sound synthesizing and so on, thus creating a new genre of 'performance art'. Still others like Chuck Close developed photojournalism, making huge larger-than-life colour photographs, with the help of the computer.

In all these forms of performance art, the computer functioned as an enabling art tool. As Steve Parker says, it emerged as an electronic paintbrush (2002: 24–25).

Computer Graphics

In the last 20 years, computer graphics have come to be used media-wide, in print as well as audiovisual media. Using the computer, it is not difficult to create a totally strange environment or creature—both of which are abundantly used in films, particularly cartoon films, outer space fantasies and odysseys. Actors mingle with animated cartoon characters. World-renowned paintings such as Leonardo da Vinci's *Mona Lisa* can be 'pixellated' for various purposes to heighten visual effects.

Progress achieved in computer technology in the 1990s led to the widespread use of the computer at home, work and school, and in public libraries, especially in the developed countries and in developed areas of poor countries. Computerization also led to e-mail and the Internet, both tools of instant communication and information sharing and retrieval in the modern world.

Electronic Newspapers and Books

Many conventional newspapers in India not only introduced the sophisticated new systems of production but also began to offer online versions on their websites. Many dot.com companies came into being, including the web newsportal Tehelka.com, which went defunct but has now restarted as a newspaper. The number of Internet users in India has risen dramatically in recent years.

Although digitalization had started in the 1980s, the 1990s saw a digital revolution worldwide, but especially in the US. Digital technology has inaugurated a fundamental change in the processing of information, and it has been applied on a wide scale in book publishing. Conventional typesetting is not needed any more. Authors can deliver a floppy disk to the publisher or send it electronically over the Internet. The editor sees the matter on the screen and edits it directly.

Electronic Book Publishing

The use of paper and ink for the preparation of a manuscript can now be dispensed with. Even the finished 'product' does not have to be in book form, if the reader has an Internet connection. The book can be obtained online from the bookseller if payment is made electronically or otherwise, and the reader does not need a conventional hard copy. Or, if the conventional book is necessary, the editor can make a camera-ready format and send the matter to the printing press, usually an offset press. These days tech-savvy publishers have dispensed with camera-ready copies (CRCs)—the final form of the book is provided to the press on a CD, which gives greater accuracy in printing.

The practice of reading books on the Web has not yet caught on in India, or indeed in other countries, because most readers prefer to physically handle books and read them at leisure. Most of us would like to be able to carry a book in our coat pocket or travel bag and turn to it whenever we get time. However, many hundreds of copyright-free classics are posted on the Web, accessible to readers. The best-known such project is the Gutenberg Project (named after Gutenberg, who popularized movable-type printing and revolutionized book production in the 15th century). Even a novel by Stephen King, *Riding the Bullet*, was made available to users of the Web in 2000. The entire novel was put online.

Although Charles Ellis, of the world-renowned publishing company Houghton-Mifflin of Boston, once said that electronic publishing would determine the future of the publishing industry, not many book readers read books on the Internet. Amazon.com calls itself the 'world's largest bookstore'. The advent of gigantic American bookstore chains such as Barnes & Noble, Borders Books and Music, and Books-A-Million is sufficient testimony for the continuance of conventional book publishing and book reading. In such megastores, book lovers are given all comforts and conveniences, and special facilities for relaxed reading from 9 A.M. to 11 P.M. every day of the year including Sundays and holidays. They also have cafeterias and comfort stations (toilets and baby-changing rooms) to attract more book lovers!

It goes without saying, however, that reading books has always been a limited activity even in literate societies. An exceptional reader can manage one book a day. Most people take a week or two to finish an average-size non-fiction book. An interesting novel may take a day or two at home or in a warehouse-sized bookstore or in a library with creature comforts. Web-reading at home involves substantial initial expenditure for installing the computer and the Internet and a regular subscription every month. The *kitaab mahals* (book palaces) described here may not charge anything, but all readers who make use of the facilities provided by them will naturally feel obliged to buy at least one book every month. Of course, there is no compulsion from anyone.

Reading newspapers and research articles on the Internet has become a fairly widespread practice in most developed sectors of the world because, in many countries, newspapers have become quite bulky. The daily edition of the *New York Times* or *Washington Post* or any major US newspaper will have at least 48 pages and the weekend editions anywhere between 200 and 500 pages! Readers do not read every page. They skim through the papers, reading only those pages which are of special interest to them. Some may like to spend more time on the stock exchange news, and other financial news. Some may devote more time to the front page and the sports pages, others to the editorials and the op-ed pieces, including letters to the editor. There is, therefore, a great deal of selective reading. Web pages are very effective at catering to the special interests of readers. There is thus a great future for the Internet newspapers.

There are unintended sociological effects of this new digital technological breakthrough. Direct sales of books through websites (without incurring heavy costs of office rent, overheads and large staff management) has its attractions and advantages. However, 'biblio dot.coms' such as Amazon.com have had to branch out or diversify. Along with books, they have begun to sell toys, music, consumer electronics and even gourmet food. McConnell points out that 'books, in the new world of digital era, have become commodities to be bought and sold like pork bellies and soybeans' (2001: 387).

In India, libraries in sophisticated institutions have introduced electronic information search. But card catalogues of books and journals are still being used in most libraries where even reprographic facilities are not available today. Web clicks and mouse movements are still quite rare in most Indian libraries, whereas even community libraries are computerized in the West. We are still far behind even in many institutions of higher learning, not to speak of small town and village libraries and schools. The index of intellectual development these days is the installation and frequent use of computerized systems of information storage and communication. While the new-age editors of the new media series in the West are creating web publications and wondering what further developments are in store for future information-seekers, libraries in India are still wondering whether the colon classification is superior to other styles of classification!

Editors of newspapers have switched to electronic publishing in both India and the US. However, the gap between the two countries is very large; whereas about three million readers of the, the *New York Times* worldwide are reading it online, and 36 million newspaper readers in the US are reading their newspapers online once a week—and that too selectively—most readers of newspapers in India read them in the hard copy form. Web reading is quite rare in India and it is mostly confined to a tiny percentage of newspaper readers in the metropolitan cities.

Nearly half of the under-30 college graduates in the US read their news online or get their news through the broadcast media, including radio and television. One can safely say that there are very few colleges in India that have large halls with dozens of computers that can be accessed by students. Having said that, there may come a time in the near future when web reading of newspapers may become a frequent activity on college campuses. The number of people obtaining news through the Web, particularly in the big cities, may also increase. However, the percentage of media users and new media users in India will continue to be small until literacy, education and the per capita income increase.

Why is this so? The answer is not hard to find. The new technology may be available in India, but its widespread use depends on many factors. All colleges must have Internet facilities together with a system that provides every student with access to computer facilities for studies and research. Many colleges in India today have a limited number of computers and access is not universal. This situation has to change. All students should be required to prepare their assignments for all classes on the computer, which means computerized library search should become essential.

Cyberology (knowledge of cyberspace use and knowledge search) must become the sine qua non of every school and college curriculum. But today, Indian schools (if at all there are enough schools in the rural areas) do not have proper school buildings with enough teachers, textbooks, blackboards and benches, not to speak of bathrooms and drinking water facilities. Boeings and bullock carts, five-star hotels surrounded by filthy *bastis*—this is the style of Indian development, which is quite unfortunate because the Indian elite have the knowledge, the technology and the means to implement new programmes. But do they have the will?

Even in those urban and semi-urban schools where some computers are available, the teaching methods are such that students do not have any curricular obligation to submit assignments prepared on a computer after a computer-based information search in libraries that have Internet facilities.

And it is unfortunate that students are not encouraged to use computers to search for knowledge on their own under the guidance of teachers (for this, teachers must themselves be fully appreciative of the use of modern technologies of information search and preparation).

Assignments are not a regular feature in many institutions except in certain departments of select universities and in the IITs and IIMs. This situation has to change. Instructors must see that students make good use of the computer. The computer culture has to be inculcated in students for personal advancement as well as social reorganization, which is essential for the overall progress of the nation.

Films

The techniques for digital imaging, recording and storing of images and their reproduction in film and television programmes first became available in the 1980s and have been used to the maximum extent from the late 1980s onwards. The longest-running prime time comedy in the US is *The Simpsons*, a television cartoon series. Cartoons became the favourites not only of children but of adults as well. By 2000, Fox, MTV, Warner Brothers and some other channels were running cartoon films, though none could reach the popularity of *The Simpsons*. Cartoons could reach perfection and earn popularity mainly because of the effective use of multimedia technology.

In India, many cartoon films that are Indian in theme are now being produced. The *Tenali Raman* series produced by the Toons Company in the Technopark, Thiruvananthapuram, Kerala, is gaining popularity because Tenali Raman is a hero from Tenali, an Andhra village, and is well known to most people in southern India. There are many folk tales surrounding the funny, sensible and adventurous escapades of Raman, the real or legendary figure. This cartoon series will appeal to both the young and the old.

Multimedia techniques have contributed a great deal to both conventional movies and unconventional (which have unusual images and extraordinary sound effects) produced in the last quarter of the 20th century. Movies employing such techniques have earned a great deal of money at the box office. They include *Star Wars*, *Jaws*, *The Godfather*, *Who Framed Roger Rabbit?*, *Star Trek*, *Rocky* and *The Towering Inferno*.

But the 'world's first entirely computer-generated feature film', namely *Toy Story*, was released in the US in 1995. It had 'no real-life actors, no models, no hand-drawn animation'. It was virtual, according to Parker. And in 1997 came Steven Spielberg's *Jurassic Park*, the story of dinosaurs where one could see real-life actors fighting with computerized, animated dinosaurs! Both films were great box-office hits; they were received avidly by film-goers not only for their special effects but for an abundant supply of related toys, games, theme park rides and other spin-off merchandise. They also had 'strong storylines, drama, sadness, humour and happy endings, the classical ingredients of popular films', according to many critics.

Other movies that captured the attention of movie fans all over the world during the late 1990s for their special effects and other qualities were *Titanic* (1997); *Star Wars Episode 1: The Phantom Menace*, a continuation of the space saga begun in 1977; and *The Truman Show* (1998), a satire on reality TV and a sad and sarcastic commentary on media manipulation. In all these movies, computer-generated imagery (CGI) was used profusely to create a fanciful and fantastic environment for the viewer.

The Digital Music Records Industry

There was no revolutionary change in the music recording industry until 1995. Some experts think that the music industry wanted to play it safe and not take risks, but it was inevitable that the changes in film-making, newspaper production and all other media activities influenced the records industry. Rock, rap, hip-hop, pop and other music cultures continued, but two new trends made headlines. The first was guitar-based bands such as Aerosmith, Bon Jovi and Van Halen, which became popular in the mid-1990s. The second trend was that of gender-based bands—all-boy or all-girl bands such as Boyzone, the Spice Girls and All Saints.

As Parker has observed,

> Through the 1990s, the media of television and popular music continued to feed off each other. Dedicated music channel MTV led the way.... After Princess Diana's death, Elton John's new version of 'Candle in the Wind' became the biggest-selling record ever—over 30 million copies in 37 days. (2002: 30)

The music records industry in India has been influenced by the developments and trends in the world. But it is film songs that have always acted as the staple of the music business in India. Except for musicals, such as *The Sound of Music* and *Mary Poppins*, this trend is not found in the West, where ordinary, non-musical films do not have songs and lyrics. There, records are cut by famous singers such as Elton John, Michael Jackson, Olivia Newton-John, Madonna, Janis Joplin and others.

There are music bands in India too, but because of the popularity of film music most singers prefer to join the world of films. In fact, both television and radio devote a considerable percentage of their programme time to film music and other film-based features.

Media and Sports

Media growth in all parts of the world is linked to the growth of sports and games. In addition to the telecasting or broadcasting of sports and games, there are special features on famous sportsmen and their personal lives. The number of former sports stars joining the band of media commentators is growing in all countries. The media have become great promoters of sports and games. Moreover, they have also become proponents of health and body-building exercises for men, women, boys and girls. This is certainly a good trend. If sex and violence can be eliminated with this extra attention on health, it will certainly be a welcome move. However, can the amount of time devoted to sport, in and out of season and sometimes at the expense of news and other essential programmes, be beneficial to society?

Sports events are organized around television coverage, especially under the pressure exerted by giant advertisers. Commercial-free channels lose the money from advertisers, but they serve the public in other ways, not least by ensuring that their viewers do not become 'couch potatoes'. There are sports channels such as ESPN and Ten Sports, huge commercial networks which enter into cut-throat competition with other channels, as the recent contro-versy between ESPN and Zee over cricket telecast rights indicates.

Sports-mania on broadcast channels is also related to the very heavy re-muneration given to sports stars (many millions of dollars). The conception of sport as a healthy human activity has been changed by business tycoons. Sports and games are no longer looked upon as human activities but as major business propositions. Sportspersons also consider their activities purely as business. Spectators see sportspeople as gladiators out there to entertain them and, if they make a small mistake, angry viewers pounce on them or break their television sets, depending on where they are! Michael Jordan, Shaquille O'Neal (basketball), Tiger Woods (golf), Michael Schumacher (Formula One racing), and soccer wizards such as Ronaldo and Maradona get paid more in a week than most people earn in their entire livetime!

Average citizens sit in front of the television to enjoy sports and games, but do not participate in any such activities for their own physical well-being, say many critics of the new-found nexus between sports and the media.

Violence, Sex and the V-Chip

We have already touched upon the question of sex and violence in the movies during the silent era, when Gorky and Tolstoy referred to it. It is interesting that the question continued to raise ethical debates about all media, but particularly film, in the last three decades of the 20th century, which saw violence of various degrees in *The Godfather, Jaws, Star Wars, The Exorcist, Mean Streets, Death Wish, The Texas Chainsaw Massacre* and *Taxi Driver*. All these portrayed high-tech, raw violence. During the 1970s, many films from Bollywood and Hollywood portrayed mindless violence perpetrated by angry young men who, like Robin Hood, resorted to violence for a just cause—violence that was, nonetheless, unjustifiable—suggesting that directors and actors were indulging in obscene violence for the sake of the social good, and not for box office takings!

Sex was everywhere, especially after the US Supreme Court's verdict that the First Amendment to the American Constitution gave protection to the portrayal of raw sexual acts on celluloid, which was a form of free expression and free speech through images. *Carnal Knowledge, Shampoo* and *L'Ultimo Tango a Parigi* (*Last Tango in Paris*) received acclaim from critics for portraying sex in a tasteful and artistic manner, but the hardcore pornography portrayed in films like Behind the Green Door and Deep Throat produced loud protests and deep revulsion.

More than pornography, however, it is violence that engages the attention of psychologists, sociologists and communications experts. For obscenity and pornography, some measure of control is available on the part of parents and elders through a system of rating films: G for general audience, that is, viewers of all ages; PG for viewing by children only if they have parental guidance and permission; R for 'restricted to children above 13 but, if under 18 years of age, only when accompanied by an adult'; and X for films that are strictly for adults. Although this system of labelling films may not be very effective, it is at least a guideline to go by.

Pornography, one may say, has disappeared from the big screen but found its niche in videocassettes played on the VCR and TV monitor, and on the digital versatile disc (DVD), a larger and more effective version of the compact disc (CD) which one can watch in the privacy of one's home. But pornography is threatening the morals of children who are frequent Internet users at home or at private cybercafés these days. Parents protest that 'corn on the cob' has been replaced by 'porn on the Web'.

Researchers in England and the US have asserted that children are influenced by audiovisual media. Studies by George Gerbner, Hilde Himmelweit and others have found support for this viewpoint. Children's TV habits, if left unwatched by elders, may even culminate in domestic tragedy, as has happened in a few cases.

'Adult' sites on the Web have already become a billion-dollar industry. Adult magazines such as *Playboy*, *Penthouse*, *Playgirl*, *Hustler* and *Maxim* had already become billion-dollar businesses in the US by the late 1960s. Elsewhere in the world also, there are equivalents of these magazines, though not always as openly marketed as in the US. These are all available on the Internet and on CDs, DVDs and other electronic media.

'Cyber-porn' is a major headache for many parents and morality monitors. How to prevent children from viewing pornography on the Web has engaged the serious attention of many people in government and society. The US government tried to prevent cyber-porn through a hurriedly-passed Telecommunications Reform Act, which included the Communications Decency Act (CDA), in 1996. But the Supreme Court rejected the CDA in 1998, declaring it unconstitutional as it abridged the right to free speech guaranteed in the First Amendment. Preventing children's access to graphic, indecent material on the Internet was parents' responsibility, the court indicated.

Two new technologies were available at the beginning of the millennium to block pornography and obscenity on the Internet: a filtering software that could block access to sites containing words or phrases associated with sexually explicit material; and a rating system that enabled service providers to label a particular programme as fit or unfit for children by displaying a small rating label on the screen.

Despite the availability of all these devices, parents and other elders are the best resource for monitoring what their wards are watching on television and the Internet. The V-chip and other devices can protect children from television violence but there is no foolproof method of protecting children from the sexually explicit and violent material that appears on the Internet.

Psychologists, sociologists and communication scholars have given some serious thought to the effects of violence and obscenity on children. Most of them agree that violent and pornographic material vitiate children's view of life and lead them to deviant behaviour or at least antisocial attitudes both at home and at school. The problem is so serious that some schools in the US ask children to observe 'No TV Weeks' to make them and their parents aware of the deleterious effects of violence and sex on unwary children who are may be led by media material into juvenile delinquency, teenage pregnancy and self-destructive drug abuse.

Many researchers have come to the conclusion that TV violence teaches aggressive and antisocial behaviour to children. Parents and professional child-minders may sometimes use the television set as a baby-sitter to keep children occupied. This can lead to children watching unnecessary violence and hence getting the distorted view that violence is normal. Children lose their ability to react to violence—they become narcotized. Some children become scared of the outside world and suspicious of every stranger. Of course, the media affect different children differently. However, watching about 8,000 murders and 100,000 other acts of violence, including rape, by the time a child completes elementary school, as Gerbner has calculated, is not a healthy trend from any angle. Desensitization to violence and criminal behaviour is a serious social problem.

Besides the V-chip, a rating system has been used by the television industry in the US by which a label appears on the right top corner of the television screen: TV-G for general audience including children; TV-MA for the ma-ture audience where parental discretion is advised if children are in the room; TV-Y for all children and TV-Y7 for children above the age of seven. Local stations apply local community standards. Some parents wanted more explicit description of the content of each programme and the industry came up with S for sex, V for violence and D for suggestive dialogue and bad language.

Neither the V-chip nor the content- and audience-based rating can solve the serious problems faced by society. Can they prevent juvenile delinquency and teenage pregnancy? The V-chip can only encourage parents to abdicate their own responsibility, according to some religious organizations that stress that parents have to take full responsibility for the type and content of TV programming. The real reason for all teenage problems, according to many social and religious leaders, is the breakdown of the family. In a recent news-paper cartoon, two 4-year-old children are portrayed as sitting in front of a TV set. The parents are out of the house. One child tells the other, 'Looks like the V-chip is blocking this show .... Let's go catch a smoke, yaar!'

Since 1954, there have been many attempts to sanitize comic books and cartoons. The debate between the mass media and morality is an old one, as we have already seen. A recent television show in the US portrayed the main character wearing a T-shirt with an inscription: I Love Vagina. There were arguments about the morality of this slogan. Can the V-chip block such messages? A wag asked: 'is vagina a bad word? All of us come through it!'

Gigi B. Sohn, Deputy Director of the Media Access Project, a public interest law firm in Washington, DC, argues that broadcasters have to serve

the needs of the public, particularly children, through educational programmes, since they have the free use of the airwaves. But broadcasters do
not want the government telling them what to do. Without government
regulation, certain broadcasters like the Public Broadcasting System (PBS)
show useful educational programmes for children: *Sesame Street*, for example.

There is another problem faced by viewers in several countries, including
India: Many educational programmes are shown very early in the morning
when most people are still in bed or have just risen from bed. Whatever be the
argument, children must have a choice of educational and informative programming from different sources. The National Geographic and Discovery
channels telecast many informative programmes, but there should be more
Indian channels offering programmes relevant to different aspects of Indian
life. Nevertheless, the media should not be coerced into observing their social
responsibility.

'Shockumentaries'

An important development in the world of film and television during the
1990s was the advent of what are generally called *shockumentaries*. This is a
word coined from 'shock' and 'documentaries', or shocking documentaries.
This genre of television programming emerged from the reality TV shows
that have enjoyed great popularity in recent years. When we consider the
nature of news, we realize that a substantial proportion of news is negative,
covering crimes, disasters, accidents and act of shocking inhumanity perpetrated by human beings on each other. Look at what is happening in Iraq and
Sudan, to give just two examples. The media follow up on such inhuman acts
and come up with features containing more details of shocking and bloody
acts.

Sometimes such acts of destruction take place purely within the domestic
field—a husband brutalizing his wife, or vice versa. Bizarre events are presented in print as well as electronic media via reports, televised features and
videographed accounts with gruesome details. All these media products are
shocking to readers and viewers. Although they are based on true events, all
truths are not pleasant and should not be repeated over and over again. The
media carry them because they know how to appeal to the bizarre tastes of
many media users. There is no great informational value in these media
products, only sensationalism and the exploitation of shock.

The same theme occurs in comic strips, television dramas and theatrical
productions. Since all media are interrelated, one medium nourishes as well

as feeds on other media. Murder has been written about from the time of Adam. Are the public so concerned about this shocking theme? Are not the themes in literature from all parts of the world the same? But is journalism the same as literature? We shall move on from these fundamental issues to more examples of mass mediated shockumentaries.

When critics pointed out that the modern media should be used for a socially useful purpose rather than for soap operas, media controllers turned to reality television. The trend started in the 1960s. CBS' 60 Minutes and 48 Hours, ABC's 20/20 and other similar programmes are in a way predecessors of the shockumentary. Of particular significance is the shocking treatment accorded by Mike Darnell, Executive Vice-President of Rupert Murdoch's Fox TV channel in the US, of the themes aired in his programmes entitled Alien Autopsy: Fact or Fiction (1995) and Animals Attack (1996). Some of these supposed documentaries shocked viewers with their gory and grue-some detail—animals attacking women in the most brutal manner and kill-ing their hapless and helpless victims right in front of the viewers who are aware that they were watching a real incident and not a re-enactment. Some critics call these depictions a form of pornography.

In any case, shockumentaries thrive on blood and gore, sex and violence—whether in the animal kingdom or in the world of humans. Although such depictions of violence and brutal sex are not prevalent in Indian films, they are not totally absent. Indian films show violence against women even in ordinary domestic life, when women are oppressed by wife-beating husbands and when parents abuse their children, particularly girls, either physically or verbally.

Reality TV is said to have premiered in the US with a show that presented clips of the private therapy sessions of a well-known woman who had com-mitted suicide three months before the show was aired. Shocking events in real life involving unusual circumstances of death—someone falling onto the cement floor of an empty swimming pool, for instance—were usually se-lected from accidents and natural disasters. The repeated airing of the clips of the terrorists' attacks on the twin towers in New York on 9/11, or the sudden explosion of the space shuttle Challenger are other examples of shockumentaries. Repeated exhibition nauseates viewers. The intention of the producers and network managers seems to be indulgence in violence for its own sake. Many viewers and media critics point out that such portrayal of violence is deliberately done by media managers.

The most unforgivable portrayal of violence in recent times was the unrelenting pursuit of Princess Diana in life and even after her death. There are many other real-life events that have become shockumentaries:

Michael Jackson's 'sexcapades', O.J. Simpson's trial, the unsolved Jon Benet Ramsey murder, President Bill Clinton and Monica Lewinsky's affair, and other such scandals. It is not only TV but all media that profit from other people's miseries.

For example, *Time* magazine with Princess Diana on its cover sold 850,000 copies, as opposed to its normal 650,000 copies; its commemorative issue on the princess sold 1.2 million copies. As stated in the publication *American Decades, 1990–1999*, Princess Diana's death and 'Monicagate' were commercially exploited by the media. There was even speculation that Princess Diana died in tragic circumstances because photographers were in high-speed pursuit of her car at the time of the fatal crash.

Many people, including journalists, have decried the 'tabloidization' of mainstream media these days and criticized the blurring line between tabloid journalism and mainstream journalism. News in the modern world has become sensational and shocking entertainment. The new technologies have helped in this a great deal. Journalism has become callous and uncaring towards human beings.

Similar trends are seen in India too. Under the pretext of investigative journalism, many political and public personalities are hunted down, with or without documented proof or by means of manipulated and misleading documentation. Even totally untrue incidents are presented on the front pages of newspapers or as lead stories on television. The media get away with these unethical practices because they take undeserved shelter under the constitutional protection given to them and also because they have grown into huge businesses with multimillion-rupee assets whereas the private citizen cannot fight them in court for want of money and time.

The likes of Howard Stern (self-styled 'king of all media') with the obscenities he uses on the air, Rush Limbaugh with his right-wing proclamations and Laura Schlesinger who offers simplistic and untenable solutions to the problems of listeners who call in for advice (McConnell 2001: 388) are still unknown in India now. But when private channels proliferate and a free-for-all trend in media ownership and content becomes a reality, all kinds of publications and broadcast material will appear. This is a matter to be discussed and debated by all concerned citizens of India. Totally unrestricted freedom of the private channels (who have yet to evolve a model code of conduct) is as bad for the public as restrictions imposed by the government.

PBS in the US and the BBC in the UK have proved themselves effective alternatives to private channels. The matter of building a less bureaucratic and more imaginative corporation that will address national media issues boldly has to be discussed and debated in Parliament and other fora. A middle path is advisable and all concerned have to think more seriously about this issue without political prejudice.

Public broadcasting with generous donations from corporations and charitable foundations and membership subscriptions from viewers is the method followed by the PBS. The BBC depends largely on government funding and licence fees, although recently it has started selling airtime for commercials, in a limited way. The advantage is that programming will be independent of commercials. At present both Doordarshan and other channels depend a great deal on advertising. However, there appears to be no end to advertising and no restriction on the time devoted to advertisements, much to the frustration of the viewers.

Even in the US, where there was an FCC (Federal Communications Commission) regulation that not more than six minutes in a 30-minute programme should be set apart for advertising, the deregulation introduced during the Reagan years led to broadcasters being allowed to exercise their discretion. Currently one-third of the time is devoted to advertising on all the private television networks in the US. But in India almost all the private channels advertise for almost half the time. This is especially true of the cable channels such as Zee TV, STAR and Asianet. The elite who access these cable channels, paying anywhere between Rs 200 and 300 a month, will soon be clamouring for a commercial-free channel. Many viewers are also turned off by the all-news channels because most of the time the same news is repeated endlessly!

A commission similar to the Carnegie Commission that studied viewers' demand for a commercial-free channel in the US and came out with the basic document for public broadcasting, *Public Television: A Program for Action* (1967), may be set up in India within a few years. This document, among other things, deals with educational television. Although some people were apprehensive that the public system would become a government propaganda tool, novel educational programmes such as *Sesame Street* (from 1969 onwards) and *Mr Roger's Neighborhood* won acclaim throughout the world as the best educational programmes for children. Other programmes presented by PBS are great ones too, the likes of which are not found on the commercial channels. However, the lengthy appeals from the channel managers to the public for donations every three months is becoming a nuisance to the viewers.

There seems to be no proper solution for the problem of presenting quality programming without commercials, but the broadcasters themselves have to cooperate with each other and come up with an optimum proportion of time to set apart for commercials. Perhaps a public committee to oversee this vital issue can come up with suitable recommendations in the future. However, there is no denying the fact that the Corporation for Public Broadcasting (CPB) and the British Broadcasting Corporation (BBC) are models for excellent broadcasting with popular support. In 10 or 12 years, PBS became a strong competitor for NBC, CBS, ABC and Fox in the US. Similarly, the BBC still produces the most admired news channels in the UK and its former colonies, although CNN has started weaning away some of its followers.

It will not be surprising if a broadcasting system that emulates the positive aspects of both BBC and CNN (minus commercial advertising) evolves in at least the metropolitan cities of India, where viewers are already tired of the mindless programmes and endless commercials. Classical programmes produced indigenously and those imported from abroad (classic films, for example) can be aired in India, along with educational programmes that have proved successful in other countries and dubbed into local Indian languages. To begin with, dubbing can be done in six major languages: Hindi, Bengali, Tamil, Telugu, Kannada and Malayalam. The new commercial-free channel can be supported by leading corporations, philanthropic funds and agencies of higher education, along with subscriptions and donations from the viewing public.

The Digital Revolution

We have already indicated how information in digital (number) form is recorded and how digital systems are applied to words, pictures and sounds. The recording is done in codes of numbers. The most modern systems of communication—from telephone to television, radio to virtual reality, CDs to DVDs, computer chips to V-chips—are all based on the binary system of two digits: 1 (a short pulse of electricity) and 0 (no pulse). If 1 is life, 0 is death; philosophically speaking, all communication in the modern world oscillates between life and death!

Digital versus Analogue

Instruments of communication that were in use before the arrival of modern digital systems worked on the analogue (also spelt 'analog') system which works on signals coded in the form of continuously varying up-and-down waves. Audio and video cassettes and most telephones of the previous era were analogue. It was during the 1990s that radio and television began to switch to the digital system.

Instead of waves, the signals in digital systems go out as ultra-fast streams of on-off digitals. The wonderful development, according to communications expert Steve Parker, is that 3–10 times as many television or radio channels can be squeezed into the bandwidth used for just one analogue channel (2002: 8).

All these developments were based on the technology of the integrated circuit (IC), which had already made great advances during the 1970s and 1980s. IC technology could pack millions of pieces of information on a few square millimeters of a thin slice of silicon (named the silicon chip). The central processing unit (CPU) of a computer, also called the 'brain' of a computer, doubled in speed and handling capacity every 18 months during the last two decades of the 20th century. The effect of all this progress was felt not only in the broadcast media but also in the music industry.

Sound Recording and the Music Industry

Storing of sound, as we have already seen, started in the early 20th century. The Victor Talking Machine started the mass-production sound recording industry in 1901, when it manufactured a gramophone invented by Emile Berliner that played sounds recorded or stored in the form of a long groove in a flat, rotating disk. Both the gramophone and the phonograph (invented by Edison) gathered sound waves and turned them into vibrations that were stored as a wavy groove.

By the late 20th century, sound recording was being done digitally. Digital recording and reproduction is of high fidelity, with clearer sound and sharper pictures (in the case of audio and video recording on CDs, VCDs and DVDs). The frequency of errors is much lower in the digital mode than in the analogue. Information is transferred almost perfectly from one form to another.

As we have seen, the 20th century started with recorded sound on gramophone and ended with what is known as MP3, an all-electronic storage format for computers and the Internet. The 1980s brought CDs that could carry about 75 minutes of sound stored in the digital mode. The CD code could be read by a laser beam. In the 1990s, CD technology was modified to include not only sound but pictures. Another version of the CD was the MD (mini disc) made by Sony in 1991. It was smaller than the CD but it could record as well as re-record.

The extended version of the CD was the DVD. It could hold seven or eight times more information than a CD. A full-length movie plus additional features like an interview with the director could be held in a DVD.

But more exciting than the CD and DVD was the all-digital MP3 which made it easier to send sound along telecommunication lines, such as the Internet lines, and to store sound and pictures on a computer disc. It could also be used for sending recorded sound (music or speech) over the Internet. Thus music became available online.

In this way all media—newspapers, radio, recorded music, graphics and television on the Internet—could be combined. This raised several vital questions: Is it lawful to make copyright material available to millions of Internet users almost free? The new millennium started with these controversies engendered by technological progress. Many of these issues are being debated even now.

The Internet

More than any other medium, the Internet has grown immensely over the span of one decade. Computers are not only interlinked for quick transmission of ideas, accounting data and personnel records internally, but also for communication with other businesses and factories. Schools, universities, governments, charitable foundations, in short, every organization in the world run on modern lines, and even individuals, have websites that announce their business to the world so that others can contact them if they wish.

The Internet is a worldwide system of computers interlinked by wires and cables, and by microwave, satellite and radio links of telecommunication networks. It is right to call it the Nets' Net.

The Internet links subscribers globally through the World Wide Web. Every subscriber can be reached within minutes, if not seconds. It is a supercomputer network. The universalization and democratization of news and information are made possible by it (Vilanilam 2000b: 213).

It is a technological marvel of the modern world, and it has already revolutionized the way in which people think, interact, gather and process information, do research, earn a living, educate and entertain themselves in the initial decades of the 21st century. Human institutions are going to change their style of operation and establish new relationships with citizens nationally and internationally.

History of the Internet

The Internet, like many other developments in communication, originated in the United States as a device for enhancing and streamlining the military's national defence information network. The objective was to protect the network from total breakdown even when one or two computers in the network stopped working. Since the Advanced Research Project Agency (ARPA) of the US Department of Defense was responsible for its development, the network came to be known as the ARPANET.

The ARPANET came into being in 1969. By 1989, it began to be used for non-military purposes also. Private corporations took up the network for commercial purposes.

Today, there is no single agency totally responsible for controlling the Internet. It is a decentralized system, although there is an Internet Society working globally for information exchange among users. There is also an Internet Architectural Board in charge of maintaining and updating technical standards.

The Internet, according to experts, had not been designed as 'a unitary infrastructure but as a voluntary protocol which millions had opted to use. It was an ad hoc, flexible, bottom up, chaotic phenomenon' (Kirkman 1999).

The use of the Internet has grown exponentially since the network's creation in 1969. Originally conceived as a way to connect major research organizations, it has now become the world's most important medium of interpersonal and inter-organizational communication. Since, however, it cannot reach the masses at one stroke, one cannot call it a mass medium.

It was in 1989 that the British computer scientist, Timothy Berners-Lee, created the World Wide Web (www or W3); within a couple of years, the Web became the mainstay of Internet users everywhere.

According to the Internet consulting company Nua, the Web was being used by 45 million people worldwide in 1996, of whom 30 million (two-thirds) were in North America. Today, China has 80 million users (about 8 per cent of its population). India may have 10–15 million users, the bulk of whom will be in New Delhi, Kolkata, Mumbai, Chennai, Bangalore and Hyderabad.

Some 60 million people used the Net in 1995; the number of users increased to 200 million at the beginning of 2000. It is estimated that the Internet will be used by a billion people all over the world in 2005, that is, one-sixth of the total population on earth. This may be a highly optimistic estimate. However, there is no doubt that the number of Net users is increasing fast.

John Green gives a demographic profile of Internet users. Seventy-seven per cent of Web users are male. However, a gradual gender balancing is occurring with more and more women entering the work force and sharing their male colleagues' net habits. The median income of users is $40,000 (almost 2 million rupees a year) but 28 per cent of users make less than

$20,000. This is indicative of the very bias of the Internet towards the rich and the powerful in India, if not in the world.

Because of the sudden increase in the use of the Internet all over the world, especially among adolescents and young adults, many concerned scientists and sociologists have suggested that in its present state, the Internet can create anarchy. But it has been in use for the past dozen years or more and there has not been any major catastrophe. Some people attribute the destruction of the twin towers in New York on 9/11 (11 September 2001) to the secret, speedy and unregulated exchange of information between and among terrorists. But there are many experts who believe that anarchy is a great feature of the Internet since no government authority or private corporation controls it. To them, anarchy is something to celebrate, not condemn, and cannot be equated with irresponsibility!

Another fear, as already discussed, is that the pornography on the Internet, if unregulated, will corrupt the morals of young people. Appropriate national laws against obscenity, pornography and other undesirable lapses to which the Internet is prone, can protect the morals of young people. The US Supreme Court, however, struck down the Communications Decency Act on the grounds that parents should be responsible for children's use or misuse of the media.

The general view prevailing among experts is that although the Internet may be anarchic, it is not desirable to pass hasty legislation to control it as that might potentially hurt freedom of information. Arthur Schlesinger, Jr, an eminent American writer and thinker, points to the great potential of the Internet in strengthening national and international communication, besides bringing communities within individual nations closer to each other. Communitarianism and democratic decentralization will be strengthened by the Internet, he says (1997: 8).

However, many communities in the US advocate equipping library computers with filtering software to block out offensive sites, for the protection of their children. Others promote self-regulating systems on the part of Internet service providers. The American Library Association (ALA) and the American Civil Liberties Union (ACLU) oppose such control measures as they believe that any attempt to regulate access to the Internet will have an adverse effect on the right to free speech, especially with regard to citizens' frank discussion of controversial topics like birth control, stem cell research, homosexuality and AIDS. Many people have also expressed their fear that blocking devices in libraries will lead to undesirable curbs on citizens' freedom and that political opponents will be monitored by government (Stay 1999: 145–46).

Cyberspace, Cybercafés and Cyberology

As Steve Parker (2002) says, the Internet is

an unreal or virtual world called cyberspace. It is an electronic place that exists only as tiny electrical pulses in computer circuits. Cyberspace presents endlessly flexible multimedia for use by advertisers, shoppers, businesses, public services such as libraries, special interest groups ... and anyone else.

Cybercafés are seen everywhere in India these days. In rich, developed countries, this phenomenon is not seen, mainly because many citizens have computers and Internet connections at home or at a nearby community library. But in many less affluent countries, citizens do not have computers at home and if at all there are community libraries nearby, they do not have Internet connections. Therefore, citizens go to privately-owned cybercafés send e-mails and use the Internet. These cybercafés are just like public utilities such as the post office or the telephone booth.

When TV expanded in India during the 1970s, many public places were furnished with TV kiosks so that ordinary citizens could watch programmes there for short periods of time. There were also community television sets in rural areas. Cybercafés are similar to those community efforts. An hour's use of these facilities may cost as little as Rs 20, depending on the size of the city. In certain towns and cities the charges are higher, but never above a dollar an hour. The availability of Internet facilities at cheap rates is a blessing in many underdeveloped or developing countries with a large lower middle class and many poor citizens.

Some cybercafés used to offer refreshment in the initial years along with fun on the Internet: virtual reality shows, video games and even closed booths in which to watch pornographic material. Most cybercafés now offer just Internet facilities. In most countries of the world, the majority of the population cannot yet afford the expense of installing a computer with Internet connection and printer at home. The average cost runs to almost five times the average per capita income of many countries. Nevertheless, computer facilities and Internet use are increasing in most countries, particularly in urban and semi-urban areas. Most of the users still belong to the more affluent sectors and they use the modern facilities for fun and entertainment of various kinds. Again, as Parker has observed, 'sites on the World Wide Web range from companies trying to attract more business to individuals just having a good time' (ibid.: 8). But nobody can deny that the facility for sending messages privately and directly from one person to another, and receiving replies within seconds, is the greatest single advantage of the modern system of interpersonal communication.

As Paul Gilster says in his foreword to John Green's book, *The New Age of Communications*, something 'protean and profound is happening to our world, whether we call it digital revolution, information super-highway or a grand convergence of the media' (Green 1997: 7).

Everything in the world, living and non-living, can be broken down into basic components, the elements which in turn consist of electrons, protons, neutrons and other particles. And all information can be transformed into the digital form: 1s and 0s. But we cannot ignore the fact that some very important precursors of modern digital technology—techniques and instruments—were developed before the advent of the digital era: telegraph, telephone, wireless, radio, television, mainframe computer, personal computer (PC), satellite dish, network broadcasting, cable television, photophonics, fibre-optics, miniaturization, multimedia software, voice-printing, high-speed computing and many more. Is today's digital revolution a precursor to more startling changes in the coming decades, which may lead to a resolution of eternal questions about the origins of life and life after death? Will the experts' prediction that today's digital revolution will enable us to read the secrets of life and the primordial archives of our species come true? Or, as Marshall McLuhan and Bruce Powers have said in their work, *Global Village: Transformations in World Life and Media in the 21st Century*, 'What may emerge as the most important insight of the 21st century is that man was not designed to live at the speed of light' (1998: 8).

10

communication technology with a human face: the challenge of the 21st century

a little over half the world's population lives in a wired world today, making frequent use of the means of telecommunication to gather, store, restore, transmit and receive information and entertainment. The other half have never even used a telephone. Yet, overall, the progress made over the millennia, from the capture and taming of fire and the invention of the wheel onwards is mind-boggling, especially in the field of communication. We must now consider ways to give a human face to communication.

All the latest instruments of communication currently in use are not the result of any single event in history but the products of a long process of invention, discovery and development involving many technologies and scientific principles and the work of many people in different parts of the world. Most of these people did not see their work as a means of amassing wealth or power. Instead, they had the urge to delve deep into natural phenomena and social relations and their contributions benefited humanity.

Lightning, thunder, the sun, the moon, the planets and the stars that appeared as mere specks of brilliance far away inspired our prehistoric ancestors to think of the light and fire which they saw in lightning and forest fires. Rubbing stones together, they made fire, cooked food and found it tastier than raw food. As John Green has observed, despite the fact that palaeontologists have found evidence of the human use of fire some 500,000 years ago, the earliest proof of our ability to make fire without rubbing stones together dates from just 13,000 years ago (1997: 5).

We are still searching for new uses for fire: for example, new rockets and fuels for space travel, better jet engines and non-petroleum fuel for air travel around the globe, the development of the microwave, the laser and, above all, newer versions of fission and fusion in nuclear weapons. Since the invention of the telegraph, scientists have invented many devices for telecommunication. The tiny mobile phone can now be used not only for telephony, but also for digital photography, television and radio, music recording and replay, e-mail and internet! This personalized communication device which we carry with us everywhere enables us to stay in touch with each other in several different ways. The human telephone operators of the past century have been replaced with the electronic switches that can handle hundreds of calls at once through computerized systems such as the ESS-5 of the American Telephone and Telegraph Company (AT&T)

'The ESS-5 is constantly scanning every phone line on its board, at the rate of one scan in a tenth of a second' (Green 1997: 52). It is said that if a problem develops, the computer can reload its whole operating system in less than 10 seconds! ESS-5 and similar switches can handle 190 million calls a day.

The revolution in communication has spread into every department of life for 2 billion people of the world. It will change the way half the world's people think, act, play and conduct their lives. It will affect their private and public life, because it is changing all aspects of commerce, politics, social relations, art, culture and even sexual life. As mentioned in Chapter 9, all this change owes its origin to the technology of multimedia and convergence, as evidenced by newer and more miniaturized compact computers. The latest versions are called 'palmtops' or 'personal digital assistants' (PDAs), electronic diaries that can come to life in a trice and obey all our 'commands', faithfully and digitally! This and other devices can be connected to a main computer at home or office and put to different uses.

These are also the days of CDs and DVDs, devices that can be hooked directly to a computer and operated at will. When digital devices like the palmtops came into use at the turn of the 21st century, many people thought they were mere fads that would not last long. But the use of digital equipment, including digital car radios, digital flat-screen television sets, etc., is steadily rising. (Liquid crystal technology helped in replacing heavy, glass 'tubes' with flat screens that give a better visual effect.) The advantage of the digital system over the analogue one is that the digital is less prone to error and provides clearer and crisper reproduction of sound and picture.

Interactive TV or two-way TV, that first entered the public domain in the early 1990s, was an innovation that was expected to find a large market but did not. The Full Service Network (FSN) started by Time-Warner in 1996 did not survive its two-year trial period. The expansion of the Internet and computer interaction very rapidly overtook the two-way TV.

The 1990s also saw the development of the CD-ROM (compact disk-read only memory) and the DVD (digital video/versatile disk), both of which could combine or converge all traditional media—the spoken word, graphics, script, calligraphy, typography, designs, all forms of instrumental music, singing, natural sounds, sound effects, pictures, drawings, paintings, film, video, 2-D and 3-D animation, cartoons and special effects.

CD-ROM encyclopaedias have animations and video clips on history and ancient geography in their entries wherever needed so that users get a more comprehensive idea of the topics. A single CD-ROM can contain 650 million characters—that is, the capacity of 450 high-density floppies or 500,000 pages of text with as many as 10,000 photographs.

The DVD looks like a CD but it can hold a full-length feature film of high sound and picture fidelity. It can store seven times the information content of a CD-ROM: 4.7 billion characters (4.7 gigabytes). Recent versions of DVDs from the first decade of the new millennium can store up to 20 gigabytes! John Green says in his book, *The New Age of Communications*, that the golden age of interactive multimedia is yet to develop. The process has begun and it will take hundreds of software specialists and skilled artists, graphic designers and composers plenty of time and effort. Above all it needs money— millions of dollars. Yet, the day is not far off when a team of multimedia specialists working in different countries will evolve a COMBO media system (Green 1997: 87–88).

The World Wide Web is already acting as a decentralized (even anarchic) information superhighway for millions of people. Extraordinary entrepreneurs with vision, such as Bill Gates, Steve Jobs and Steve Wozniak are known in the computer world for their farsightedness. They trod the path of ancient and modern pioneers such as Pascal, Leibnitz, Boole, Babbage, Maxwell, Weiner, Shannon and Weaver and put their ideas into practical use. One may go a step further and say that the 20th century pioneers made the computer and compunication accessible to the general public through PCs. Besides Bill Gates, there are many other names to be remembered, such as that of Douglas Engelbert, a young naval radar technician who was inspired by an article by Vannevar Bush in the *Atlantic Monthly* and worked to develop human beings' natural abilities to solve problems through the computer.

According to John Green and other writers and communication experts, if there is someone who can be called the father of the new media, it is Vannevar Bush. He influenced the growth of 20th century science and engineering more than any other person. In 1945, Bush published his seminal article, 'As We May Think', in the *Atlantic Monthly*. In this article, Bush had anticipated the fax machine, xerography, the polaroid camera, microfilm, speech recognition technology and the speech-to-print typewriter, the personal computer, multimedia and even virtual reality. Bush's visionary article challenged the intellect of two generations of computer scientists. His article can be compared to the science fiction of another great visionary, Sir Arthur

C. Clarke, who wrote about space odysseys in the same year, 1945. (Clarke wrote the screenplay for his own novel, *2001: A Space Odyssey*.) Many of the visionary projects which these two men conceptualized have actually been realized in the last three decades, particularly in space travel and the widespread use of the computer.

Another very important name in modern science and technology is that of Nicholas Negroponte, a digital expert who spoke and wrote about the post-MTV generation.

A very important name associated with the mathematical theory of communication is that of Claude Shannon, who died in March 2001. A professor at MIT, Shannon worked with Warren Weaver on theoretical aspects of communication, particularly mathematical, engineering and digital aspects. He was one of the earliest (in the late 1940s) to predict that every gadget in communication, both audio and video, would work on the binary or digital system instead of the analogue system.

The present decade, the first decade of the new millennium, is seeing a new generation of film and tape editors who easily convert video signals into digital bits which can be stored, recalled, edited and rearranged, all on the computer. Today's film and television products, as already indicated, are the products of computerized editing systems. Editing of digital video images has become as easy as the editing of printed matter on the computer. And miniaturization is also progressing at a fast pace.

Can Technology Make
Mass Communication Two-Way?

Despite all these new developments, is not mass communication still a one-way process? In the 1970s, cable television raised the hope that people would be able to send messages in return instantaneously. But even today, mass communication remains one-way. The most successful experiment so far in two-way communication was the QUBE two-way cable service that was started by Warner Communications in Columbus, Ohio, in 1977. The QUBE helped the television audience register its views on poll topics. Even today, some cable channels ask viewers to e-mail their opinions on certain topics of current interest. But the topics polled, in 1977 and now in the 21st century, are often not very significant ones and do not relate to the basic problems facing the large majority of the people.

There are two basic drawbacks in such polls. First, the polls conducted by the cable channels in developing countries like India can ascertain the views only of the elite; just 10–15 per cent of India's population can afford cable channels. Second, the channels concentrate on issues of interest to the rich and the privileged.

Two-way communication has become more practical in videogames, video shopping, bill-payment, virtual education, and so on, but interactive cable television such as QUBE did not thrive. Not all television sets are hooked to videogames, home shopping or online banking. These are certainly marvellous innovations, but ordinary set owners (and they are the majority) look upon television as a mere instrument for entertainment. Many of them use it primarily for viewing feature films and programmes based on popular films and film music. Going to the movies or other centres of entertainment has become expensive, particularly for a family of three or more members. Most people, therefore, take maximum advantage of their TV set for *manoranjan* (entertainment), and nothing else. This may be true of people in the developed world as well.

Although online banking, shopping and other services save people a lot of time and effort, they often miss the face-to-face interaction and personal contact with others. Therefore, whatever the merit of online shopping, most people look upon it as their predecessors looked upon the electric toothbrush two or three decades ago. Marketing firms, factories and financial institutions, however, use online communication very effectively. Ordinary people do not make use of it to a great extent. This is perhaps the reason for the discontinuation of Time-Warner's 1994 experiment in virtual shopping after two years. It was too expensive.

Some people in India are enamoured by virtual schooling or virtual education. This would require expensive infrastructure for every student. It is a great idea, no doubt, but when we consider the vast number of young people in India who are to be educated, the infrastructure needs that will have to be met to enable them all to access virtual education become huge both in terms of equipment and cost. There is still no substitute for proper buildings and basic facilities such as electricity, water and drainage in every school district.

To receive virtual education, or even education via satellite in all our villages, proper housing with an uninterrupted supply of electricity is essential. Electricity is at the base of every modern technology. India is still short of such basic necessities.

Technology without a human face is what is progressing in many countries. Millions of human beings all over the world are dying of hunger, disease and war. Technology is being used to augment the production and distribution of weapons of war and destruction. The plight of almost one-third of the world's population is yet to attract the serious attention of technologists, scientists, national leaders and international experts. Once in a while, certain world organizations—the United Nations, the IMF, the World Bank—refer to the plight of the poor, but nothing substantial is being done to design appropriate technology to improve the lives of millions of the poor. While capital-intensive high technology is galloping ahead, the socioeconomic condition of the poor progresses at the pace of a disabled mule.

Let us now reflect on the most recent effort by India to use a satellite to educate people on a massive scale.

EDUSAT and Human Development

The Indian Space Research Organisation's (ISRO) geosynchronous satellite launch vehicle (GSLV) took off from the Satish Dhawan Space Centre in Sriharikota, Andhra Pradesh, at 4.01 P.M. on 20 September 2004. The 1,950-kilogram satellite, appropriately named EDUSAT (Educational Satellite) is India's first satellite exclusively for educational services.

EDUSAT is expected to revolutionize distance education, as it will beam signals from a central television studio, where a teacher will lecture on a particular subject, to educational institutions equipped with signal reception facilities. The idea is that all students in schools or colleges with television monitors specially adapted for receiving the signals can learn new things simultaneously.

Space technology can thus help solve a serious problem faced by educationists in India, namely, the lack of good teachers and effective teaching methods. When it becomes fully operational in the coming months, EDUSAT will reach 1,000 classrooms and 50,000 students to begin with. More classrooms and students are expected to benefit in the future.

EDUSAT is, in a way, the offspring of ISRO's (and perhaps the world's) first major effort to instruct thousands of villagers via satellite, SITE (Satellite Instructional Television Experiment), conducted for one year between 1 August 1975 and 31 July 1976. As described in Chapter 8, hundreds of programmes on topics including health, hygiene, communicable diseases, family planning and language learning were re-transmitted from a geosynchronous satellite, ATS-6, donated by the Ford Foundation.

SITE was very successful especially in proving that a geosynchronous satellite that received signals from the Space Applications Centre (SAC) under ISRO in Ahmedabad could re-transmit them to thousands of villages in several states. For SITE, 2,400 villages were selected in the six Indian states of Andhra Pradesh, Karnataka, Orissa, Madhya Pradesh, Bihar and Rajasthan.

The hardware aspects of SITE were found to work excellently. The most important hardware goal of SITE was realized on 15 August 1982. When the Indian National Satellite (INSAT) series was inaugurated. That led to a significant expansion of television in India. It is no exaggeration to say that SITE brought India onto the world map of television (Vilanilam 1996: 62–90).

For the past three decades, however, there has been no major effort on the part of Indian space scientists to utilize the results of SITE to explore the educational potential of television (except the limited UGC and IGNOU programmes telecast for students in the distance education stream).

Despite the fact that TV signals can reach almost 95 per cent of the geographical area of India, they have not been fully exploited in changing the sociocultural attitudes of the people, especially in rural areas—notwithstanding the SITE findings that TV could change villagers' attitudes to agricultural practices, high-yield varieties of seeds and so on. Following SITE, what received major attention was the provision of entertainment programmes to the villagers, especially televised epics (the Ramayana and Mahabharata, for example), thus underlining the *manoranjan* potential of television. The deleterious effects of the revivalism triggered by such shows was seen five years later when some among the unwary and illiterate millions were misled by crafty politicians and fundamentalists into a dangerous and vicious interpretation of religion, resulting in warped notions of *Bharatiyata* (Indian-ness or nationalism) and Hindutva.

TV's potential in highlighting the socioeconomic problems of the country and thus making both the elite and the masses aware of the real priorities of the country has not been explored, despite the positive findings of the scientists involved in conducting the satellite experiment. The ahistorical and unscientific approach to the social aspects of modern science culminated in the destruction of the Babri Masjid on 6 December 1992 and more recently led fanatics to perpetrate the Godhra massacre in February 2002 and the consequent pogrom in Gujarat during March–May 2002.

Mindless entertainment provided by television can be exploited by communal forces and people with an axe to grind, especially in a highly volatile environment in a region where thousands of the illiterate, poor and disgruntled are led by hypocritical leaders who have no qualms destroying men, women and children in different ways. The optimism of secular national leaders such as Jawaharlal Nehru and scientists like Vikram Sarabhai, who believed that modern means of telecommunication could create a scientific temper among the people has been shown to be unfounded. However, EDUSAT—properly utilized—can educate not only students in some universities and colleges but also the general masses about a number of practical measures that can change the face of India through concerted action. The 'global village' concept can be harmonized with the basic needs of the large majority of India's population. Advanced technology (including satellite communication) can be made to serve the basic needs of the masses, such as mass education, information about health and hygiene, technical aspects of modern living, self-employment and economic development.

It is not too much to hope that the historical development gap between rich and poor nations can be leapfrogged with the help of appropriately designed technologies. EDUSAT, it is said, is designed to serve for at least seven years, during which period 'it will transmit five spot beams covering the northern, northeastern, southern and western regions ... (using) radio frequencies known as the Ku-bands' (Gopal Raj 2004: 10). But it is the higher education sector that is the main target of EDUSAT.

The Visvesvaraya Technological University (VTU) of Karnataka, the Yashwantrao Chavan Maharashtra Open University (YCMOU) and the Rajiv Gandhi Technical University (RGTU) in Madhya Pradesh have been provided with studios where 'classes' can be filmed and uplinked to the satellite, which then re-transmits the signals to ground terminals in various colleges in the catchment area. Some receiving stations will be interactive so that teachers can clear the doubts of the students even as the teaching session proceeds. Educational experts are of the view that EDUSAT will be quite useful especially in catering to the needs of advanced engineering and technology students. Higher education in other disciplines will also eventually benefit from it. Medical students, for example, will benefit from telemedicine through EDUSAT programmes.

However, the problems faced by more than 13 million high, middle and lower primary schools in the country are likely to continue unresolved for at least the next 25 years, mainly because there are many millions of young students living in very poor circumstances and without the advantage of even basic facilities at school or at home, not to speak of advanced facilities such as distance education through satellite or terrestrial television! To most such students, electric connections are not available at home or school. Thousands among them may not live in properly-built houses. Their parents may be unemployed or under-employed throughout the year. Above all, the absence of proper school buildings in many villages, which is already well-documented (Oommen 1999), will restrict all modern schemes of education.

Even 57 years after Independence, India has not been able to build permanent school buildings in its 560,000 villages. Is it so difficult for political leaders and administrators to draw up a plan to build one primary, one secondary and one higher secondary school for a cluster of three villages, and one college for a cluster of 30 villages? Perhaps successive governments have not considered education, especially at the school level, a national priority. All attention seems to have been concentrated on the tertiary level of education, particularly engineering and medical colleges, the graduates of which often leave the country at the earliest opportunity to train or study and ultimately live and work abroad. In effect, engineering and medical colleges in India and other developing countries have become training institutes for the UK, USA and other advanced countries that have a shortage of young engineers, computer programmers, medical doctors and healthcare personnel.

It is true that thousands of India's graduates are getting jobs abroad. But the majority of Indians do not live abroad! Who will take care of their basic needs? Don't the young men and women of India have an obligation to serve their own country for at least a short period, especially after utilizing all the facilities provided for their higher education at nominal cost, compared to the cost of higher education in the developed world? Is serving other countries the primary goal of national education?

What will be the content of programmes televised by EDUSAT? Will they be focused on the basic requirements of development in India? Will they pay enough attention to the present and future needs and priorities of the country? Or will they be based on the needs and priorities in rich countries?

The benefits of EDUSAT should reach the people of India and other South Asian countries where, for historical reasons, the socioeconomic and technological problems are almost the same. For more than three decades—since SITE—there has been no attempt to use satellite technology in education. However, better late than never. Attention must be bestowed on the basic needs of the school-going population: school buildings with separate classrooms, blackboards, drinking water and toilets, qualified and committed teachers who are aware of the goals of education. This should not be overshadowed by the glitter of the high-tech education championed by the elite and mass media of India which, with a few exceptions, have all along de-emphasized the real priorities of the nation.

Electronic learning or virtual education can become universal only when the availability of electricity becomes universal and electronic gadgets are housed in proper buildings. Is there any modern nation on the face of the earth where there is as much disruption in the supply of electricity as there is in India? No building can stand safe if the foundation is not safe. Electricity is the foundation of all modern systems and hence of all modern nations.

The hope that the fundamental needs of all will be met in a phased manner has been belied by actual events and experiences in the past 57 years.

Perhaps the needs of people living in metropolitan cities, state capitals and large towns have been met to some extent, but 'India lives in her villages' is not a mere slogan. By meeting the needs of a tiny minority living in islands of prosperity in a sea of misery where a billion people struggle to stay afloat and escape the clutches of misery, India cannot lay a firm foundation for sustainable development.

Some of the problems in basic educational development requiring immediate solution are identified in the following questions and observations.

- Will pre-primary, primary, middle and secondary school students of all states and villages of the country have core courses of study so that movement from one area of the country to another will not cause any great hardship to students and their parents?
- What is the assurance that all children receiving school education will be able to secure a job?
- Will 12 years of schooling be made uniformly available to students of all states and villages?
- Will the last four years of schooling be occupational and craft-oriented so that school graduates will be employable upon leaving school? Will all high schools be properly equipped with workshops, laboratories and libraries with computerized systems?
- Will admission to higher education be strictly based on merit? And certainly without 'donations', a convenient euphemism for bribery. The anxiety of securing admissions, even at the kindergarten level, is really the beginning of 'bribing wisdom' in society, or the realization that bribes can buy everything.
- Will EDUSAT programmes be linked to the regular syllabi already prescribed at various levels? Are there enough agencies to coordinate the syllabi at various levels of education?
- Will degrees be delinked from jobs? Why should Ph.Ds become bus conductors?
- Will there be a quality control supervising agency for high school education similar to the National Assessment and Accreditation Council that looks after colleges, to ensure that all schools have basic minimum requirements and amenities?
- Will all schools be assessed and accredited, especially the pre-primary, primary and middle schools?
- How many schools have an uninterrupted supply of electricity and running water, and proper sanitation?
- How many schools have playgrounds and other recreational facilities, besides computers and libraries?

- How many schools have working television sets? Are class hours set apart for television viewing, discussions and presentations based on the programmes watched? Presentations are not the privilege of college students at the postgraduate level; schoolchildren should be trained in presenting and explaining their ideas.
- Do students get an opportunity to observe the functioning of local government and democratic, legislative institutions?
- Do they get a chance to visit nearby places of historic importance?
- Are they motivated to go out into the community during spare hours and help in community work, including cleaning up the environment and sharing information with fellow citizens on matters of social, economic and political importance?
- Will a team of selected students and teachers participate in literacy programmes for the less fortunate citizens in their community? Young people can do a better job of instructing their illiterate grandparents than regular teachers who want special remuneration for literacy programme participation.
- Will there be an expert team in each region to design special programmes for teachers who can utilize them later for the people of the region? Will such programmes be given publicity through the media?
- What is the mechanism to monitor the drop-out rates in each school? And what is the method to attract dropouts back to school?
- Are students exposed to an interdisciplinary system of education, so that science majors in future will know the fundamentals of the social sciences and humanities, and vice versa? Similarly, will non-science students in colleges be given an opportunity to get exposure to the fundamentals of major scientific developments in the world?
- Can students who, for various reasons, discontinue education after passing the high school examination be permitted to take up higher education on a part-time basis so they can also earn their livelihood simultaneously?
- Will computerized systems be introduced in all schools from the primary level so that students are exposed to computers from a very early age? Computers are quite essential for living in the modern world, but they should not be confined to the urban areas. Schools in rural areas must also have a few computers so that rural students will get familiarized with it and become computer-literate.
- Will senior students get an opportunity to learn the basic facts of life through sex education and also the need for maintaining a proper sex

ratio in society for the well -being of all? The declining sex ratio in many states of India is alarming and will lead to more sex crimes. Adequate knowledge about the functioning of the family and society has to be imparted to students. The relevance of knowledge in one area for students who major in other fields has to be stressed by teaching at least the fundamentals of economics and sociology, for example, to students of science and the humanities. The interdisciplinary nature of knowledge has to be stressed in education. Mere scientific and technological information is not sufficient for students of IT, engineering and medicine. Similarly, arts and humanities students should have an opportunity to choose fundamental courses in science and social science.

All modern technological visionaries are optimists. They believe, like their mentors and gurus did, that computers will change the world. They also believe that everyone on Earth should have access to the computer, e-mail and the Internet. They hope that the children of the 21st century will communicate through the computer. Gates and others believe that the computer will become the universal tool of all young people for communication in the 21st century.

However, there are millions of people in the world who have no access to drinking water, not to speak of the telephone, television or computer. And more than 40,000 children die every day of malnutrition and various preventable diseases caused mainly by hunger and improper food. It is a highly imbalanced world we live in.

Communication through the mass media continues to be one-way. Modern systems of interactive, interpersonal communication, such as the telephone and the Internet are affordable only to a tiny percentage of the national population.

Another vital factor affecting the mass media is the relationship between content and ownership. The media tend to become manipulators of the mind because they are owned and operated by people whose primary objective is making huge personal profits for the owners and not the betterment of society.

Given the ownership pattern today, a dozen media behemoths can determine what the world should know, whom the world should turn to for advice and guidance, and what the world should take as the truth. And whoever shouts loudest will be able to sell his wares at the quickest pace. Loudness here is determined by circulation; frequency of repetition of certain pieces of information; and highlighting of information through appropriate size and colour and illustrations in print, and through video-clips, graphics and so on.

The freedom of the individual is trampled upon by the media proprietors who make use of the airwaves—a public good—for private benefit, in the form of huge profits and social prestige and influence. Even cyber systems have come under increasing monopoly pressures. It seems that every system of mediated communication (mass and interpersonal) has been monopolized by a handful of worldwide conglomerates whose ultimate goal is the establishing of a mega-market. Bill Gates in his book *The Road Ahead* says:

> Markets from trading floors to malls are fundamental to human society, and I believe the new one will be the world's central department store. It will be where we social animals will sell, trade, invest, haggle, pick stuff up, argue, meet new people and hang out. (quoted in Green 1997: 71)

But can we ignore the big imbalance prevailing in the world today between the haves and the have-nots? Markets for computers and electronic goods, entertainment gadgets and telecommunication devices, weapons of warfare and personal protection, do not care about this cruel imbalance. What matters is control of the market by conglomerates that are more powerful and financially stable than even some large, politically independent states.

Poverty will continue to affect more than 1 billion people (more than one-sixth of the world's population). Sudden displacement from ancestral land due to war, famine and large development projects causes untold misery to millions. The market becomes absorbed in profit and loss calculations but ignores the millions who suffer. Technology bypasses the millions who bear the brunt of wars and the market-driven engines of mindless 'development'.

In this grim atmosphere, is it not fair to devote some attention to real communication strategies that motivate people of all persuasions to think about the plight of human beings bowed by the weight of centuries of oppression, poverty, unbalanced development, joblessness, famine, hunger and disease?

It looks as though the mass media and the instruments of interpersonal information and communication technology (ICT) unwittingly spread the false impression that the world has already solved the basic problems faced by the millions. They give the impression that they have forgotten the socio-economic picture of the so-called global village.

In 1974, *Fellowship*, the magazine of the Fellowship of Reconciliation, drew the world's attention to the fundamental nature of the global village. Close to 70 of the 100 residents of their imaginary village, representing all the people in the world, lived sub-standard lives; about half were illiterate and suffering from various kinds of misery—poverty, malnutrition, ill-health, illiteracy and ignorance. More importantly, the entire income of the village was controlled by just six of the 100 villagers!

Thirty years on, the global village is still much the same. The United Nations Human Development Reports in recent years have indicated that poverty reduction ought to remain the most important priority of the global village, since of the 6 billion total population, nearly a quarter are absolutely poor and earn less than a dollar a day.

India has perhaps the largest number of people affected by both income poverty and human poverty. Out of the 1.5 billion absolutely poor people in the world, almost one-third are in India, which also has more blind, illiterate and disease-stricken people than any other country in the world. Women, children and the old and the infirm suffer the most.

There has been great improvement in many indices of development during the past 30 years. For example, infant mortality has been reduced from 236 per 1,000 in 1970 to 115 in 1995. Life expectancy has doubled to 62 now. But the absolute number of infant deaths in India is still close to 2.5 million each year.

Grain production has increased and, for the five years till 2004, bumper harvests raised the hopes of all. But India is still facing a paradox. In an incisive article in the *Wall Street Journal,* Thurow and Solomon have said that 'despite its overflowing granaries, India has more hungry people than any other country—as many as 214 million'. This is one-fifth of India's population. It is possible that the figure is closer to 315 million, since people who get one square meal a day are not considered hungry by many statisticians.[1] Hunger is defined differently by different organizations. Parts of Uttar Pradesh, Madhya Pradesh and Orissa frequently experience famine, especially the hilly and mountainous regions.

Perhaps India has enough food for all her people, but many of the poor cannot afford to buy it. Perhaps the point raised by the Nobel Prize-winning economist Amartya Sen regarding the Bengal famine of 1943 is still relevant today as far as hunger and poverty in India are concerned: many Indians do not have the purchasing capacity to buy the food that is available in the vast Food Corporation of India (FCI) godowns. The stored grain rots and becomes inedible while people starve.

India's annual production of wheat alone recently exceeded 70 million tons. This is greater than the wheat production in the United States. Yet, almost half the children under five years of age are malnourished.

---

[1] The different governments in India in recent years have considered the provision of employment for all able-abodied persons for 100 days a year as a great and noble goal—not full employment throughout the year!

According to the latest data from the Food and Agriculture Organization (FAO) quoted in Thurow and Solomon's article, the number of undernourished in the poor quarters of the world increased by 18 million in four years (1997–2001), to almost 800 million. The undernourished of Asia, Africa and Latin America are worse than hungry. They are getting something to eat— just enough to eat and die!

Some 300 million children are among the world's hungriest people. They form almost one-third of the total number of the hungry on Earth. Building rural schools, giving children at least one full midday meal, providing clean drinking water and at least one nutritious beverage a day during school is as necessary in India as building roads and bridges.

All these data clearly underline the importance of job creation, to enable people to earn enough to buy food. India, China and Brazil, the three most populated countries of the world, are now 'suffering from a famine of jobs and livelihoods', Thurow and Solomon conclude (2004). Will IT or ICT jobs alone do the trick?

If the ICT experts fail in creating employment avenues for the ordinary millions (and not just for those trained in computers, electronics and information processing), the basic problems that worry the majority of the people and also the planners are likely to continue.

It is important for communication scholars to differentiate between growth and development. It is equally important for them to distinguish between communication and mass communication. To assume that haphazard, elite-oriented, lopsided and foreign-financed growth will lead to development is as unrealistic as to equate social communication with mass communication. Mass communication often divides rather than unites people in poor countries; only social communication, interpersonal and through small groups, can lay a lasting foundation for social cohesion, provided the process of communication takes place on a socially just and equal footing.

In the 1960s, the dominant ideas that propelled the engine of development were 'growth in the GNP', 'higher per capita income', 'massive injections of foreign investment', 'higher investment in hi-tech industries', 'modernization', 'Westernization', 'industrialization' and 'urbanization'. In the 1970s, the primary objectives were 'development', 'eradication of poverty' and 'higher investment in mass communication'. But in neither case was there any great benefit to the poor; the number of people in poverty has grown and so has the social control of the rich.

In the 1980s, even the idealism of the two preceding decades of development received a setback, and the concept of development gradually fell into the background. Growth at any cost replaced all human considerations.

Greed seems to have led the mighty nations to a condition characterized by the drying up of the milk of human kindness. The 1990s saw the total disappearance of all slogans of equality and socialistic ideas; countries that swore by socialism, particularly the Soviet Union and the Eastern European countries, either disappeared from the world map or were divested of socialistic ideas. The market became supreme.

The last decade of the 20th century also saw the rapid expansion of telecommunication and the advent of new systems of quick interpersonal and mass communication. In the new millennium the technological marvels of the late 20th century are being taken even further. The current mantras are 'transformation through telecommunication', 'connectivity through electronics', and 'liberalization, privatization and globalization'.

The philosophical foundation of all these ideas has been the same: strengthen the markets through mass communication that will lead to mass consumption. The same connection is made in W.W. Rostow's model, the basis for the development models of Lerner and Schramm, who took six Middle Eastern countries as testing grounds for their mass media and development paradigm. What has been happening in those countries has not led to their development but to their destruction. The philosophy of development propounded by communicologists in the 1960s and 1970s has been drowned in the noise of gunfire in some of those countries. The late 1980s and early 1990s reverberated with a new philosophy, first expressed in Samuel Huntington's article titled 'The Clash of Civilizations', in *Foreign Affairs*. Should the world aim at a *clash* instead of *cooperation* and *consanguinity*.

Perhaps the mass markets were not useful to the majority of the target audience. Or, even if useful, they were not accessible to all except the very rich. The experts of the previous era, such as Walter Rostow, identified the last stage of economic growth as the stage of *mass consumption*. But the mass markets created by economic growth and mass communication were accessible, in 'developing' countries, only to the rich. The rich in these countries run into millions and exceed the population of many countries of the world. Mass communication is really meant for them.

What products are available in plenty in the global market? Are these goods going to help reduce poverty, hunger and malnutrition, and promote the creation of jobs and environmental safety, increase the availability of safe drinking water and fulfil the basic needs of the absolutely poor of the world (APW)?

There is nothing wrong with strengthening markets through mass or interpersonal communication, provided there is consideration for goods that are most essentially needed for the APW. The rich countries and the rich in the poor countries have been marketing goods for the last three centuries. A slightly reoriented production and marketing strategy which keeps the APW in mind will work wonders for the poor. Poverty, injustice and inequality are also causes of terrorism. Democracy based on equality of citizens and equal opportunities for jobs and other essentials of life has to be established by the people themselves, striving for communitarian democracy based on their own history and socioeconomic and cultural milieu. No military might can succeed in imposing democracy from outside.

The world has seen, for the last six decades or so, intense psychological and physical efforts to spread the idea that mass production and the mass marketing of goods through mass communication will usher in an era of wealth and prosperity for all. It has also been assumed that wealth generated this way will trickle down within society, in a natural manner. Distributive justice has to be part and parcel of development action to make development sustainable. Social justice implies meeting the basic needs of at least the majority of the people who are struggling to survive on less than a dollar a day.

Is private industry interested in meeting the basic needs of the poor? History has shown time and time again that democratic governments, governments of, by and for the people, at the state and village level took upon themselves the responsibility of providing the most essential things for the people. Defence, police protection, hospital services, basic educational facilities, etc., are provided by all democratic governments, including those of the US and UK. If education and healthcare are left to private entrepreneurs, they will become huge businesses solely interested in profit-making. This has been proved in certain developed countries where, since the 1980s, greed has motivated private industry to get into providing basic services. The healthcare and insurance industries in these countries are now in private hands, which has had disastrous consequences for the majority of the citizens. For instance, poor American senior citizens who are unable to buy essential medicine that has suddenly gone up in price are forced to travel to Canada and Mexico where the generic (non-branded) medicines are safe and economical, thus clashing with their own government.

A glaring omission in the literature on development and communication is the lack of focus on the ruthless exploitation of the natural and human resources of the colonized countries by means of private corporations. This was an early stage in the development of now-rich countries, but it is conveniently omitted from development literature. This is a wilful rejection or obfuscation of historical truth. The historical intervention by the military forces of rich countries in the affairs of poor countries, allegedly to modernize, civilize and democratize them, is also usually omitted in discussions of communication and development.

Frequent mention of the need to urbanize India is made by all development experts. But bringing rural people into urban centres without providing jobs and occupational avenues in the countryside can never be helpful to either rural- or urban-dwellers. Most development thinkers speak of the need for making the rural people more active and positive in attitude. But without a livelihood, how can rural people have any self-esteem, any desire for life-sustenance and freedom (the three major ingredients of social change and development)? Why did (and do) hundreds of farmers die in the major IT- and ICT-promoting states of India? How can positive thinking be nurtured when the very advocates of positive thinking commit, through negative actions, crimes against humanity?

Land reforms are essential in India since the arable land is, to a great extent, in the hands of absentee landlords in the large states of Uttar Pradesh, Madhya Pradesh, Andhra Pradesh and Rajasthan, and even in some smaller states, such as Tamil Nadu, Karnataka and Orissa. Without land reforms that will enable small cultivators to come together in co-operatives to cultivate on a large scale using modern, mechanized systems of farming and irrigation, high-yielding variety of seeds and direct and efficient marketing of grain and other agricultural products on a large scale, along with agri-based and rural industries, poverty and joblessness will continue in India.

What kind of information is being spread by the media? How many media programmes deal with the basic issues of production and distribution? Information about electronic devices and their use in sophisticated offices or call centres cannot put food in the mouths of the poor. Cultivation of the land using modern techniques is essential; so is the great need for keeping the large number of currently unemployed and able-bodied persons occupied. Ail media attention seems now to be on IT and ICT. While these are important, how can India ignore the development of agriculture? What plans are there to link IT and ICT with agriculture? Similarly, what importance is given in our basic educational communication to the reduction of drudgery and manual labour? All of us know that computers can count sacks of grain but they cannot produce grain! We need people to plan the production of grain as well as people to till the land using modern equipment. Technical education relating to agriculture is essential.

In India, where close to 80 per cent of the population is rural, emphasis has to be given in education to rural law and rural sociology for people from these areas to understand how administrative and legal systems, social practices and conventions work and how they can be used or changed.

Only when educational institutions and their stakeholders (students, teachers, parents and managements) become aware of the essential link between national goals and educational practices will education become really useful to the people. Rejecting all thoughts of elitism, teachers and students have to look upon education as the true means of democratizing the country and its systems of governance.

EDUSAT and other modern equipment for education must serve not only those who are already educated but those who have never had any chance of acquiring even literacy, not to speak of a familiarity with computerized systems of communication. Literacy, the basis of reading, writing and comprehension, is most essential. The constitutional goals of building a literate society as the basis of an egalitarian society can be realized only by ensuring universal primary education for all children under 14 (it should actually be 18, since it is recognized now that people under 18 years of age are still children). This universal basic education is a must and it should be the sine qua non of national education policy for the following reasons.

1. Human resources are the most important deciding factor in national development.
2. All citizens must participate in some national development work during the early years of their schooling.
3. Human resources have to be properly prepared, with a systematic employment of their total potential, through a comprehensive system of education made available to all without considerations of caste, creed, sex, financial background or family social status.
4. The educational policy has to be based on the following considerations:

    (a) All human beings are equal.
    (b) Every individual has a right to dignity and respect.
    (c) Education should help in the building of a society of free and equal citizens.
    (d) Every educated person should believe in the dignity of labour.
    (e) Education should help the educated to observe and uphold their civic duties and responsibilities.
    (f) Education must help the educated to rely on themselves and live honourably without compromising their basic principles.
    (g) Education should help the educated to live in dignity and let others live in dignity.

The first priority in most poor countries (or countries with a very large number of poor people) should, therefore, be the betterment of economic life through fulfilment of basic needs including literacy and education of the large majority. However, development is not purely an economic phenomenon; it must encompass more than the material needs of people. Development must embrace the total human personality, including the needs of the spirit which usually find outlets in artistic creativity, spiritually uplifting experiences and in close communion with nature and humanity at large. As Mahatma Gandhi said, development should open the path for people to realize their total human potential. But Gandhi himself admitted that to a starving man, God appears in the form of bread. This existential factor has to be given priority in the development philosophy of all countries (Vilanilam 1992: 190–224).

One last point about ICT and development. According to many media sociologists, the new technologies of information and communication are directed at creating a global shopping centre and not at benefiting the poor with better systems of education, healthcare or fulfilment of basic needs. Schiller, the doyen of communication science in the US, said two decades ago that all the new technologies have begun or been developed for military use.

He, and others, have highlighted the collusion among national governments, private corporations, communication technologists and the mass media (see Schiller 1983:18). Can the new technologies serve in the empowerment of the common people and small communities? Can they revitalize democracy by making possible the active participation of all people and make the elite aware of the real priorities and basic needs? Will they help in restructuring the world for the establishment of small communities that are free to decide their own way of living without hurting other communities and co-operating with others for the benefit of all? Will they help in removing the present situation in which the proliferation of the mass media has made media institutions rich but democracy poor (McChesney 1999)?

glossary

Anglo-Indian newspapers Newspapers in English started by Englishmen (settlers and officials of the East India Company). The first Anglo-Indian newspaper was *Hicky's Bengal Gazette or the Calcutta General Advertiser*, started by James Augustus Hicky in 1780.

binary system The binary system is the basis of all modern systems of communication, including telecommunications. Unlike the digital system based on 10 and the vigesimal system based on 20 followed by some ancient tribes, the binary system has a base of 2—the 'yes, no' or '1, 0' system.

bit In computer language, *bit* is another name for 'binary digit'. Scientists refer to 'bits' of information, that is, the number of pieces of information that the computer stores in 'yes, no', '1, 0' or 'on, off' fashion. Eight bits form a *byte*.

chain ownership The pattern of ownership where the same publishing company owns different newspapers or newspaper editions, or the same media company owns several units of the same medium, in the same state or in different states.

coaxial cable A cable used in the cable television system (also called community antenna television or CATV). It has the capacity to carry from several dozen to unlimited spectra. This system has no spectral limitations and it can provide combined TV–Internet–e-mail access. It can also be used in telebanking and teleshopping with minor modifications.

communication This is the process of exchanging ideas for better understanding between and among people, with the aim of promoting peace, love and better living conditions for human beings. The word is derived from the Latin roots *communis* and *communicare*, both of which imply sharing and mutual understanding.

conglomerate media ownership Some media companies have major/controlling shares in non-media companies. Media are just a part of their business interests. Some such companies own media companies to promote their non-media interests. This type of ownership is called conglomerate ownership. (See also *vertical integration*.)

cross media ownership Some newspaper companies, especially in the West, own—apart from newspapers—magazines, radio and television stations, and publishing, film and other media companies. Recently, many publishing companies have developed web-publishing in addition to other forms of publishing. This type of ownership pattern is called cross media ownership, signifying that the same media company owns different media units.

digitalization Information can be gathered, processed, stored, retrieved and transmitted digitally using a '1, 0', 'yes, no' or 'on, off' binary system. Converting all information into this binary mode is called digitalization. *Digitus* in Latin means 'finger'.

dysfunctions The media not only have functions, they also have dysfunctions, about which media users must be made aware (see Chapter 1). Some of the dysfunctions are: status-conferral, ethicizing, narcotization and desensitization.

editionalization Large, successful newspaper chains in India are nowadays bringing out their newspapers from six or more cities or towns, altering the contents of one or two pages so that the editions serve the local population to that extent. The contents of the other (usually six, eight or 10) pages remains the same. This practice is called editionalization, and its main objective is to increase circulation and advertising revenue.

feedback One of the major components in the process of communication. Without feedback, there is no communication. Communication is a continuous process mainly because there is feedback between the source and the destination, between the communicator and the communicatee, between the sender and the receiver. Other components are the medium, the message and noise.

hypodermic needle model This is also known as the *magic bullet model*. It is another name for the Stimulus–Response (SR) Model. A person injected thus subcutaneously (hypodermic, or 'under the skin') will behave under the stimulus of the message, says this erroneous but convenient assumption.

Indo-Anglian newspapers Newspapers in English started by Indians. For example, the first Indo-Anglian newspaper was the English magazine called the *Brahmanical Magazine*, started by Raja Rammohan Roy.

interpersonal communication Communication between and among individuals and small groups, or between one person and a small group of people.

intrapersonal communication Communication taking place within the mind of each person. It encompasses the flow of ideas occurring in the mind as a result of the five senses—sight, sound, smell, touch and taste—corresponding to the five sense organs—eyes, ears, nose, skin and tongue.

journal Etymologically, a record of events, almost a diary, where the journal-keeper enters salient points of daily occurrences.

journalism This is the name given to any reporting of events, issues or personalities—in writing, film, photography or videography—for a large or small group of human beings, to inform, educate, entertain or enlighten them for individual or social benefit.

magic bullet model See *hypodermic needle model*.

mass Usually, a large, heterogeneous, amorphous, anonymous and undefined group of people. After many countries experienced successful social revolutions in the 19th century, the term *mass* acquired the positive sense of ordinary people engaged in movements for political, economic and social equality, and for liberty. (See also *the masses*.)

mass communication Communication through the mass media, between a central source of organized messages and a very large, anonymous and heterogeneous group of people across the world, using modern print and electronic technologies for rapid transmission. It involves the mass production and dissemination of messages (words, images and sounds) by organizations managed by large numbers of trained professionals. Mass communication is a one-way process; there is very little exchange between the producer of messages and the receivers of the messages. The most significant meanings of this term are based on the ideas of *mass* and *the masses*.

the masses The term commonly carries the connotation of 'the lower class'— often assumed to be ignorant, illiterate, uneducated, unruly, irrational and even violent groups of people. Generally, 'the masses' indicates a large, aggregate, undifferentiated group of people lacking order and bearing mainly a negative image. 'Mass' here can also mean 'mob', unruly and defiant, as in the phrase 'mob violence'.

mass media Different media of communication transmitting messages of all kinds simultaneously to large, heterogeneous and anonymous masses of people living in different localities, nations or parts of the world. Such media transmit messages rapidly and instantaneously. Large groups of people receive information from the mass media in the same language (such as English) or translated into local languages, in print or voice, with or without pictures, through either radio or television (audio or video).

media convergence Different media, generally print and electronic, are used to produce messages for the audience. The methods used to be different for different types of media but, from the late decades of the 20th century, all media produce messages using the electronic processing of news, information and entertainment. Thus, all media converge electronically. The media are said to converge because the process of production is basically the same. The message may be produced using different media in the same production unit.

new journalism A new type of writing, originated by journalist-writers such as Tom Wolfe, Truman Capote, Norman Mailer and Gay Talese in the late 1960s and early 1970s; they wrote non-fiction novels based on actual events reported in newspapers.

new media With advancements in technology have come many improvements in the media's variety and performance. The new media include digitalized media based on computerized systems, and the World Wide Web of interlinked global networks. Electronic production of newspapers, books, films, television and radio programmes has become the order of the day. CD-ROMs, cyberology, digitalized systems, the music industry, V-chips, DVDs, Internet reading of news and fiction, reality shows, 'shockumentaries', etc., are all by-products of the new computer-based media.

photojournalism Journalistic writing in which the contents are illustrated with the help of photographs. Pictures may tell a fuller story with fewer words. This branch of journalism developed with the technical attainments achieved in photography during the 19th and 20th centuries. Journalism that benefits from photographs and photographs that tell a story are both essential ingredients of photojournalism.

pixel, pixel array A pixel is defined as a tiny point of light or 'picture element' displayed on a monitor. A typical colour monitor may have a 640-by-480 pixel array. The colours of the original picture are converted into picture elements, pixels of different shades or colour levels. A single picture is built up out of thousands of pixels.

pyramid of communication Mass communication occupies only the apex of the 'pyramid of communication' (see Figure 1.3). The base of the pyramid is *intrapersonal* communication. The bulk of it is *interpersonal* communication represented by a (husband–wife) couple or dyad; family; classroom; corporate, governmental or religious group, etc.

Satellite Instructional Television Experiment (SITE) SITE was the largest national television experiment of its kind in the world. With the help of the National Aeronautics and Space Administration (NASA) of the US, the UN Development Programme (UNDP), the International Telecommunication Union (ITU) and the United Nations Educational, Scientific and Cultural Organization (UNESCO), ISRO succeeded in launching SITE using the US-supplied Applications Technology Satellite, ATS-6. SITE is the progenitor of the TV system in India and the INSAT series of satellites.

statement journalism An unflattering term used to denote the practice prevalent among many newspapers and some electronic media organizations which publish every statement that comes to them with or without authentication. The media publish one statement and then subsequent statements in response without checking the accuracy of the first statement itself.

Stimulus–Response (SR) Theory Communication was seen by early theorists, in the 1940s, as the process of stimulating a response in the receiver. In other words the message was supposed to induce an action by the receiver. The audience had no will of its own; the message receiver was motivated to act according to the effect of the message. This was a psychological approach to the practice of communication and it was the basis of hundreds of 'effects research' projects in the early decades of communication research, particularly in the US. (See also *hypodermic needle model*.)

Universal Model of Communication (UMC) A representation of the process of communication, showing five components: sender (S), receiver (R), medium (M1), message (M2), feedback (F). Some theorists add a sixth component, noise (N), which obstructs the process.

vertical integration Some media companies also own companies that produce the most essential ingredients which go into the production of media. For example, some newspaper companies own thousands of hectares of land where bamboo is cultivated on a large scale so they have a captive source of newsprint for their own needs and can monopolize its production. Similarly, some companies monopolize the production of raw stock for the film industry—and produce hundreds of films for the cinema industry.

references and select bibliography

Abramson, A. 1995. 'The Impact of Television', in A. Smith (ed.), *Television: An International History*. New York: Oxford University Press.

Agee, W., P.H. Ault and E. Emery. 1979. *Introduction to Mass Communications*, 6th ed. London: Harper & Row.

Allen, D. 1991. *Media without Democracy: And What to Do about It*. Washington, DC: Women's Institute for Freedom of the Press.

Anderson, J.A. (ed.). 1994. *Communication Yearbook*, Vol. 14. New Delhi: Sage Publications.

Arora, S.K. and H.D. Lasswell. 1969. *Political Communication*. New York: Rinehart & Winston.

Avery, R.K. and D. Eason (eds). 1991. *Critical Perspectives on Media and Society*. New York: Guilford Press.

Bagdikian, B.H. 1997. *The Media Monopoly*, 5th ed. Boston: Beacon Press.

Baker, E. 1994. *Advertising and a Democratic Press*. Princeton, NJ: Princeton University Press.

Barnes, M. 1940. *The Indian Press: A History of the Growth of Public Opinion*. London: Allen & Unwin Ltd.

Basinger, J. 1999. *Silent Stars*. New York: Alfred A. Knopf.

Baughman, J.S., V. Bondi and V. Tompkins (eds). 2000. *American Decades 1990–1999*. Detroit: Thomson Gale.

Baughman, J.S., M. Bruccoli, V. Tompkins, R. Layman and V. Bondi (eds). 1995. *American Decades 1920–1929*. Detroit: Thomson Gale.

Baughman, J.S., R. Layman, V. Tompkins and V. Bondi (eds). 1994. *American Decades 1960–1969*. Detroit: Thomson Gale.

Bhatnagar, R.R. 1946. *The Rise and Growth of Hindi Journalism, 1826–1945*. Allahabad: Kitab Mahal.

Bhattacharya, S.N. 1965. *Mahatma Gandhi, the Journalist*. Bombay: Asia Publishing House.

Biagi, S. 1994. *Media/Impact: Introduction to Mass Media*. Belmont, CA: Wadsworth Publishing.

Bianculli, D. 1992. *Teleliteracy: Taking Television Seriously*. New York: Continuum.

Boyd-Barrett, O. and T. Rantanen (eds). 1998. *The Globalization of News*. London: Sage Publications.

Bruccoli, M., V. Tompkins, R. Layman, V. Bondi, J.W. Hipp and J.S. Baughman (eds). 1996. *American Decades 1900–1909*. Detroit: Thomson Gale.

Bryson, L. (ed.). 1948. *The Communication of Ideas*. New York: Harper & Bros.

Burgoon, J.K. 1994. 'Nonverbal Signals', in M.L. Knapp and G.R. Miller (eds), *Handbook of Interpersonal Communication*, 2nd ed. New Delhi: Sage Publications.

Carlson, R. and B. Goldman. 1994. *Fast Forward: Where Technology, Demographics and History Will Take America and the World in the Next Thirty Years*. New York: Harper Business.

Carnegie Commission on Educational Television. 1967. *Public Television: A Program for Action*.

Chatterji, P.C. 1991. *Broadcasting in India*. New Delhi: Sage Publications.

Chatterji, S.K. (ed.). 1956. *The Cultural Heritage of India*, Vols I–IV. Calcutta: R.K. Mission Institute.

Cherry, C. 1959. *On Human Communication*. Cambridge, MA: MIT Press.

Chomsky, N. 1988. *Manufacturing Consent*. New York: Pantheon.

––––––. 1989. *Necessary Illusions*. London: Pluto Press.

Collins, L. and D. Lapierre. 1978. *Freedom at Midnight*. New Delhi: Vikas Publishing House.

Curran, J. and M. Gurevitch (eds). 1991. *Mass Media and Society*. London: Edward Arnold.

Dahlgren, P. and C. Sparks (eds). 1993. *Communication and Citizenship: Journalism and the Public Sphere*. London: Routledge.

Davis, D. 1995. *The Five Myths of TV Power (or, Why the Medium is Not the Message)*. New York: Simon & Schuster.

DeFleur, M. 1970. *Theories of Mass Communication*. New York: David McKay.

DeFleur M. and E.E. Dennis. 1986. *Understanding Mass Communication*, 2nd ed. Boston, MA: Houghton Mifflin Co.

Dennis, E.E. 1992. *Of Media and People*. New Delhi: Sage Publications.

Dordick, H. and G. Wong. 1993. *The Information Society*. New Delhi: Sage Publications.

Ebert, R. (ed.). 1997. *Roger Ebert's Book of Film*. London: W.W. Norton & Co.

Fournoy, D. and R. Stewart. 1997. *CNN: Making News in the Global Market*. Luton: University of Luton Press.

Fox, R.F. 1996. *Harvesting Minds*. London: Praeger.

Freedman, D. 1994. *Brainmakers: How Scientists are Moving beyond Computers to Create a Rival to the Human Brain*. New York: Touchstone.

French, D. and M. Richards. 1996. *Contemporary Television: Eastern Perspectives*. New Delhi: Sage Publications.

Galtung, J. 1984. 'Social Communication and Global Problems', paper presented to the IAMCR Conference at Prague.

Gandhi, M.K. 1950. *Satyagraha in South Africa*. Ahmedabad: Navajivan Publishing House.

––––––. 1954. *The Collected Works of Mahatma Gandhi*, Vol. XX (April–August 1921). New Delhi: Publications Division, Ministry of Information and Broadcasting.

––––––. 1958. *An Autobiography: The story of My Experiments with Truth*. Ahmedabad: Navajivan Publishing House.

Gerbner, G. 1985. 'Mass Media Discourse: Message System Analysis as a Component of Cultural Indicators', in T.A. Van Dijk (ed.), *Discourse and Mass Communication: New Approaches to the Analysis of Mass Media Discourse and Communication*. Berlin: Walterde Gruyter & Co.

––––––. 1996. 'Invasion of the Story Sellers', Foreword to Roy F. Fox, *Harvesting Minds: How TV Commercials Control Kids*. Westport, CT: Praeger Press.

Gerbner, G., L.P. Gross and W. Melody (eds). 1975. *Communications Technology and Social Policy*. New York: Wiley.

Gerbner, G., H. Mowlana and H.I. Schiller (eds). 1996. *Invisible Crises: What Conglomerate Control of Media Means for America and the World*. Boulder, CO: Westview Press.

Giannetti, L. 1982. *Understanding Movies*, 3rd ed. Englewood Cliffs, NJ: Prentice-Hall.

Gopal Raj, N. 2004. 'A Satellite to Serve Students', *The Hindu*, 22 September.

Government of India. 1997. *Doordarshan*. New Delhi: Ministry of Information and Broadcasting.

Green, J. 1997. *The New Age of Communications*. New York: Henry Holt & Co.

Greenfield, P.M. 1984. *Mind and Media: The Effects of Television, Videograms and Computers*. Cambridge, MA: Harvard University Press.

Habermas, J. 1990. *The Structural Transformation of the Public Sphere*. Cambridge: Polity Press.

Head, S.W. 1982. *Broadcasting in America*. Boston, MA: Houghton Mifflin.

Headrick, D. 1981. *The Tools of Empire: Technology and European Imperialism in the 19th Century*. New York: Oxford University Press.

Jacker, C. 1964. *Man, Memory and Machines: An Introduction to Cybernetics*. New York: Dell Publishing.

Karney, R. (ed.). 1999. *Chronicle of the Cinema: 100 Years of Movies*. London: Dorling Kindersley.

Khurshid, A.S. 1956. *Newsletters in the Orient*. Assen: Royal van Gorcum.

Kirkman, B. 1999. 'Governance of the Net', *The Hindu*, 23 May.

Kittross, J.M. and C.H. Sterling. 1978. *Stay Tuned: A Concise History of American Broadcasting*. Belmont, CA: Wadsworth Publishing.

Krishnamurthy, N. 1966. *Indian Journalism*. Mysore: Mysore University Press.

Kurzweill, R. 1990. *The Age of Intelligent Machines*. Cambridge, MA: MIT Press.

Lampton, G. 1991. *Telecommunication: From Telegraphy to Modems*. New York: Franklin Watts/Venture.

Lambert, S. and S. Ropiquet (eds). 1986. *CD-ROM: The New Papyrus*. New York: Microsoft Press.

Lasswell, H. 1948. 'The Structure and Function of Communication in Society', in L. Bryson (ed.), *The Communication of Ideas*. New York: Harper & Bros.

Lazarsfeld, P. and E. Katz. 1955. *Personal Influence*. New York: Free Press.

Lazarsfeld, P. and R. Merton. 1948. 'Mass Communication, Popular Taste and Organized Social Action', in L. Bryson (ed.), *The Communication of Ideas*. New York: Harper & Bros.

Lee, P. (ed.). 1984. *Communication for All: The New World Information and Communication Order*. London: World Association for Christian Communication.

Leebaert, D. 1991. *Technology 2001: The Future of Computing and Communication*. Cambridge, MA: MIT Press.

Lent, J.A. 1971. *The Asian Newspapers' Reluctant Revolution*. Ames, IA: Iowa State University Press.

————. 1990. *The Asian Film Industry*. Bromley, UK: Christopher Helm Publishing.

Lent, J.A. and J.V. Vilanilam (eds). 1979. *The Use of Development News: Case Studies of India, Malaysia, Ghana and Thailand*. Singapore: AMIC.

Lerner, D. and W. Schramm (eds). 1967. *Communication and Change in Developing Countries*. Honolulu: East-West Center.

Lichtenberg, J. (ed.). 1990. *Democracy and the Mass Media: A Collection of Essays*. New York: Cambridge University Press.

Lippmann, W. 1922. *Public Opinion*. New York: Harcourt Brace.

MacBride, S. et al. (eds). 1980. *Many Voices, One World: The MacBride Report*. Paris: UNESCO.

McChesney, R. 1999. *Rich Media, Poor Democracy: Communication Politics in Dubious Times*. Urbana, IL: University of Illinois Press.

McConnell, T. (ed.). 2001. *American Decades 1990–1999*. Detroit: Thomson Gale.

McLuhan, M. 1962. *The Gutenberg Galaxy: The Making of Typographic Man*. Toronto: Toronto University Press.

———. 1994 [1964]. *Understanding Media: The Extensions of Man*. Cambridge, MA: MIT Press.

McLuhan, M. and B. Powers. 1989. *Global Village: Transformation in World Life and Media in the 21st Century*. Oxford: Oxford University Press.

McNair, B. 1998. *The Sociology of Journalism*. London: Arnold.

McQuail, D. 1969. *Towards a Sociology of Mass Communication*. London: Collier-Macmillan Ltd.

———. 1975. *Communication*. London: Longman.

———. 1994. *Mass Communication Theory: An Introduction*, 3rd ed. New Delhi: Sage Publications.

Merton, R.K. 1957. *Social Theory and Social Structure*. Glencoe, IL: Free Press.

Miller, G.R. (ed.). 1994. *The Handbook of Interpersonal Communication*, 2nd ed. New Delhi: Sage Publications.

Mishra, Dasarathi. n.d. 'Advertising in *Hicky's Gazette*: An Analytical Study'. *Indian Journal of Communication*, II (2–3): 3–12.

Moitra, A.N. 1969. *A History of Indian Journalism*. Calcutta: National Book Agency.

Munshi, K.M. 1948. *Gandhi: The Master*. Delhi: Rajkamal Publications.

Murthy, N.K. 1966. *Indian Journalism*. Mysore: Mysore University Press.

O'Malley, L.S.S. (ed.). 1968. *Modern India and the West*. New York: Oxford University Press.

Oommen, T.K. 1999. 'Evolving the Real Nation'. *The Hindu*, 18 July.

Orlik, P.B. 1992. *The Electronic Media: An Introduction to the Profession*. London: Allyn & Bacon.

Panicker, P.N. 2004. 'Media and the Public Sphere'. *The Hindu*, 12 January.

Parker, S. 2002. *The History of Communication and Information Technology*. New York: Gareth Stevens Publishing.

Philip, A. 1932. *India: A Foreign View*. London: Sidgwick & Jackson Ltd.

Postman, N. and S. Powers. 1992. *How to Watch TV News*. New York: Penguin.

Price, M.E. 1996. *Television, the Public Sphere and National Identity*. Oxford: Clarendon Press.

Primrose, J.B. 1939. 'The First Press in India and Its Printers', *The Library*, 20 (3).

Priolkar, A.K. 1958. *Printing Press in India*. Mumbai: Marathi Samsodhaka Mandala.

Raj, Mohan D.R. n.d. 'Journalism and Fiction: Gay Talese and Tom Wolfe', *Indian Journal of Communication*, III (1).

Rao, V.D. 1987 [1964]. 'The Beginning and Growth of the Marathi Press', in S.P. Sen (ed.), *The Indian Press: A Collection of Papers Presented at the Fourth Annual Conference of the Institute of Historical Studies*. Calcutta: Institute of Historical Studies.

Rheingold, H. 1991. *Virtual Reality: The Revolutionary Technology of Computer-generated Worlds—and How It Promises to Transform Society*. New York: Touchstone.

———. 1993. *The Virtual Community: Homesteading on the Electronic Frontier*. New York: Addison-Wesley.

Roszak, T. 1994. *The Cult of Information*. Berkeley, CA: University of California Press.

Sainath, P. 2004. 'When Farmers Die', *The Hindu*, 15 June.

Schechter, D. 1998. *The More You Watch, the Less You Know*. Edison, NJ: Seven Stories Press.

Schiller, H.I. 1973. *The Mind Managers*. Boston, MA: Beacon Press.

———. 1983. 'The Communication Revolution: Who Benefits?', *Media Development* 30 (4).

Schiller, H.I. 1989. *Culture, Inc.: The Corporate Takeover of Public Expression*. New York: Oxford University Press.

———. 1996. *Information Inequality: The Deepening Social Crisis in America*. New York: Routledge.

Schlesinger, A., Jr. 1997. 'Has Democracy a Future?', *Foreign Affairs*, 76 (5).

Schramm, W. 1964a. *Mass Media and National Development*. Paris: UNESCO.

———. 1964b. *The Process and Effects of Mass Communication*. Urbana, IL: University of Illinois Press.

———. 1988. *The Story of Communication: Cave Painting to Microchips*. New York: Longmans.

Sen, S.P. (ed.). 1987 [1964]. *The Indian Press: A Collection of Papers Presented at the Fourth Annual Conference of the Institute of Historical Studies*. Calcutta: Institute of Historical Studies.

Shannon, C. and W. Weaver. 1949. *The Mathematical Theory of Communication*. Urbana, IL: University of Illinois Press.

Shaw, M. 1996. *Civil Society and Media in Global Crisis: Representing Distant Violence*. New York: Printer Publications.

Siebert, F.S., R. Paterson and W. Schramm. 1956. *Four Theories of the Press*. New York: Free Press.

Signorielli, N. and M. Morgan (eds). 1990. *Cultivation Analysis: New Directions in Media Effects Research*. New Delhi: Sage Publications.

Sinclair, J., E. Jacka and S. Cunningham (eds). 1996. *New Patterns in Global Television: Peripheral Vision*. Oxford: Oxford University Press.

Sklar, R. 2002. *A World History of Film*. New York: Harry N. Abrams.

Smith, A. 1980a. *Goodbye, Gutenberg: The Newspaper Revolution of the 1980s*. New York: Oxford University Press.

———. 1980b. *The Geopolitics of Information: How Western Culture Dominates the World*. New York: Oxford University Press.

———. (ed.). 1980c. *Newspapers and Democracy: International Essays on a Changing Medium*. Cambridge, MA: MIT Press.

———. 1991. *The Age of Behemoths: The Globalization of Mass Media Firms*. New York: Twentieth Century Fund.

———. (ed.). 1995. *Television: An International History*. New York: Oxford University Press.

Solomon, N. 1999. *The Habits of Highly Deceptive Media: Decoding Spin and Lies in Mainstream News*. Monroe, ME: Common Courage Press.

Solomon, N. and J. Cohen. 1997. *Wizards of Media Oz: Behind the Curtain of Mainstream News*. Monroe, ME: Common Courage Press.

Stark, S.D. 1997. *Glued to the Set: The Sixty Television Shows and Events that Made Us What We are Today*. New York: Free Press.

Stay, B.L. (ed.). 1999. *Mass Media: Opposing Viewpoints*. San Diego, CA: Greenhaven Press.

Stephens, M. 1998. *The Rise of the Image; the Fall of the Word*. New York: Oxford University Press.

Strat, L., R. Jacobson and S.B. Gibson (eds). 1996. *Communication and Cyberspace: Social Interaction in an Electronic Environment*. Cresskill, NJ: Hampton Press.

Thurow, R. and J. Solomon. 2004. 'An Indian Paradox: Bumper Harvests and Rising Hunger', *The Wall Street Journal*, 25 January.

Thussu, D.K. 2000. *International Communication: Continuity and Change*. London: Arnold.

Traber, M. and C. Christians (eds). 1997. *Communication Ethics and Universal Values*. New Delhi: Sage Publications.

216   mass communication in india

Traber, M. and K. Nordenstreng (eds). 1993. *Few Voices, Many Worlds: Towards a Media Reform Movement*. London: World Association for Christian Communication.
Vanden Bergh, B.G. and Helen Katz. 1999. *Advertising Principles: Choice, Challenge, Change*. Lincolnswood, IL: NTC Business Books.
Van Dijk, T.A. (ed.). 1985. *Discourse and Mass Communication: New Approaches to the Analysis of Mass Media Discourse and Communication*. Berlin: Walter de Gruyter & Co.
Vaughan, T. 1994. *Multimedia: Making It Work*. Berkeley, CA: Osborne/McGraw-Hill.
Vedalaukar, S. 1987 [1964]. 'The Orgin of the Hindi Press', in S.P. Sen (ed.), *The Indian Press: A Collection of Papers Presented at the Fourth Annual Conference of the Institute of Historical Studies*. Calcutta: Institute of Historical Studies.
Vijayan, K. (ed.). 1997. *Ramayana in Palm Leaf Pictures* (Citraramayana). Thiruvananthapuram: Oriental Research Institute and Manuscripts Library, University of Kerala.
Vilanilam, J.V. 1984. 'Rural Press in India', *Media Asia*, 11(4).
———. 1985. *Education and Communication*. Trivandrum: Kairali Books International.
———. 1987. *Religious Communication in India*. Trivandrum: Kairali Books International.
———. 1989. *Reporting a Revolution*. New Delhi: Sage Publications.
———. 1992. *Science Communication and Development*. New Delhi: Sage Publications.
———. 1996. 'The Socio-Cultural Dynamics of Indian Television', in D. French and M. Richards, *Contemporary Television: Eastern Perspectives*. New Delhi: Sage Publications.
———. 2000a. *Human Rights and Communication: Towards Alternative Systems of Development and Education*. Bhubaneswar: NISWASS/CEDEC.
———. 2000b. *More Effective Communication—A Manual for Professionals*. New Delhi: Response Books.
———. 2003a. *Aa Lokam Mutal e-Lokam Varei* (Malayalam). Thiruvananthapuram: Kerala Bhasha Institute.
———. 2003b. *Growth and Development of Mass Communication in India*. New Delhi: National Book Trust.
Volker, I. 1999. *News in the Global Sphere: A Study of CNN and Its Impact on Global Communications*. Luton: University of Luton Press.
Whitehouse, G.E. 1988. *Understanding the New Technologies of the Mass Media*. Englewood Cliffs, NJ: Prentice-Hall.
Wordsworth, W.C. 1968. 'The Press', in L.S.S.O'Malley (ed.), *Modern India and the West*. New York: Oxford University Press.
Worsely, P. 1964. *The Third World*. Chicago: University of Chicago Press.
Wright, C.R. 1959. *Mass Communication: A Sociological Perspective*. New York: Random House.

about the author

J.V. Vilanilam was formerly Vice-Chancellor, University of Kerala, and served as Professor and Head, Department of Communication and Journalism, at the same university. He is currently Professor Emeritus of Communication. During a rich and varied career, Professor Vilanilam has been Member, Adjunct Faculty, Temple university; Visiting Scholar and Lecturer, University of Pennsylvania; Research Associate, Rutgers University; and Senior Travel Fellow, Association of Commonwealth Universities, London.

Dr Vilanilam has two doctoral degrees (Ph.D in Mass Communication from the University of Amsterdam, 1986, and D.Litt. from Bhagalpur University, 1981) and two master's degrees (M.S. in Communication, Temple University, Philadelphia, 1975, and M.A. in English from Banaras Hindu University, 1958). Extensively published, Dr Vilanilam has contributed to top journals in his field, and is the founder-editor of two journals, the *Indian Journal of Communication* and the *Journal of Communication Studies*. He is the author or co-author of two dozen books, among which are *Evaluation of Press Performance in India: Through Content Analysis of Four Newspapers* (1977), *Reporting a Revolution: Iranian Revolution and the NIICO Debate* (1989), *Science Communication and Development* (1992), *More Effective Communication: A Manual for Professionals* (2000), and *Advertising Basics! A Resource Guide for Beginners* (2004).